IMPACT OF GLOBALISATION AND RETAINING STRATEGIES FOR LABOUR AND EMPLOYMENT

IMPACT OF GLOBALISATION AND RETAINING STRATEGIES FOR LABOUR AND EMPLOYMENT

Edited by
A. BALAKRISHNAN

PUBLICATIONS

KALPAZ PUBLICATIONS
DELHI-110052

Impact of Globalisation and Retaining Strategies for Labour and Employment

Rs. 950

ISBN: 81-7835-602-3

Published in 2007 in India by
Kalpaz Publications
C-30, Satyawati Nagar,
Delhi-110052
E-mail: kalpaz@hotmail.com
Phone : 9212729499

Lasser Type Setting by: Rudra Computer Graphics, Delhi
Printed at : Salasar Imaging System, Delhi

Contents

SECTION-B : WOMEN AND AGRICULTURAL LABOURERS

SECTION-C : ISSUES OF TEXTILE LABOURERS

SECTION-D : MIGRANT LABOURERS IN VARIOUS INDUSTRIES

Foreword

Globalisation of the economy implies universalisation of the process of production and trade. It has become a dominant feature of the world economy over the last two decades. The world nations are becoming integrated into the global economy through trade and capital flows. This trend has emerged as an after effect of globalisation and the impact is likely to be experienced in the field of industry, labour, employment, industrial trades, business and laws relating to employment and individual vocations.

It is necessary to obtain sufficient growth and create employment opportunities to provide productive employment to the growing labour force and it is widely regarded as one of the major problems that the country faces. In India, growth rates of employment have been relatively high in urban areas, but the employment opportunities are meager in rural areas. There are also wide variations in the unemployment rates among different states in the country over the past few decades. There are concerns that the processes of liberalization and globalisation are creating an environment which is not conducive to expanding employment in the organised private sector. The existing industrial units are shedding excess labour in order to remain competitive and are introducing new technology which is essential to ensure competitiveness. Therefore, it is important to focus our attention on the impact of globalisation and the responses that are necessary to enhance the image of our country and improve her economic activities. Efforts should constantly be made to create more organised employment opportunities in a healthy environment.

There is a need to obtain a minimum level of protection and welfare for workers in all sectors of the economy – organised as well as unorganised.

The Department of Applied Research of Gandhigram Rural University has undertaken a number of studies related to labour problems. It has been observed that there is a paucity of research on various labour related issues, employment and globalisation. Against these backdrops, seminar on the "Impact of Globalisation and Retaining Strategies for Labour and Employment" was conducted. The seminar profiled the existing situation and the impact of globalisation on rural economy through presentation of papers and careful deliberations. It further helped to trace the effect of globalization on labour management and migration. The factors influencing the growth of labour force in the informal sector were also identified. It also helped to highlight the socio-economic conditions of organised and unorganised labourers, problems of agricultural and plantation labourers, labour issues in textile industry and migrant labour.

I have no doubt that this book, based on the seminar papers, will be read widely and will be useful for academicians as well as activists. I am sure the book will help to popularize research perspectives on labour and employment and shall pave the way for the framing of policies and initiating programmes.

Dr. T. Karunakaran
Vice-chancellor
Gandhigram Rural University

Preface/Acknowledgement

Globalization refers to increasing global connectivity, integration and interdependence in the economic, social, technological, cultural, political, and ecological spheres. Globalization is the convergence of prices, products, wages, rates of interest and profits towards developed country norms. Globalization of the economy depends on the role of human migration, international trade, movement of capital, and integration of financial markets.

The scenario that has emerged after globalisation and the impact that it has witnessed and the impact that it is likely to be experienced in the field of industry, the "labour market" employment, industrial vocations and laws relating to employment and individual vocations.

The need to ensure adequate growth and employment opportunities and providing productive employment for the rapid increase in the labour force is widely regarded as one of the most important problem facing the country. There is a widespread concern that the acceleration in GDP growth in the post reform period has not been accompanied by a commensurate expansion in employment. Public sector withdraws from many areas. There are fears that the processes of internal liberalization and globalisation are creating an environment which is not conducive to expanding employment in the organised private sector. Existing industrial units are shedding excess labour in order to remain competitive and new technology which is essential to ensure competitiveness. Therefore, it is essential to concentrate our attention on the impact of globalisation and the responses that are necessary to improve the competitiveness of our country and economic activities, to ensure a regime of harmonious industrial relations, to ensure increasing opportunities of employment, to ensure at least a minimum level of protection and welfare for workers in all sectors of the economy-organised as well as unorganised. It is the right time to organise a state level seminar to discuss the issues of globalisation on labour and employment.

Objectives of the Seminar

- To trace out the impact of globalisation on labourers in various trades
- To find out the type and rate of labour migration
- To analyse the factors of growth of labour force in the informal sector
- To develop suitable strategies for the welfare of the labourers.

Sub Themes of the seminar

1. Socio Economic Conditions of Organised and unorganised Labourers
2. Problems of Agricultural and Plantation Labourers
3. Labour issues in Textile industry
4. Migrant labour.

Prof.V.G.Dhanakumar, Indian Institute of Plantation Management, Banglore, in his keynote address, spoke of the world class strategy for the management of labour quality in Agri-business sector and he pointed out some component of HRD indicators with special reference to grassroot resources which continue to log behind the improvements. India's ranks in terms of Human Development Index (HDI) stood in 127 out of 177 countries and 103 in Gender Development Index (GDI) out of 144 countries during 2004. Employment in the organized sector declined by 0.8% in 2003 due to a decline of public sector by 1%. Several initiatives are being taken to improve the quality of labour resources and skill through management training and development.

The inaugural session was chaired by Dr.G.Palanithurai, Professor and Head, Department of Political science and Development Administration, Gandhigram Rural University; Gandhigram. His informative inaugural speech focused on the merits and demerits of globalization in a developing economy.

Mr.J.Paul Baskar, Chairman, Peace Trust, Dindigul, in his special address, pointed out that the issues related to the labour migration and trends due to globalization and also he stressed the need to control the rural-urban migration. The welcome address was given by Prof.M.A.Sudhir, Head, Department of Applied Research, Gandhigram Rural University, Gandhigram. He explained the need and purpose of the seminar. Further he added the relevance of the seminar during the globalised era. Dr.S.Gunasekaran, Reader, Department of Applied Research, proposed the vote of thanks.

There were three technical sessions namely : i) Issues in organised and unorganised sector; ii) Issues of Agriculture and plantation labourers; iii) Issues of textile and other industrial labourers and iv) migrant labourers. 50 papers were presented by academicians, experts from Non-Governmental agencies and researchers in the above technical sessions.

The papers presented in the seminar were based mostly their on research and focused on the main issues of labourers in the globalised situation. There were also a number of papers focusing on the nature of employment, working and living conditions of unorganised workers working in certain specific industries. The informal sector is delinked from the formal sectors, and it has to create employment opportunities to ensure the survival of the people engaged in it. Issues concerning women labourers working at exploitative wage rates and miserable working conditions were also covered by the seminar. The impact of globalization on the labour and employment in various trades were discussed at length.

Delivering the valedictory address, Prof.N.Narayanaswamy, Dean, Department of Rural Development, Gandhigram Rural University, expressed the view that the globalization should bring prosperity to the labourers who are suppressed, paid low and working in hazardous environment. The question of migration is also needed to be addressed while discussing the emerging perspectives in development in the urorganised sector. For the valedictory session welcome address was given by Dr.C.Sivapragasam, Reader, Department of Applied Research, and the seminar outcome was presented by Dr.M.Hilaria Soundhari, of the Department of Applied Research, and the formal vote of thanks was extended by the seminar Director Dr. A. Balakrishnan.

I take this opportunity to express my indebtedness to our Vice-Chancellor Dr.T.Karunakaran, who encouraged and supported to conduct the seminar and to bring the papers in the form of a book. I express my sincere thanks to University Grants Commission, New Delhi which provided financial assistance to conduct the seminar and also supported to publish the seminar papers in a book form.

I am extremely grateful to Prof. M.A. Sudhir, Head, Department of Applied Research, Gandhigram Rural University for his constant encouragement and support in organizing the seminar and to disseminate the seminar papers in the form of book.

I am extremely grateful to Prof. R. Murugesan, Director, Centre for Rural Development, Annamalai University, for his expert opinion for publication and his encouragement in my academic endeavours.

I convey my thanks to chairpersons who chaired the three technical sessions and their valuable suggestions during the seminar.

I am thankful to my colleagues in the Department, Prof.R.Sreerangarajan, Mrs. A. Mumtaj, P.G. Balasubramanian, A. Ingarsal, R. Elango, G. Jayesh and P.R. Sucheth for their support in completing the academic assignment.

I am also grateful to our publication division and members in the publication committee for their approval and support to bring this book. I also extend my thanks to Kalpaz Publications, New Delhi for publishing the book.

(A. BALAKRISHNAN)

List of Contributors

Dr. M.A.Sudhir, Professor and Head, Department of Applied Research, Gandhigram Rural University, Gandhigram, Dindigul, Tamil Nadu – 624302.

Dr. A. Balakrishnan, Reader, Department of Applied Research, Gandhigram Rural University, Gandhigram, Dindigul.

Dr. L. Rathakrishnan, Reader, Department of Rural Industries and Management, Gandhigram Rural University, Gandhigram, Dindigul, Tamil Nadu – 624302.

Dr. M. Soundarapandian, Professor, Department of Economics, Gandhigram Rural University, Gandhigram, Dindigul, Tamil Nadu – 624302.

Ms. N. Prabha, Research Scholar, Department of Rural Industries and Management, Gandhigram Rural University, Gandhigram, Dindigul, Tamil Nadu – 624302.

Mrs. S. Lakshmi Ganapathy, Sr. Research Fellow, Tamil Nadu Agricultural College, KIllikulam. Thoothukudi Dt.

Mr. D.Kathiravan, Lecturer in Economics, St. John's College, Palayamkottai, Thirunelveli – 627002

Dr. S. David Amirtha Rajan, Reader and PG Head, Department of Commerce, The American College, Madurai.

Dr. Mrs.P. Gnana Soundari, Reader in Economics, Lady Doak College, Madurai – 2.

Dr. S. Kumar, Lecturer of Economics, Government Arts College (Autonomous), Coimbatore – 18.

Dr. G. Chandra Kumar, Reader and Head, Department of Economics, AVC College (Autonomous), Mayiladuthuarai-609001.

Ms. C. Suguna, Research Scholar, Department of Economics, AVC College (Autonomous), Mayiladuthuarai-609001.

Dr. N. Meenakshisundaram, Professor and Head, Department of Rural Industries and Management, Gandhigram Rural University, Gandhigram, Dindigul, Tamil Nadu – 624302.

Ms. R. Renganayaki, Research Scholar, Department of Rural Industries and Management, Gandhigram Rural University, Gandhigram, Dindigul, Tamil Nadu – 624302.

Dr. D. Kumar, Sr. Lecturer and Research Adviser, PG and Research Department of Economics, Jamal Mohammed College (Autonomous), Trichy -20.

Mr. A. Saleem Batcha, Sr. Lecturer and Research Adviser, PG and Research Department of Economics, Jamal Mohammed College (Autonomous), Trichy -20.

Ms. P. Poongodi, Assistant Professor, Kongu Arts and Science College, Erode-638 107.

Dr. C. Swaminathan, Principal, Kongu Arts and Science College, Erode -638107.

Ms. G. Barani, Lecturer, Management Studies, Kongu Arts and Science College, Erode -638 107.

Mr. A. Abdul Rahman, Research Scholar, Department of Cooperation, Gandhigram Rural University, Gandhigram.

Mr. R. Bagavathi Muthu, Guest Lecturer, School of Economics, Madurai Kamarajar University, Madurai.

Ms. T. Indra, Guest Lecturer, School of Economics, Madurai Kamarajar University, Madurai.

Ms.S. K.Sathya Prabha, Research Scholar, Department of Political Science, Madurai Kamarajar University, Madurai.

A. Chandraprabha, Research Scholar, Department of Rural Industries and Management, Gandhigram Rural University, Gandhigram, Dindigul, Tamil Nadu – 624 302.

Mr. N. Mukundan, Lecturer in Economics, PG and Research Department of Economics, AVC College (Autonomous), Mayiladuthurai.

Mr. S.Thiyagarajan, Lecturer in Economics, PG and Research Department of Economics, AVC College (Autonomous), Mayiladuthurai.

Prof. M. Perumal, SGL in Economics, Urumu Dhanalakshmi College, Thiruchirapalli.

Mrs. A.Inigo Antony Beaula, Research Scholar, Department of Rural Industries and Management, Gandhigram Rural University, Gandhigram, Dindigul, Tamil Nadu – 624 302.

Ms.V.Mangaiyarkarasi, Lecturer in Sociology, Pondicherry University, Pondicherry - 605 014.

P.G. Balasubramanian, Research Scholar, Department of Applied Research, Gandhigram Rural University, Gandhigram, Dindigul, Tamil Nadu – 624 302.

Dr.S. Baluchamy, Reader, Department of A&CE, Gandhigram Rural University, Gandhigram, Dindigul, Tamil Nadu – 624 302.

Mr. C. Senthil Kumar, Research Scholar, Department of A&CE, Gandhigram Rural University, Gandhigram, Dindigul, Tamil Nadu – 624302.

Ms.K. Praveena, II M.A. Economics, Lady Doak College, Madurai.

Ms.M. Mahalakshmi, II M.A. Economics, Lady Doak College, Madurai.

Dr. N. Lalitha, Reader, Department of Rural Development, Gandhigram Rural University, Gandhigram, Dindigul, Tamil Nadu – 624 302.

Mr.M.K. Badrinarayanan, Research Scholar, Department of Rural Development, Gandhigram Rural University, Gandhigram, Dindigul, Tamil Nadu – 624302.

Dr.A. Thomas William, Faculty Member, Department of Rural Development Science, Arul Anandhar College (Autonomous), Karumathur, Madurai – 625514.

Dr. G. Albin Joseph, Faculty Member, Department of Rural Development Science, Arul Anandhar College (Autonomous), Karumathur, Madurai –625514.

Ms. A. Chandraprabha, Research Scholar, Department of Rural Industries and Management, Gandhigram Rural University, Gandhigram, Dindigul, Tamil Nadu – 624302.

Ms.S.Kasi, Research Scholar, Department of Economics, University College, Kerala University, Trivandram.

Dr.R.Sundaresan, Reader, Department of Economics, University College, Kerala University, Trivandram.

Mr.S. Sathes Kumar, M.Phil Scholar, Department of Applied Research, Gandhigram Rural University, Gandhigram.

Ms.G. Bhuvaneswari, M.Phil Scholar, Department of Economics, Madurai Kamaraj University, Madurai.

Dr. A.Venkatachalam, Reader in Commerce, GTN Arts College, Dindigul.

Ms.S. Siyamala Devi, Senior Lecturer in Commerce, MVM Arts College, Dindigul.

Mr. J.Paul Baskar, Chairman, Peace Trust, Dindigul.

Fr. Soosaiappan, PG Student, Department of Rural Development Science, Arul Anandar College (Autonomous), Karumathur, Madurai – 625514.

Dr. M. Karuppanalagu Lecturer and Head, Department of Economics

Yadava College, Thiruppalai , Madurai – 625014.

Ms. Anitha, Project Staff, Peace Trust, Dindigul.

Dr. K.Ravichandran, Reader, Department of Cooperation, Gandhigram Rural University, Gandhigram, Dindigul, Tamil Nadu – 624302.

Mr. K.Dhevan, Research Scholar, Department of Cooperation, Gandhigram Rural University, Dindigul, Tamil Nadu – 624302.

Dr. Samwel Kakuko Lopoyetum, Senior Post- Doctoral Research Fellow, Department of Cooperation, Gandhigram Rural University, Gandhigram, Dindigul, Tamil Nadu – 624302.

Mr. S. Alagu Marimuthu, Lecturer in Economics, Yadhava College Madurai.

Mr. P. Selvamani, Project Fellow, Department of Political Science and Development Administration, Gandhigram Rural University, Gandhigram, Dindigul, Tamil Nadu – 624302.

Mr. D. Gopalsamy, Lecturer in Economics, PG & Research Department,Gobi Arts and Science College, Gobichettipalayam – 638453.

Mr. G. Sathis Kumar, M.Phil Scholar, Department of Economics, MC College, Thambaram, Chennai.

T.Saravanan, Research Scholar, Department of Rural Industries and Management, Gandhigram Rural University, Gandhigram, Dindigul, Tamil Nadu – 624302.

Dr. S. Dhanasekaran, Principal, RVS college of Education, Dindigul.

Mr. Well Howrae, Lecturer, Department of Rural Industries and Management, Gandhigram Rural University, Tamil Nadu – 624 302.

Mr. R. Anandarasu, Lecturer, B.Ed. Programme (Integrated), Department of Applied Research, Gandhigram Rural University, Gandhigram, Dindigul, Tamil Nadu – 624302.

Dr. R. Seerangarajan, Professor, Department of Rural Industries and Management, Gandhigram Rural University, Gandhigram, Dindigul, Tamil Nadu – 624302.

Mr. K. Karnan, Joint Director, Department of Handlooms and Textiles, Kuralagam, Govt. of Tamil Nadu, Chennai.

Kishor Bhanushali, Assistant Professor, Mahathma Gandhi Labour Institute, Ahemadabad.

Mr. R. Albert Christopher Dhas, Lecturer in Economics, The American College, Madurai.

Ms. M. Helen Mary Jacqueline, Lecturer in Economics, Lady Doak College, Madurai.

Dr. A. Selva Kumar, Reader in Commerce, Pope's College, Sawyerpuram – 628256.

Dr. G. Karunanithi, Prof. and Head, Dept. of Sociology, M.S. University, Tirunelveli – 627 012.

SECTION – A

ORGANISED AND UNORGANISED SECTORS

1

Globalization and its Impact on Labour and Employment

M.A. Sudhir

Globalization has become a very popular term and it has set in a process of far-reaching consequences (ILO, 2004). It has been the most debatable issue worldwide and is considered as the process of an economy getting integrating with that of the world economy. This phenomenon draws countries out of their insulation and makes them join the world in its march towards a new world order. According to Nayyar (2002) globalization is an expansion of economic transitions and the organization of the economic activities across the political boundaries of nation state. IMF (1992) depicts globalization as an increasing integration of economics around the world particularly through trade and financial flows. The entire world becomes a single marketed and a corporate strategy is followed for a global market environment. It is not a new phenomenon, but the globalization today is market by its speed and reach over the entire world. It has been represented in two forms today. In the first case, it encompasses all types of economic and cultural transfers of nations and, on the other hand it simply refers to economic exchange of goods and services internationally. Its key effects are to enhance the international integration of market for goods and services, technology, financial, capital and labour. The economic globalization manifests in three forms such as an increase in international trade, financial flows and foreign direct investment (Loots, 2002). It is a well known fact that the process of globalization does not evolve equally world wide. The developing nations, therefore, must integrate into the global trading network – by adopting policies and forming partnerships within multinational corporations (Vyas, 2002). With this end in view, India liberalized its market economy over a decade ago dismantling the complex network of industrial controls, liberalizing the foreign trade and facilitating FDI inflows through several measure. These trade reforms aimed at exposing Indian firms to global markets and compelled them to produce better quality goods and also the currency transactions enabled them to import better quality materials and technology. Globalization has become a buzz word in India since 1990s and the good effect of globalization is envisaged in the next few decades especially in sectors like human and physical resource development, entrepreneurship, domestic and foreign markets, labour and employment.

Impact on Labour Force

Globalization has a definite impetus on the empowerment and mobility of the labour force. This is also associated with consequential impact on economic growth and development. The out migration as a part of globalization helps to curtail unemployment, reduce poverty and earn foreign remittance. The benefits can also be reflected in terms of transfer of technology, skill upgradation and migrant by integrated workers. The United Nations Global Commission on International migration setup in 2003 advocated for integrated policies and strategies for effective management of labour migration at the global level. Poverty is a major directing force behind migration. Aspiration for better economic empowerment is another causal factor emerging in all cases of migration. This is evident in the case of migrant Indians dominant presence; people from Kerala in Gulf Countries, from Tamil Nadu in Singapore and Malaysia, and from Punjab in Canada and East Africa. The migrates desire to take an opportunity to improve their living standards, enhance income and accumulate wealth.

Employment Perspectives

Majority of the migrant workers towards Middle East and Gulf countries are unskilled and semi-skilled workers. Those migrating to developed countries are mostly skilled and professional workers from the fields of information technology, electronics, medicine and nursing. The extent of migration from India has fluctuated dropping from 438,000 persons in 1993 to 199,500 persons in 1999 and rising again to 368,000 persons in 2002. There are estimated 3.6 million Indian migrants workers in six Gulf countries. According to the ILO Report and that of Department of International Development, 25 per cent are semi-skilled and the rest of 5 per cent are unskilled. Out migration is a male dominated phenomenon in India. Women migrants often suffer prone to vulnerable situations and are from exploitation, sexual harassment, work related diseases and even HIV/AIDS of course, there are significant growth in terms of reducing unemployment earning foreign exchange and enhancing migrants skills and interrelationships leading to empowerment. In the state of Kerala, the return of remittance amounts to 22 per cent of the state income and there is a lot of development in rural areas funded by remittance both in Kerala and Punjab. Migration has a positive impact on family life. The living standard of the family, children's education, salary and investment are possible indicators showing favourable trends. According to Juan Somavia, Diretor General ILO (2001) "Migrant workers provide valuable services with their labour and furnish often factories, produce food, provide domestic service, staff in hospitals and contribute part to a wide range of basic needs, often for low wages, and with little recognition of the value of their contribution". The percentage of remittance has shown gradual increase sharing GNP of 3.07 in India. In addition the informal system of remittance through the Hawala or Huundai system is also prevalent.

Human and Labour Rights

The recruitment of migrant workers involves the Government and private agencies, and even the local and national intermediaries. The unscrupulous recruiting agencies are the target of criticism against the manipulation, exploitation and discrimination. Migrant workers face diverse forms of harassment in the work place and in the host society. This includes low or non-payment of wages, insufficient medical facility and death benefits while on duty. Domestic migrants often complaint about harassment, unpaid salary, break of contract and lack of protection or security in job. They are also faced with innumerable problems emerging from social, religious and cultural barriers. The typical issues facing migrant workers are reported as follows:

1. Bad working and living conditions
2. Retention of Travel documents and transfers
3. Problems related to contract deals unable to file complain against the employers and their agents.
4. Problems arising from ethnic and religious differences
5. Health problem resulted from poor living and working conditions
6. Fraudulent practices – excessive cost of recruitment and service restrictions
7. Lack of legal awareness
8. Social isolation and its favorable effects such as STD/HIV/AIDS
9. Erosion of talents and resources to the urban and influential areas
10. Depletion of man power in rural areas.

Trade Union Intervention

Trade Unions do not have a common strategy or stand on migrant labourers. Trade Union interventions usually take place on adhoc basis. Due to lack of initiative and effective leadership, the cases are left to the individuals or courts to settle. In few cases there are instance of exploitation and letting down the workers at the hands of the mighty employers.

Also, there is a paucity of research works undertaken on various issues of labour and unemployment. The publications based on field research on the effect of globalization on the trade union issues are conspicuous by their absence.

2

Emerging Concerns in Wage, Employment and Income in the Globalised Era

A. Balakrishnan

The emerging economic environment involving rapid technology changes, requires response in terms of change in methods, trade and services, globalisation of economy, liberalization of trade and industry and emphasis on international competitiveness and the need for bringing the existing laws in tune with the future market needs." It is, therefore, necessary for us to examine changes that have taken place in recent years in the world, changes in our economy and in our economic policies and to study their impact on the economy in general, and industry and labour in particular.

Alan Rugman (2000) gives considerable importance to the role played by multinationals and therefore, he defines globalisation as "the world wide production and marketing of goods and services by multinational enterprises."

Anthony Giddens, Director of the London School of Economics (1999) feels that with globalisation, social relations are no longer local, but stretch across time and space. It is often said that a global capitalist culture is being promoted by the powerful multinational enterprises. This global culture is being further speeded up by global mass media and communication technologies.

Globalisation promotes economic growth and prosperity to all nations. It promotes technology, creates more quality jobs for the community, the free foreign investment supplements domestic savings and encourages more investment in the community. The FDI – receiving countries are in a better position to benefit from international integration; increase in international trade is good for economic growth.

They feel that globalisation will destroy employment and local communities, that the third world is not likely to benefit by this process, and that family, community and democracy will have the last word. In a brilliant review of the international economic relations in the 20th century, Ian Clark (1997) argues how fragmentation of communities and countries are interlinked with globalisation.

The Human Development Report on South Asia 2001, released by UNDP is perhaps the strongest critic of globalisation. The benefits of globalisation have remained limited to a small minority of educated urban population. As a result, income inequalities have increased." The report also concludes that South Asia, which is the home of the largest number of poor people in the world (515 million), did not make much progress towards poverty reduction as a result of globalisation. The balance sheet of gainers and losers in the globalisation process shows the uneven burden borne by the poor within and among the nations. The report comes to the conclusion that "the number of people in poverty have increased. The poor are being marginalized. The resource allocations to the poverty alleviation programmes are declining, reducing their effectiveness." The report also comments on the growth rates of countries in South Asia and says that in most countries growth rates are declining. All these make one wonder whether globalisation has promoted growth and brought prosperity.

At the threshold of liberalized economy, the Labour market forces, wages, income security and employment situation were normal. After implementation of L.P.G. and W.T.O. agreement, these two policies had effect on Labour market, there has been drastic changes in the form of employees lay out. In formal sector wages have been converted into informal (unorganized) workers, such as Labour contract, under employment and also the agricultural wages have been reduced to meager amount of wage rate.

This paper makes an attempt to elicit details on how to overcome the problems of existing wages, employment generating enterprising and income in Labour market particularly in the Globalised era .It is necessary to find out how the existing and changing structures are needed to meet out the emerging issues in areas like, income, wage, employment and Labour market.

According to National Commission on Labour, 60 percent of the workers in unorganized sector are self employed or home based and thus remain outside the purview of Minimum Wage Act. With new era of globalization, the size of unorganized sector is on rise, unorganized sector is the largest employment provider.

Employment

The need to ensure adequate growth in employment opportunities to provide productive employment for the continuing increase in the Labour force is widely regarded as one of the most important problems facing the country. There is widespread concern that the acceleration in GDP growth in the post-reform period has not been accompanied by a commensurate expansion in employment. Public sector employment is expected to fall as the public sector withdraws from many areas. There are fears that the processes of internal liberalization and globalization, inevitable though they may be, are creating an environment which is not conducive to expanding employment in the organized private sector. Existing industrial units are shedding excess Labour in order to remain competitive, and new technology, which is essential to ensure competitiveness, is typically more automated and it leads to reduction in employment level. The net result of these forces, it is feared, could be a very slow expansion in employment opportunities in the organized sector, with a rise in unemployment rates and growing frustration among the youth. The problem is perceived to be especially severe for educated youth, who have high expectations about the quality of employment opportunities that should come their way.

The vast majority of Indian workers are employed in the informal or unorganized sector where jobs are unprotected and uncertain and labour market competition keeps wages low.

Job seekers of all categories registered in the Employment exchanges in India (in thousands)

Year	*Registration*	*Placement*	*Vacancies notified*	*Submission made*	*Live Register*	*% of placement to submission*	*% of placement to vacancies notified*	*% increase in live register over previous year*
1994	5927.3	204.9	396.4	3723.4	36691.5	5.5	51.7	1.1
1995	5858.1	214.9	385.7	3569.9	36742.3	6.0	55.7	0.1
1996	5872.4	233.0	423.9	3605.9	37429.6	6.5	55.0	1.9
1997	6321.9	275.0	393.0	3767.8	39139.9	7.3	70.0	4.6
1998	5851.8	233.3	358.8	3076.6	40089.6	7.6	65.0	2.4
1999	5966.0	221.3	328.9	2653.2	40371.4	8.3	67.3	0.7
2000	6041.9	177.7	284.5	2322.8	41343.6	7.7	62.5	2.4
2001	5552.6	169.2	304.1	1908.8	41995.9	8.9	55.6	1.6

Source: DGE & T. Ministry of Labour.

Wage

The most remarkable feature of the wage structure in India is the enormous wage differential between the organized and unorganized sectors. In the context of the ongoing debate in North-South trade and wage inequality, it would be interesting to investigate how the skilled-unskilled wage differential has changed in the last two decades.

Organized-unorganized sector wage inequality has generated concern for distributional reasons. It is a widespread belief that government protection of labour and product markets has contributed to the isolation of the factory sector from the rigors of the market. This generates two concerns. First, a concern with inequality created by "undeservedly" high wages. Second, a concern with "excessively" high wages discouraging labour demand in the organized sector. Adherents of this view demand policy reforms that curb union power and revoke job security legislation. Indeed, these demands are currently central to the controversy over India's new economic policies which, so far, have concentrated on product market deregulation. It is important, in this context, to understand wage determination and how it ties in with the determination of employment, productivity and growth.

Implications for Policy Reform

The results carry the following relevant implications. Labour markets in India are severely segmented along both industry and state lines. Improvements in productivity are shared with workers and to extent; do not translate into increases in employment in the short run. In the long run, however, the existence of insider wage setting is expected to have no implications for the employment effects of technical change if the product market is competitive. This is because competitive forces will ensure that these gains are eventually spread through the population via their impact on product prices. What is clear from the analysis, however, is that wages are not market clearing irrespective of government interventions. Therefore, analyses that recommend the removal of all state machinery in the labour market as a cure for its ills are likely to be barking up the wrong tree. Although unemployment does not drive wages down to the competitive level, it does exert a dampening force.

Efficiency Wages

In an efficiency wage model, the additional revenue reaped by the payment of wages in excess of the supply price of labour offsets the additional cost incurred. This simple fact affords a direct test of the efficiency wage hypothesis which can be implemented by estimating a production function that includes wage-dependent effort.

The fact that higher wages induce higher productivity will generate a positive employment effect, the size of which depends upon demand elasticity. The role of policy here is not straightforward. For instance, if efficiency wage considerations are the driving insider force, there is not much scope for direct policy intervention. If, instead, factory unions are driving rent-sharing, policy initiatives aimed at job creation will have to consider carefully whether economic reforms that alter product market structure are not more important than interventions designed to curtail union power.

Conclusion

The shift in workforce composition from self-employment to casual wage employment that has been in progress since the 1970s continued through the 1990s. The unemployment rate increased at this time but it is unclear whether this signifies a lengthening of unemployment spells and a worsening of job opportunities or whether it simply denotes a greater degree of transitional or frictional unemployment as labour is reallocated towards the more productive sectors. Average daily earning per person per annum in the economy increased at a significant pace in rural and urban areas and for men and women.

The National Commission on labour (2002) included "Suggest any umbrella legislation for ensuring a minimum level of protection to the workers in unorganised sector. But, contrarily, wage system is not equal to their productivity and not even for place to place. In the light of better quality of informal labourers' productivity, their income earning must be hike.

At present scenario of Labour Market in informal sector, productivity increased but wage rate is decreased as well as not stable in the nature of work. During 1980-2000, the real wage has actually declined. Proportion of total value added in informal wage system. Subsequently 21% of value added increasingly in manufacturing sector. Income earnings are very low in informal sector rather than manufacturing and IT sector. Because of legislative measures, tax reforms are favourable and support for globalization polices, i.e trade union's rights, privileges are not consider by informal sector employment. Therefore, drastically changes in informal sector when we compared with formal sector wages and income earnings. The status of employment is changing from permanent to contract. The above changes are taking place in all the trades, especially in the labour and employment due to globalization.

References

1. Agarwal, R.N and Goldar, B., "Economic reforms and employment in India projections for the year 2001-02", *Indian Journal of Labour Economics,* Indian Society of Labour Economics, Delhi, Vol. 38, No. 4, pp. 577-95, 1995.
2. Aggarwal,A., "Estimates of Fixed Capital Stock in the Registered Manufacturing Sector in India", *Working Paper No. 937*, Indian Institute Of Management, Ahmedabad, 1991.
3. Banerjee, B., "The Role of the Informal Sector in the Migration Process: A Test of Probabilistic Migration Models and Labour Market Segmentation in India," in *Oxford Economic Papers,* Oxford University Press, Oxford, pp. 399-422, 1983.
4. Bhagwati, J. and Srinivasan,T.N., *Foreign Trade Regimes and Economic Development: India*, Macmillan, Delhi 1975.
5. Economic Intelligence Service, *The Liberalisation Process,* Center for Monitoring of the Indian Economy (CMIE), Bombay, 1991.
6. Ghose, A.K., "Employment in organized manufacturing in India", in *Indian Journal of Labour Economics,* Indian Society of Labour Economics, Delhi, Vol. 37 (2), April-June, pp.141-62. 1994.
7. National Labour Commission Report II), www.labour.nic.in, 2002.

3

Employment Opportunities in Organized Sectors of Poultry Farms

M. Soundarapandian and N. Prabha

The poultry industry has also got good marketing potential and has got huge developmental possibilities as well. We may stress that per capita consumption of eggs and poultry meat is on the increase and this would enrich the developmental potentialities. Much has been done in the field of developing the industry, still the industry need a planned strategy for its development. Seeing the labour and employment potentialities involved, the industry has great employment possibilities as well.

Labour Employment: Domestic Labour and Hired Labour

The labour involved in the poultry industry may be of two types: domestic and hired labour. The domestic labour may be used for maintaining and looking after the birds. It is also used for disposing-of the poultry products. Hired labour is also needed. Hired labour may be for full time or part time. Full time labour is needed for maintaining the birds on a regular and daily basis. A part time hired labour is required for preparation of sheds, transportation of poultry feeds and poultry products and for performing the marketing process relating both eggs and poultry meat.

Types of Labour Requirements

The skilled labour used in the poultry farms mainly undertakes the work requiring work of responsibility and those jobs which need technical knowledge. The skilled work may be veterinary services, feeding the birds, purchasing of the birds, medicines, equipments etc. and selling the eggs and poultry meat etc. For all those jobs poultry experts be engaged.

The jobs unskilled labour may undertake may involve the watering services of birds, cleaning the poultry equipments, and litter, preparation of sheds and poultry house, transportation work involved and the sweeping work etc. These jobs may be undertaken even by any illiterate and experienced man too.

Labour Welfare Measures and Working Conditions

In the India region mainly the poultry units are in organized farms employing only a limited number of persons on wages basis, most on a casual job. And it was found that all the poultry farms-mini, small, medium or big ones-do not provide good working condition to the labour employed on them.

In a number of cases the persons employed, have to stay twenty four hours a day on the farms situated in remote-areas and out-skirts of the towns/cities. As regards the facilities for their betterment and better working conditions, what they enjoy is the natural atmosphere alone with almost no physical facilities. That is why in a number of cases they do not acquire proficiency in their work and they regard their job purely as a temporary one with no security of job ensured to them. In a number of cases, when these persons go on leave to their places/home towns, they do not come back to the farms to resume their usual duties. This would not only benefit the employees but also the entrepreneurs of the farms on a long run basis, solidifying the base of poultry industry on the whole.

Labour Welfare Activities

Labour welfare activities mean work for improving the health, safety, general well-being and industrial efficiency of the workers beyond the minimum standard laid down by the Factories Act and other labour legislations. Workers' welfare should be understood as meaning such services, facilities and amenities. At present, the labour welfare Central Government; (2) The State Government; (3) The Employers and their organizations; (4) Trade Unions; and (5) Voluntary organizations. In order to activate the government, the employers; and the workers' organisation for the welfare of labour class, the following suggestions may be offered.

- A machinery should be set up to create harmony and mutual understanding between capitalists and laborers.
- A feeling of fraternity should be the basis of relations between employers and employees.
- The activities should be undertaken on joint-venture basis.
- Welfare work should be considered the responsibility of the community.

Naturally, there arises a need for providing welfare measures and better working conditions to the employees of the poultry units, statutory in some sort of social minima, indicating the responsibility for carrying out the welfare services offered by the three agencies, i.e., the State, the employers, and the workers' organisation.

Role of the Government in Encouraging Employment Opportunity in Poultry Sector

India lives in villages and at present the Government is laying an added stress on the development of villages with rural reconstruction. For the rural development a number of schemes have been enunciated by the Government, specific mention may be made of IRDP, TRYSEM; NREP; DPAP; CAD; SFDA; CDP; and Panchayat Raj schemes etc. All the schemes for Rural Development and Rural Reconstruction have two under lying objectives and strategy: (a) Higher employment generation throughout the year to the maximum persons; and (b) An adequate and regular income to the rural folk for maintaining an average level of living.

Table 1 reveals that the state-wise employment in organized sector in India. The state wise employment in organized sector in the year 2003 was ranging from 14.5 to 3593.2. The lowest employment opportunity in organized sector was Damon and Diu and highest employment opportunity in organized sector was 35.93 in Maharashtra.

Table 1 : State-wise Employment in Organized Sector in India (As on 31st March, 2001 to 2003) (In '000)

State/UTs	*2001*	*2002*	*2003*
Andhra Pradesh	2075.3	2050.7	2100.8
Arunachal Pradesh	-	-	-
Assam	1116.4	1063.9	1079.2
Bihar	1613	1613	1613
Chhatisgarh	348.1	354.3	354.3
Delhi	841.1	836	836.5
Goa	110.2	60.8	60.8
Gujarat	1696	1584	1630.9
Haryana	652.7	665.4	635.5
Himachal Pradesh	304.5	297.2	297.2
Jammu & Kashmir	210.1	210.1	210.1
Jharkhand	@	@	@
Karnataka	1849.7	1855.9	1850
Kerala	1241.7	1220.9	1211.4
Madhya Pradesh	1179.1	1141.6	1109.7
Maharashtra	3694.6	3634.6	3593.2
Manipur	83	82.8	82.8
Meghalaya	81.9	81.9	81.9
Mizoram	41.5	41.5	41.5
Nagaland	77.7	77.3	70.6
Orissa	828.8	777.7	750.2
Punjab	847.2	836.2	800
Rajasthan	1248.3	1205.8	1179.9
Sikkim*			
Tamil Nadu	2505.8	2516.4	2402.2
State/UTs	*2001*	*2002*	*2003*
Tripura	123.3	123.3	123.3

(Contd.)

(Contd.)

State/UTs	*2001*	*2002*	*2003*
Tripura	123.3	123.3	123.3
Uttaranchal	270.4	265.3	262.3
Uttar Pradesh	2223.8	2173.9	2143.8
West Bengal	2324.7	2263.9	2263.9
Andaman and Nicobar Islands	38.1	40	39.6
Chandigarh	91.3	90.8	90.4
Dadra and Nagar Haveli	-	-	-
Daman and Diu	15	14.5	14.5
Lakshadweep			
Pondicherry	25.8	25.8	51
India	27789.2	27205.5	27000.3

Note : * : No Employment Exchange is Functioning in this State.

@ : The Figures for Jharkhand were included in Bihar.

Source : Rajya Sabha Unstarred Question No. 2548, dated on 24.03.2005.

For developing rural India more and more stress be laid on the development of poultry farming with dairying and other rural industries on scientific lines for ensuring higher employment generation and adequate earning to the rural poor. Poultry industry by nature has got both the potentialities. No enterprise of rural economy may be kept at par with poultry and dairying in the present day economic conditions and in the light of increasing pressure of population on agriculture. In developing poultry industry not only in the Region but in the country as a whole, the role of the Government seems to be of immense value.

Conclusion

Demand for poultry increasing and production reaching 37 billion eggs and 1 billion dollars, this sector now employs around 1.6 million people. At least 80% of employment in the poultry sector is generated directly by these farmers, while 20% is engaged in feed, pharmaceuticals, equipment and other services required by the poultry sector. Additionally, there may be a similar number of people roughly 1.6 million who are engaged in marketing and other channels servicing the poultry sector.

Reference

V.K. Agarwal, *"Production and marketing poultry products in India"* Mittal publications, NewDelhi, 1994.

www.poultrysite.com

www.indiastate.com

4

Economic Globalization and its Implications for Employment in India

S. Kumar

Globalization means integration of the economies of the world with one another. Integration takes place when product and factors move about freely as among the different countries. Conceived thus the world economy become a one single economy. In concrete terms there are no restrictions (like quotas, licenses, high tariffs, administrative barriers etc.) on the movement of products and factors. In brief globalization implies: being able to manufacture in the most cost effect way possible anywhere in the world: being able to procure raw materials and drawing management resources from the cheapest source anywhere in the world; having the entire world as a market.

Factors Leading to Globalization

- The forces that lend momentum to the process of globalization have been identified by Michael porter to include the following:
- Growing similarities of countries in terms of available infrastructure, distribution channels and marketing approaches.

- Fluid capital markets-national capital markets are growing in to global capital markets because of the large flow of funds between countries.
- Technological restructuring-the reshaping of competition globally as a result of technological revolutions such as in micro electronics;
- The integrating role of technology-reduced cost and increased impact of products have made them accessible to more global consumers;
- New global competitors-a shift in competitors from traditional country competitors to emerging global competitors.
- End of the Cold war in 1990s-it set the stage for most developing countries to liberalise their economies and undertake structural reforms aimed at higher growth of their economies and create a climate for attracting foreign investments to supplement domestic resources.

Globalization and Its Impact

According to the data provided by the World Bank, India's share in World exports rose from .54% in 1990 to .67% in 1999. It would also be desirable to consider the export of services. India's share in world service export was .69 % in 1990 and it rose 1.15 in 1999 indicating significant improvement. Globalisation did not help India to the same extent as it helped China and Mexico. The average annual growth rate of export of goods and services increased by 8.9% during 1990 and 1999 for India, but the increase was much higher for Mexico (13.4%) and China (13.5%) during the same period.

Another major commonly claimed benefit of globalization is that it should lead to a greater inflow of foreign investment which should help to increase the productive capacity of the economy. The total average inflow of foreign investment during the six year period (95-96 to 2000) was $4.85 billion which is just half the level targeted by the order of $10 billion. India has not benefited from foreign direct investment to the extent to which the globalisers had made us to believe that it would.

There is a wide gap between the level of investment approved and actual flows. There is no doubt that sometime lag between the approvals and inflow of investment is inevitable. In the initial years of economic reforms this was undesirable. This explains the fact that during 91-95 actual inflow of investment was only 21.3% of the total approved investment. However the situation started improving there after and during the 5 years period, 1996-2000 actual inflow of investment was 40.8% of total approved investment. Increase of imports for greater than increase of exports. Globaliser advocated the acceptance of new strategy on the plea that India will be able to access foreign markets more effectively. It would be of interest to examine this claim during 2000-01, when exports grew to a level of 13 % of GDP. Gaurav Dutt, Valeriekozel and Martin Ravallion of the world bank in their paper "A model based assessment of India's progress in reducing poverty in 1990" suggest that the key determinants of the rate of poverty reduction at the state level are agricultural yields, growth of non farm sector development spending and inflation. This model has given the following findings. The rate of poverty reduction in the 1990 is slightly lower than that in 1980s. The main reason for the slow decline in poverty is the pattern of growth that was promoted following the policies of liberalization, privatization and globalization have helped already industrialized states much more as compared with less industrial states and their neglect of agriculture has been responsible for the skewed pattern of distribution in post reform period.

A major fallout of policies of globalization is the decline in the growth rate of employment. During the period 1983-94 the annual growth rate of employment was 2.04%, but it came down to 0.98 % during 1998-2000. As a consequence the unemployment rate went up from 6.03% in 1993-94 to 7.32 % in 1999-2000. This was despite the fact that rate of growth of labour force declined to 1.3 % during the period 1993-94 to 1999-2000. This was largely the result of deceleration in employment in agriculture and community and personal services. These sectors account for nearly 70 % of the total employment, but they recorded virtually no growth in employment

From a review of decade of performance after the introduction of globalization, it became evident that globalization policies had not be able to deliver the intended benefits in terms of macro indicators: GDP growth, poverty reduction, employment generation, boost to investment, export of merchandise.

Steps in Globalization

Need to promote competitiveness of Indian producers through the higher productivity growth, better quality products and innovations in products and process technology. Companies have to enter into the strategic alliances not only for bringing in state of art technology but also to reduce costs, improve efficiency and penetrate the global markets with joint efforts.

Self reliance in technology is the major determinant for achieving competitive advantages like demand conditions, supplier industries, and domestic competition and supporting infrastructure. Global competitiveness can be sustained only through the upgradation of technology and the development of human skills.

We have to set up new institutes for improving a wide range of human skills, from computer software to aircraft maintenance. The march of technology in manufacturing and services require not large amount of cheap unskilled people. But skilled persons needed drastically to cope with demanding in coming days.

The planning commission constituted a task force in concentrating on the enlargement of organized sector employment as the main vehicle of employment generation.

The Govt. provides much higher amount of credit as indicated by Nayak committee on development of small scale enterprises, it would go a long way in enlarging employment.

Information technology (IT) sector provided 2.2 million jobs to computer professionals and other related personnel engaged in IT sector. NASSCOM-MC Kinsey report (1999) has estimated that by the year 2008, IT enabled services will provide 11 million jobs and generate revenue of US$17-18 billion. In this sense, IT industry has great future in expanding employment opportunities.

WTO which bears upon trade in goods and services besides trade-related matters such as investments, intellectual property rights etc. Removal of several tariff and non tariff barriers imposed by other countries on exporter. These hurdles have taken on many forms in those countries. For example, certain products in some countries are heavily subsidized

In the case of exports, as also of imports, infrastructural facilities (like ports, aerodromes, storage etc) need to be adequate and modernized. These are related to the foreign exchange market, which should remain free from the manipulators.

Special efforts are required to induce Indian settled abroad to transfer to the maximum their savings to India.

Revolutionary improvements in transportation networks are reducing the cost of moving goods across the countries. That is the improvement of transport facilities will fetch more employment generation and economic development.

Conclusion

Globalization of the domestic economy of India will take us on the path of developmental at a more rapid rate than ever before. It may also state that India is already globalised to an extent. This more towards globalization got further strengthened, in fact was made almost inevitable, because of the powerful sources that in recent times were promoting this phenomenon on a world wide scale.

References

P. Jagadish, *Globalised Indian Economy*, Himalaya Publications, New Delhi, 2004.

Ruddar Datt and K.P.M. Sundaram, *Indian Economy*, S. Chand and Company Ltd, New Delhi, 2005.

Rudddar Dutt, *Second Generation Economic Reforms in India,* Deep & Deep Publications Pvt. Ltd., New Delhi, 2002.

5

Issues on Social Security under Organized and Unorganized Sector

G. Chandra Kumar and C. Suguna

The term unorganized labour has been defined as those workers who have not been able to organize themselves in pursuit of their common interests due to certain constraints like casual nature of employment, ignorance and illiteracy, small and scattered size of establishments, etc. As per the survey carried out by the National Sample Survey Organization in the year 1999-2000, the total employment in both organized and unorganized sector in the country was of the order of 39.7 crore around 2.8 crore in the organized sector and 36.9 crore (about 93%) in the unorganized sector. out of 36.9 crore workers in the unorganized sector, 23.7 crore workers are employed in agricultural sector, about 1.7 crore in construction work, 4.1 crore in manufacturing, 3.7 crore in trade and 3.7 crore in transport, communication and services. The need was felt, therefore, to take urgent steps in consultation with the unorganized sector and to bring them under various social security schemes available to the labourers in the organized sector. This research paper attempts to analyse Issues on Social Security under Organized and Unorganized sectors.

The concept of social security works on the principle of social partnership for a social cause. It is a dynamic concept that widens the scope and dimension of responsibility of protection of individuals against eventualities that on load to physical, financial or emotional distress. In other words, social security aims at improving the quality of life of productive workers through a well planned, deliberate and sustained social effort and involvement, while also caring for the old and the infirm. A life free from want, misery and deprivation is the goal. The success of any social security system, thus, depends on the extent to which it negates the ill-effects of death, disease or disability besides other contingencies leading to destitution or deprivation. It helps to create a more positive attitude to the challenge of globalization and the consequent structural and technological changes. Social security measures draw their strength from the Directive Principle of State Policy and also the Concurrent List of the Constitution of India.

With changing time the working class has greater expectations from the social security apparatus to provide the necessary safeguard. Social protection is increasingly viewed as an integral part of the development process. Social Security programmes vary according to the needs of the people depending on their employment and income status. The crucial factor to be kept in mind while assessing our social security arrangements is the deep diversity in the external circumstances and needs of workface and its dependants.

It is estimated that globally there are over two billion people who are not covered by any form of social security protection. This is a major challenge to the existing social security system that has evolved in the last century in the form of institutional support required by all persons in order of losses due to sickness, injury, loss of income and inability to work.

Organized and Unorganized Sectors

The organized sector includes primarily those establishments which are covered by the Factories Act, 1948, the shops and Commercial Establishments Acts of state governments, the Industrial Employment Standing Orders Act, 1946 etc. This sector already has a structure through which social security benefits are extended to workers covered under these legislations. Institutionalized social security cover is provided through the EPFO and ESIC schemes.

The unorganized sector on the other hand is characterized by lack of labour law coverage, seasonal and temporary forms of employment, High labour mobility, discretionary wages, dispersed nature of operations, casualization of labour, lack of organizational support, low bargaining power, etc. all of which make it vulnerable to socio-economic hardships. The nature of work in the unorganized sector varies between regions and also between rural and urban areas, which may include remote rural areas as well as sometimes the most inhospitable urban concentrations. In the rural areas it comprises landless agricultural labourers, small and marginal farmers, share croppers, persons engaged in animal husbandry, fishing, horticulture, bee-keeping and toddy-tapping, forest workers, rural-artisans, etc. Whereas in the urban areas, it comprises mainly manual labourers in construction, carpentry, trade transport, communication etc. and also includes street vendors, hawkers, head load workers, cobblers, tinsmiths, garment makers, etc.

Keeping in view the social security needs of the workers, Government set up the second National Commission on Labour to suggest rationalization of existing labour laws in the organized sector and an umbrella legislation to the workers in the unorganized sector. The commission was mandated to recommend improvements in the effectiveness of the measures relating to social security, occupational health and safety, minimum wages, the linkages between wages and productivity. And also to recommend safeguards and facilities required for women and handicapped workers. Social security to the organized workforce, continued to be government's priority even in the era of liberalization.

6

Developing Labour Cooperatives under the Reigns of Globalization

Samwel Kakuko Lopoyetum and P. Selvamani

An Overview of Liberation and Labour Cooperatives

Labour Cooperatives are highly potential instrument for socio-economic growth and development especially in rural, semi-urban and tribal areas. It is necessary to strengthen the performance of labour cooperatives to ensure better utilization of available and scare resources and to ensure stable employment opportunities at fair wage rate to the unemployed and underemployed working population in the country. It is disheartening that, the plight of unskilled labourers is serious rather than skilled labourers. It is estimated that, nearly 37% of the rural population of India consists of unskilled workers, economically weak and most of them are living below poverty line. They are financially weak, but quantitatively large in number and mostly found in both rural and urban areas.

Liberalization and Labour Cooperatives

Liberalization simply means to remove quantitative controls from the market. It would mean that, a market is liberalized if there are no restrictions controls, quantitative or other imposed restrictions on either the buyers or sellers or in the market environment. Hence, Labour cooperatives must take advantage of this particular environment and make their businesses more effective and efficient.

Most of the developed countries are nowadays facing and experiencing hardships to retain and gain higher employment growth of their economies. Most of the developing countries are mainly emphasizing on the economic reforms and stressed on the gradual growth on the business expansion, diversification, technological upgradation, disinvestments, privatization and foreign trade, with the intention to capture the world market. The contribution of Labour cooperatives in the economic reforms and liberation must also be felt from time to time.

The prospects of human resource potential in India are strong and formed the component of direct promotion of economic growth and development. But the rate of unemployment in developing countries are ever increasing, even though there is upsurge in development of manufacturing sector and higher growth in the service sectors, ICT, is very particular unique in this respect. Therefore, Labour cooperatives have greater role to play in the long-run.

After a splendid 15 years of economic reform in India, the unemployment rate has risen at the alarming rate. Undoubtedly, there is growth in economical terms, but at the cost of labour and labour market. Hence, there is need for the formation of labour cooperatives to provide gainful employment for the population.

Need for Labour Cooperatives in the Era of Globalization

There is an imperative need to develop labour cooperative movement in the country to promote social justice and eliminate exploitation by the middlemen or labour contractors. Moreover, the labour cooperatives may be an important channel for generation of employment/jobs opportunities to mass on the long-term basis. The labour cooperatives can involve themselves in road and house constructions, forestry projects, rural projects, and creation of public assets and in urban areas to create enormous employment opportunities in the present changing environment. However, they can do various public works and job works of routine nature which are to be completed at places like railway stations, docks, etc.,

Therefore, the formation of labour cooperative organizations can assist to serve needed employment agencies and opportunities particularly in the changing environment. Labour cooperatives can ensure maximum and optimum utilization of available scarce resources, which leads to develop more number of employment/ jobs to the weaker section of the community. In this regard, the State and Central Governments should provide positive support and facilities to them in terms of financial and non-financial assistance, strengthening their working operations, ensuring efficient and effective management administration.

Labour cooperatives are required especially at the grassroots levels to promote employment opportunities and protect the interest of rural poor and other weaker sections of the community especially those persons based in the rural areas. Further, labour cooperatives can provide a simple, viable and dynamic ownership structure for business, which would eventually to capture and build an active entrepreneurial skill among its members. As a result, labour cooperatives can distribute the fruits of Democratic management and control, ownership, financial and non-financial benefits equitably to them and it can be proud of itself in providing adequate services to the community, workers, and members in the present changing environment.

Further, there is an urgent need to sensitize Government functionaries, agencies, organizations and leaders at various level to formulate strategies to promote labour cooperatives and help them to achieve their objectives with concerted efforts.

Labour Market and Labour Force in the Present Environment

Labour force is divided into four segments based on their activity statuses viz: Self-employed, wage and salary earnings, casual and unemployed. Of these, self employed are most loosely connected to labour market, because of the possibilities of work sharing and work spreading in a self-employed enterprise discussed in detail by the Dantwala Committee (1970). According to NSSO, 55th round survey-report No.458 depicts that nearly 52 percent of the Indian Labour Force was self-employed, a little less than one-third was casual labour, about 14 percent wage and salary earning and a little over 2 percent unemployed. Hence, there is scope for the formation of labour cooperatives in the present economic environment.

Economic Growth and Labour Market in the Present Environment

In urban India, the deceleration and decline in organized sector employment is one the most disturbing features of the period after 1990's, especially given that industrial output increased manifold and the service sector was the most dynamic element in national income growth. This was due to the collapse in public sector employment, since private organized sector employment did not increase fast enough to compensate. In such situation, cooperative sector and Labour cooperatives can be roped in to mitigate the problems faced by the economy.

There are several reasons why the pattern of growth are different over the 1990s and did not generate sufficient employment even in the urban areas. Economic measures worked against the interests of most small producers, who accounted for not only the most labour intensive forms of urban production but also the dominant part of urban manufacturing employment.

Manufacturing experts strove to become or remain competitive in an increasingly difficult international environment, they were forced not only to find various ways of making labour more "flexible" that ever but also to adopt relatively capital intensive new technologies that could ensure the quality and consistency that were required in world markets. This is a typical case of present environment.

Labour market in the context of New Economic Environment requires a lot of labour market flexibility and integration. In the post-liberalization economy the labour market and work force may require a lot of reforms large numbers of workers are displaced and the pattern of employment has changed as a result of liberalization. Some previous studies indicate that the formal sector employment is lost as a result of policy reforms. At the same time the informal sector labour force and productivity has increased. Labour cooperatives must take advantage of this present environment.

The labour market is taking longer time to accelerate itself with the changing environment. Therefore, labour market and Labour cooperatives should be given top priority in all the planning and policy orientation in the New Economic Environment. The excess rigidity in labour laws is not supporting employment creation. The redeployment of labour must be provided and supported through some tangible programmes and schemes which can be implemented through Labour cooperative organizations. There is need for substantive policy intervention and promotion in the rural and urban labour market. The significance of informal labour in the New Economic Environment must be given extra focus due to insecurities and vulnerability existing in the present Environment.

In manufacturing sector, substantial number of employees have shifted from one place to another and from regular to contract basis. This has extremely interfered with the employees structural system. It mainly aimed at cost reduction; reduction of overhead charges and innovative technology and upgradation leading to employees lay out. There is also insignificance importance given to labour unions. For example in Tamilnadu (Tirupur) more than 264 dying factories were closed; as a result 25,000 workers lost their jobs (Dinamalar Daily 11.11.2005). They can easily form labour cooperatives or Workers cooperative society to mitigate their problems.

Employment Opportunities through Labour cooperatives the New Economic Environment and Contemporary era of Privatization, Liberalization and Globalization in the New Economic Environment, more opportunities are existing in the informal and formal sector and therefore, it needs to be enhanced and channeled through Labour cooperative sector. The Indian development plan and employment scenario must meet the requirement of backlog of unemployed persons and promote the productivity of employment, particularly in the cooperative sector and Labour cooperatives. Because in the present environment, the wage system is controversial, hence there is need for synchronizing action. Suppose, the seasonal workers, contract workers who may not be getting uniformity in treatment and appropriate wage structure can be synchronized in a scientific manner and their problems mitigated through Labour cooperative organizations .

By and large economic reforms have aimed at labour intensive production and manufacturing system. The labour force participation rate declined in 1999 – 2000 as compared with 1993 – 1994, which is reflected in a sharp deceleration in the growth of the labour force from 2.29 percent per annum in 1987 – 88 to 1993 – 94, to 1.03 percent per annum in the period 1993 – 94 to 1999 – 2000. The deceleration in employment is therefore also associated with a sharp decline in the growth of the labour force and poor response in the labour market. Hence, there is imperative need for the formation of the Labour cooperative societies.

In rural and urban areas, large number of self and wage employment can be promoted and encouraged through Labour cooperative organizations. Even the major programmes which are meant to eliminate poverty and generate employment opportunities can be implemented through Labour cooperative societies. The programmes such as: Jawahar Gram Samridhi Yojana (JGSY), Swarnjayanthi Gram Swarozgar Yojana (SGSY), Employment Assurance Scheme (EAS), Sampoorna Grameen Rozgar Yojana (SGRY), National Social Assistance Programme (NSAP). Pradhan Mantri Gramodaya Yojana (PMGY), Swarna Jayanti Swa Rozgar Yojana (SJSRY), Indira Awaas Yojana (IAY), Food and Work Programme (FWP), Annapurna, Krishi Shramik Samajik Suraksha Yojana, and Shiksha Sahayog Yojana are all aimed at achieving this objective. Hence, there is paramount need to have clear policy note and objective on Labour cooperatives and its role in the elimination of poverty and creation of gainful employment.

Also, these programmes are implemented as target support measures and to offer re-employment services. The problem of regional employment imbalances are very common in India. These programmes must support on the attainment of efficiency goals, higher productivity to enable job seekers make good use of their skills and knowledge. Labour cooperatives must ensure a balancing environment in both formal and informal sector labour potentiality, skill development and skill upgradation in the new economic environment in the present changing environment.

Fine tuning of the Formal Sector and Informal Sector Enterprises through Cooperative Sector and Labour Cooperative

Societies Generally, organized sector labours have social protection and must get safeguarded from eternal environment in their working conditions. But at the same time, liberalization and globalization which have influenced the overall paradigm shift and change of job opportunity and employment scenario is prevailing in the Indian economic system. Here, there is imperative need for the formation of the labour cooperative societies. In fact, most of the Government sector organizations and industries were undergoing privatization process which have thrown out large number of workers. This workers can gainfully from Labour cooperative societies. In this context, the job environment and structure has entirely changed till now which can pave way for the provision of labour cooperatives. Things must change in favour of the formal and informal sector labour cooperative enterprises in the present changing environment.

Paradoxically, Indian Industrial sector has drastically changed and infact increasing productivity is being witnessed. At the same time, labour productivity and efficiency is also increasing in informal labour sector. Hence, there is need for fine-tuning the formal and informal sector through labour cooperative enterprises in the new economic environment.

Upgradation of Labour Force through Labour Cooperative Societies in the New Economic Environment In the labour market, a large number of labour contribution and usage are mainly found involved in industrial, agriculture, manufacturing, casual work etc., They can be upgraded by the formation of the labour cooperative societies. We can have upgradation of labour force in all these areas, which lead to increase of income, job security etc., If their working hours and overall duty arrangements and responsibility is fixed on cooperative contract basis they could survive in the long-term goal achievement and job satisfaction in the present new economic environment. But, simultaneously, their working efficiency, skill, responsibility should be measured in order to make better quality of work output in the labour cooperative society.

A paradigm shift in labour market in the new economic environment is mainly focusing on efficiency and productivity of labour force in both formal and informal sector through labour cooperative societies. It is essential to adopt practical reform measures in labour force, labour market, labour productivity to embrace the structural change taking place in the new economic environment. The shift must mainly dwelt on higher productive employment, enhancement of social security measures, marginal contribution, incremental income and comprehensive rural industrialization leading to synergistic approach of organized and unorganized sector through cooperative sector in the 21st Century.

Table – 1: Performance Indicators of Forest Labour Cooperatives for Weaker Sections (Primary level) in India (Rs. In Million)

S. No.	*Particulars of indicators*	*1998-1999*	*1999-2000*
1	No. of Forest Labour Cooperatives	3401	3408
2	Membership	0.74043	0.7395
3	Share capital	52.8	53.57
4	Working capital	1607.3	1751.6
5	Business Turnover	521.3	521.4
6	Assets	1381.8	1538.1
7	Value of Forest Contract taken up	234.9	407.2
8	Value of Contract Awarded by Govt.	91.5%	95.5%
9	Value of Forest Produce Collected	260.3	390.6
10	Value of Sales	389.4	459.9
11	Societies in Profit Making	40%	39%

Source: Indian Cooperative Movement-A Profile 2002, National Cooperative Union of India.

This table presents the status of labour cooperatives for the weaker sections at primary level in India during 1998-1999 and 1999-2000. The performance indicators used to assess the status are; number of forest labour cooperatives, membership, share capital, working capital, business turnover, assets, values etc.,

During 1998-1999, societies in profit constitute 40% and during 1999-2000 it constituted 39%. Simultaneously, though the value of contract awarded by Government increased from 91.5 percent to 95.5 percent. There is ample scope and potentiality of the Government to award contracts to the labour cooperatives in the present changing environment.

Table – 2 : Progress of Labour Contract and Construction Cooperative Societies in India (Rs. Millennium)

Year	No. Contract Labour	Membership (Contract Labour)	No. Forest	Membership (Forest)
1990-91	18411 (----)	10211 (----)	3269 (----)	4022 (----)
1991-92	20121 (9.78)	11126 (8.96)	3346 (2.36)	3471 (-13.70)
1992-93	22535 (12.00)	10031 (-9.84)	4418 (32.04)	6502 (87.32)
1993-94	23382 (3.76)	13104 (30.64)	3648 (-17.43)	6003 (-7.67)
1994-95	24457 (4.60)	13194 (0.69)	3738 (2.47)	6275 (4.53)
1995-96	27099 (10.80)	13670 (3.61)	3854 (3.16)	7638 (21.72)
1997-98	28958 (6.86)	15136 (10.72)	3401 (11.75)	7404 (-3.06)
1998-99	29779 (2.84)	15936 (5.29)	3401 (0.00)	7404 (0.00)
1999-2000	30428 (2.18)	16718 (4.91)	3408 (0.21)	7395 (-0.12)

Source: Indian Cooperative Movement-A Profile 2002, National Cooperative Union of India.

At the moment, there are 34,744 primary labour/construction and forest cooperative located in 146 districts and 14 state level federations which are working for the betterment of labourers, with a total membership of 24.10 lakhs in India. The above table depicts the progress of labour contract and construction cooperatives in India. The progress and growth is indicated interms of their growth rate. Also, this table indicates that there was fluctuation in the growth and progress of labour contract and construction cooperative societies and its membership. The study reveals that, the number of labour contract cooperatives reduced by 7.6 fold from 1991-1992 (9.78) to 1999-2000 (2.18) and the number of forest cooperative also reduced by 2.15 fold in 1991 (2.36) to 1999-2000(0.21). The outcome of the analysis indicates "declining trend and slow growth in the labour contract and construction cooperatives in India". Hence, there is imperative and urgent need for the State and Central Government for taking appropriate measures to make labour contract and construction cooperatives and forest cooperatives more vibrant, viable, productive, profitable and survive and sustain in the changing environment.

Management of Labour Cooperatives in the Present Globalization Environment

Generally, labour cooperatives are managed by the elected Board of Directors (BOD's). The Board of Directors are the supreme authority to take and handle all issues concerning the operations, working and management of labour cooperative including policy and decision making process. They handle programme scheduling and implementations, framing rules and regulations, and allotment of funds etc., But, unfortunately at present, In Tamilnadu, labour cooperatives are fully managed and controlled by the Special Officers (SO's), even in the Centenary celebration of cooperative movement in India, the entire cooperative sector is stuffed and strangulated by the Government.

Progress, Growth and Development of Labour Cooperatives

In the globalization environment and changing environment, there are issues emerging with regards to the growth and development of labour cooperatives which should be considered as components and yardstick/instrument for socio-economic, cultural development as well as human advancement in the present changing environment. Labour cooperatives helps in improving the social conditions, economic up-liftment and cultural situations of rural people and encouraging their spirit of initiative. The progress, growth and development of labour cooperatives are presented in tables.

Table – 3 : State-wise Labour Contract/Construction and Forest Labour Cooperatives

Name of the State	*No. of Labour Construction Cooperatives*	*No. of Forest Labour Cooperatives*
Tamilnadu	226	40
Pondicherry	2	1
Andhra Pradesh	4520	59
Karnataka	296	55
Kerala	592	56

Source: Indian Cooperative Movement - A Profile 2003, National Cooperative Union of India.

An analysis of the State-wise labour contract/construction and labour cooperatives during 2003 reveals that Andhra Pradesh had the largest number of forest labour cooperatives (59), followed by Kerala (56) Karnataka (55) and Tamilnadu state (50). Whereas the number of labour construction cooperatives was highest in Andhra Pradesh (4520), followed by Kerala (592) Karnataka (296) and Tamilnadu state (226). Tamilnadu, Andhra Pradesh, Karnataka and Kerala states and Union Territory have been taking keen interest in the development of labour cooperative movement in their states. It heartening that, Kerala state Government has decided to provide a maximum of 20% contract value as advance to these cooperative societies, subject to a maximum value of Rs. 20, 000/- in respect of all works. There is imperative need to make them more effective and efficient in the present changing environment. They can apply principle of management and professionalization of their operation to compete with other organizations.

Structure of Labour Cooperatives

The structure of labour cooperatives consist of Primary Labour Cooperatives, District Labour Cooperatives, State Labour Cooperative Federations and National Labour Cooperative

Federation of India. The National Labour Cooperative Federation of India aims protecting the economic and social interest of the weaker section/community and to work for the advancement/ betterment of labourers in India. In order to achieve this purpose, these structural arrangements are mainly geared to organize, promote, coordinate, assist and develop working and operations of labour cooperatives organizations. The District level federation can hope to become self-reliant, self-reliance and self-sufficient to provide goods and service for the betterment of members- labour cooperatives in the long run.

Impact and Effect of Globalization on Labour Cooperatives

As per the IMF Staff Report, "Globalization refers to the increasing integration of the economies around the world, particularly through trade and financial flows". The term some times also refer to the movement of people (labour) and knowledge (technology) across international borders. Further Globalization is a reality which means that different things may happen to people (labour) in different situations or environment.

In the present changing environment Globalisation produces benefits as well as threats or even negative impact to labour cooperatives. One of the threats is loosing of its own local identity, primarily in terms of socio-cultural values and philosophical-moral values of cooperatives and many other threats are plainly prevailing in an environment which is "creative destruction". The foremost benefit is financial and economic growth and development of labour cooperatives. Because of the international competition the general trend is how to attain the reduction in the cost of commodities and cost of production. Multi-nationals are more willing to provide technology transfer, knowledge management, Information and Communication Technology (ICT) which was not the case a couple of decades ago, hence this is a new changing environment for the labour cooperative societies.

By adopting the Globalization process and economic reforms measures the number of Multinational companies, Private corporations and enterprises have emerged and even providing housing and other construction loans to people at a very cheaper price with required amount is the most common scenario in the present economic environment. But, at the same time, Government also has not provided a funds/loans/financial packages to labour cooperatives in the wake of new economic reform and changing policies. As a result, the labour cooperatives cannot provide loans to its members at a very reasonable price/ rate of interest for different construction purposes. So, it is very difficult to manage labour cooperative in the presence of private competitors especially in the post liberalization and Globalisation (changing) environment.

Even though, in the globalization environment, labour cooperatives are facing large number of threats to survive in the present conditions, it has chances to achieve sustainable progress, growth and development by cost reduction of production, tools, equipments, technology transfer, information through media and they can make use Internet, and they can sign Memorandum of Understandings (MoU's) with other types of cooperative business organizations.

Further, survival in the global competitive environment with less and less Government policy support would call for restructuring of labour cooperatives for better democratic representation, participation of members, faster decision-making process in implementation of business plans and contracts in the present changing environment.

Labour Cooperatives and Employment Creation

In India, labour cooperatives were introduced for protecting the economically weaker sections of society against exploitation by private contractors or private enterprises. At present, there are nearly 29,000 labour contract and construction cooperatives working for poor people, of which 12.1% represent tribal labour cooperative and 87.9 % non-tribal labour cooperatives. These cooperatives are involved in the primary process of making and creating employment opportunities for labourers to remove the low level coverage of labour force and promote gainful employment opportunities for the labourers.

Further, the Government of India is extending its financial assistance to labour cooperatives through a central sector scheme to empower the weaker sections through labour cooperative societies, which can promote more employment opportunities in the long-run.

Social Protection and Organizational Sustainability of Labour Cooperatives

Even in the era of globalization, most informal labourers remain unprotected and do not have any social security measures or protection. In order to ensure social protection for informal labourers, the labour cooperatives must organize informal laboureres and bring them under the umbrella of cooperative fold. They can achieve their aim/goals by organizing various programmes in a sustainable manner, they can even introduce different insurance scheme and service to members. Further, labour cooperatives have to build concrete alliances and relationship with other cooperatives and even local progressive NGO's.

Labour cooperatives can achieve organizational sustainability by ensuring effective member participation and proper representation of informal labourers/workers in making the policy formulation needs and its effective and efficient implementation. There are possibilities for labour cooperatives to become sustainable organization by stable funding, payment of labourers for their services, involving themselves in the savings, credit and adopting innovative financing methods.

Capacity Building and Bargaining Strength of Labour Cooperatives

Labour cooperatives should have dynamic capacity building programmes and policies for formal and informal labourers to survive and sustain in the era of globalization and changing environment. The capacity building measures should include various managerial skill developments programmes including organizing, leadership training programmes, technical and decision-making methods and programmes.

Labour cooperatives have to create collective bargaining strategies for both statutory and adhoc, for labourers and to develop a strong and viable informal labourers net work through creating pressure for collective bargaining strategies and measures.

Major Problems of Labour Cooperatives in the Globalization Environment

At present, labour cooperatives are facing financial constraints, which leads to them not able to fulfill their financial requirements. They cannot meet the financial requirements of the members with in a stipulated time period. The Government has not arranged any skill up-gradation and development training programmes for the employees of labour cooperatives.

Mal-practice and mis-utilization of funds by the employees of labour cooperatives. They could not get any construction contracts from the Governments (both Central and State). As a result, labour cooperatives may not be able to manage competition from private contractors. Even in the globalization and new economic environment, labour cooperatives have not been maintaining proper and good relationship with other forms of cooperatives business organizations.

Most of the labour cooperatives are fully dependent on surplus funds available with District Central Cooperative Banks (DCCB's) for its working capital, financial needs and loans. There are diversified sources of funds for the labour cooperatives. There is hardly any provision for long-term financing for purchasing of heavy equipments required by construction industry.

Labour cooperatives are also facing constrains in the form of paying heavy rent for acquiring services of costly equipments like road-rollers etc. The socio-economically weaker section who are also considered to live below poverty line, village artisans, Agricultural labourers, forest labourers, beedi workers, construction workers, and fishermen have been exploited in terms of human resources and labour efforts. They are mainly exploited in terms of more working hours, low wages, and inadequate health and welfare facilities. There are adequate indicators that, all these groups of people still are unorganized, even there are innumerable changes taking place in the present economic environment.

Labour cooperatives and its member's performance have not been satisfactory for a long period of time. Their meager performance is a result of large number of untrained, unskilled and unqualified labourers etc. The financial resources of labour cooperatives have become poor and poorer everyday. The main reason is poor financial base and low level of share capital contribution by the Government, members and more often, they are being prevented to raise funds from other (external) sources.

Large number of labour cooperative members are uneducated, tradition bound, conservative and superstitious, therefore you cannot expect higher efficiency and effectiveness in their business transactions. Labour cooperatives, especially at the primary level are frequently appointing mediocre and professionally untrained personnel and unqualified staff members to manage their affairs. This would lead to mis-management and mal-administration of the business activities of the society.

The primary level labour cooperatives are becoming dormant due to inadequate financial transactions and dismal managerial support from the Government.

Measures for Strengthening the Structure of Labour Cooperatives

The prospects of labour cooperatives can become brighter if the Government takes right measures to reserve all the forest products for forest labour cooperatives and protect all the tribal community from exploitation emanating from nook and corner of the society.

The Government should also ensure "commercial exploitation of forest to be entrusted to cooperative sector (labour cooperatives) rather than private contractors". Because it serves larger interest in term of the community in the long-run. There is paramount need to promote growth and development of labour cooperative by initiating positive policies, extending adequate concessions and facilities, and financial assistance viz., this can be done by means of subsidy and share capital participation.

The Government should give more than 10% of tender works/construction works to labour contract and forest labour cooperatives over the lowest tender of private contractors. In this way, they will feel motivated and encouraged. The policy makers, administrators and Government functionaries should give all unskilled and skilled works to be undertaken by the labour cooperatives without assigning any type of pre-conditions or limitation.

The state Government should extend adequate support not only in the form of financial and administrative but also in the form of reorganization, re-engineering, remodeling, revitalization, rejuvenation and diversification of business activities to improve their operational efficiency and management.

Further, the State Government should make adequate provision in the budgetary provision for share capital, working capital and different type of subsidy for purchase of tools, equipment, machineries, setting up of complete infrastructure etc.

Most of the members of labour cooperatives are living below poverty line. Hence, there is limited scope for contributing adequately to build-up the financial base for labour cooperative society. Therefore, it is essential for the Government to extend adequate financial concession to these societies in the form of payment of "Earnest Money" and "Security Deposit" and / or any suitable arrangement to boost up their financial standing in the open market economy.

The State Government should make arrangement for amending their Act, Rules, and Regulations of labour cooperative for ultimately ensuring that the actual workers become members even including their wife's as independent members. Moreover, these aspects can be treated and taken as the basic qualifications for entering into labour cooperative societies.

Besides the Government support, there are large number of apex level cooperative business organizations such as, NCUI, NCDC, NABARD and Cooperative Banks which should make comprehensive arrangements for providing adequate financial assistance to labour cooperatives, particularly in the era of economic Liberalization and Globalization.

The Government may opt for revising their reform policy with regard to labour cooperatives and sufficient works may be awarded to them, so as to make the labour cooperatives become economically viable and financially sound. The Government should implement the "National Rural Employment Guarantee Scheme" through labour cooperative societies.

The Government should also provide adequate share capital and financial assistance to enable the labour cooperative federations to rightly perform it's promotional and developmental activities, particularly in this era of economic reforms. The work awarding agencies should ensure regular work and employment to the members of labour cooperatives. The work awarding agencies should interact with the District federation in the event of awarding the contract.

It is necessary to install efficient information and communication system, the strong will of the state Government can assist to involve in the execution of works at the district level and primary level and ensure better method of Information and Communication Technology (ICT).

The Government may consider and think in terms of promoting insurance for unorganized workers and forest labourers through labour cooperative set-up. Even the promotion of micro-insurance system through labour cooperatives might seem imperative in the era of economic liberalization and Globalization.

Labour cooperatives can be encourage by the Government to provide and implement the various welfare schemes related to healthcare and family care, crèches, pure drinking water and educational facilities to labourers and its members.

Further, it is highly essential to strengthen the structure of labour cooperatives to ensure maximum utilization of all available scarce resources in a proper way for the creation of public assets creation of employment opportunities, which in turn provide continuous gainful employment opportunities to unemployed and under employed working population, especially in the area of operation of primary level cooperative societies. Also, they can strengthen their structure by providing skill development training programme and latest knowledge management skill to its employees both on-the-job training and off-the-job training. Governments both Central and State should provide maximum financial and non-financial promote progressive growth and development of labour cooperatives in the present changing environment.

Suggestions for Enhancing Labour Cooperatives in the Present Changing Environment

There is an imperative need to enhance labour cooperative in the present changing environment. The authors have provided the following suggestions:

- Labour cooperatives should disseminate and improve their members knowledge in terms of its principle, methods, possibilities of competing with private agencies administration, management, nature, importance etc., in line with the present changing environment.
- Labour cooperatives should take suitable measures to ensure proper auditing of its accounts within a stipulated period of time, which eventually should indicate the real picture of labour cooperatives to members, people and create good image among the community.
- In order to increase thrift and saving habits of its members, labour cooperatives can enhance its funds (financial) position. Also, the governments should facilitate credit guarantee schemes for all labour cooperatives.
- Labour cooperatives should take certain work projects associated with greater labour participation. Through implementation of these project works, there is high possibility to promote and generate employment opportunities to labourers.
- Both Central and State Governments should provide and extend their financial and non-financial (technical) assistance for labour cooperatives in order to improve socio-economic conditions of poor and weaker sections.
- Labour cooperatives should also make concerted efforts to promote leadership-training programmes among skilled and unskilled workers, which can promote the welfare of weaker sections of the society.
- In order to compete with private and multinational contractors, Governments, NCDC, NCUI and NABARD have to provide financial package for strengthen the financial health (base) and soundness of labour cooperatives in the present changing environment.
- Labour cooperatives have to organize frequent skill development training programmes among unorganized labour, which would make labour cooperatives to become more sound, viable and profitable. Further, promotion of skill development among its members social justice and empowerment of weaker section of society in the long-run.

- Labour cooperatives should be exempted from paying Income Tax and Government should give due preference in allocation of contract works to labour cooperatives, which enable them to improve the socio-economic of people, empower the local community and to ensure their participation in labour cooperatives.
- National and State Federation of labour cooperatives have to create revolving funds for purchasing heavy equipments, machines and tools by labour cooperatives.
- Governments should provide and create suitable and conducive environment (social, legal and political etc.,) for the large-scale creation of sustainable job/work opportunities to labourers.
- The National Labour Cooperative Federation may undertake functions as agency for export of labour to overseas (abroad) through ministry of labour, which may lead to reduce unemployment and underemployment problem in the country in the long-run.
- Special attention may be paid and given through imparting technical skills to the members of labour cooperatives to become financially viable, technically strong in the Globalization and present changing environment.
- The labour cooperatives have to take special measures and efforts for improving the working conditions of women labourers and general exemption from payment of earnest money and security deposits in the labour cooperative societies.

Conclusion

It is sad that even in the era of economic liberalization, globalization, and changing economic environment there is no line of credit to meet the financial requirements of labour cooperatives. Therefore, concessional finance through cooperative banking structures, Governments and NABARD may be essential for the growth and development of labour cooperatives organizations in the present globalization environment. Also needs preferential treatment to labour cooperatives are essential for survival of labour cooperatives. There is need for effective and efficient management and administration of labour cooperatives, outlook towards labour cooperatives as balancing center for growth and development of the Indian economy. Moreover, labour cooperatives are highly essential and indispensable under the reigns of globalization.

Selected References

Kamat, *"New Dimensions of Cooperative Management"*, Himalaya Publishing House, New Delhi, 2002, Page No. 405 - 411.

Kapadia, Karin etc., *"Worlds of Industrial Labour"*, Sage Publication, New Delhi, 1999, Page No. 18 -30.

Bhagwati Pradad etc., *"Labour Contracting Cooperatives and Employment Generation"*, The Cooperator, No. 7, Vol. 38, Page No. 399, January - 2001.

Pandey, *"Labour Cooperatives: Some Issues"*, The Cooperator, No. 5, Vol. 42, Page No. 226 – 228, November – 2004.

Samwel Kakuko Lopoyetum and Selvamani P., *"A Paradigm shift of Cooperative Leadership in the era of Economic Liberalization and Globalization"*, The Cooperator, No.11, Vol. 41, Page No. 456-463, May 2004.

Samwel Kakuko Lopoyetum etc., *"Fundamental Management Dimensions of Cooperatives: An Analysis of Major Imperative issues"*, Indian Cooperative Review, No. 4, Vol. 40, Page No. 245, April - 2003.

Rodger and Gerry etc., *"The Creation of Employment in Segmented Labour Markets: A General Problem and its implications in India"*, Indian Journal of Labour Economics, No. 1, Vol. 36, Page No. 39, 1993.

Ruddar Datt, *"Economic Reforms, Labour and Employment Generation"*, Deep Publication Pvt. Ltd., New Delhi, 2003, Page No. 13-31.

12th Indian Cooperative Congress, *Labour cooperatives – Progress and Problems*, National Cooperative Union of India (NCUI), New Delhi, Page No.1-10, 29 – 30th December, 1992.

Bhagwati Prasad, *"Human Resource Development for SCBs, DCCBs, and PACBs"*, The Cooperator, No.1, Vol. 42, Page 9 -14, July 2004.

Mahalingam S., *"Human Relations and Productivity in Cooperatives"*, Tamilnadu Journal of Cooperation, No. 4, Vol. 4, Page 5-8, February – 2004.

Bhagwati Prasad, *"Human Resource Management and Development in Cooperatives"*, The Cooperator, No.2, Vol.43, Page 66-68. August - 2005.

Sharma S.D., *"Human Resource Development Utilization in Cooperatives: Experience of South Asia"*, The Cooperator, No.7, Vol.38, Page 293- 95, January - 2001.

Prabhakar Sharma & Joglekar, *"Upgradation of Handloom Cooperatives"*, Indian Cooperative Review, No.3, Vol. 39, Page 235-240, January - 2002.

Khurana M.L., *"Human Resource Management in Housing Cooperatives"*, Cooperative Perspective, No.1, Vol. 38, Page 1–5, April -June, 2004.

Samwel Kakuko Lopoyetum and Selvamani P., *"Strategies for Sustainability of Dairy Cooperative Business Organizations in the Present Environment"*, Indian Cooperative Review, No.4, Vol.43, Pages 653 – 662, May 2004.

7

Social Security for Women Workers in the Unorganized Sector

N. Meenakshisundaram and R. Renganayaki

Social security for all citizens has always been a priority in India. The concept of social security is derived from the provisions of Article 38 of the constitution of India, which requires that the state should promote the welfare of the people by securing and protecting a social order in which justice – social, economic and political-shall inform all institutions of national life.

Today the informal sector accounts for nearly 96 per cent of the workforce. Women particularly are confined to unorganized sector employment, with 96 percent of all female workers being in this sector. Women are concentrated in the lower end of the spectrum, in low paying and insecure jobs. Their work is insecure, irregular and often unrecognized. Her work contribution not only to her own family but also to the development of her village, town and to the country as a whole.

Social Security for Women Workers

1. Child care

The women worker plays the triple role of a worker, a housewife and a mother and child care is often considered as the sole responsibility of the mother. The working mother is often bogged down by the burden of child care. This leads to the decline in the productivity of the mother as well as negative impact on the health of both the mother and the child.

A women worker works for long hours, often seven days a week. She often has to walk long distances by foot or travel in crowded public transport to reach her place of work. A working mother remains exhausted and often very anxious about her child's welfare. Child care provisions relieve the women of one of her multiple burdens, creates time and space and work opportunities for women and support her empowerment. In the absence of adequate child care facilities, a working mothers has no option but to leave the child with a slightly older sibling. A large part of sibling caregivers are girl-children-many of them not above the age when they need care and nurturing themselves. Provisions of child care facilities enable the girl child to attend school and enjoy their own childhood.

2. Maternity Benefits

The most productive years of a women's life are also the reproductive years of her life. In the absence of any provision for maternity leave, a women worker often has to leave her job to have a child. Poor health, additional medical expenses along with loss of employment make the women worker economically vulnerable during the period of childbirth, plunging her into a crisis of borrowing and high interest expenses. She does not take adequate rest and starts working soon after childbirth with adverse effect on her health. This repeated neglect of a women's health during pregnancy and child birth manifests itself into high maternal mortality rate, anaemia and poor health of the women worker.

3. Sickness

Lives of women workers in the unorganized sector are replete with different kinds or risks including personal, occupational and family derived from sickness. Sickness of herself or of immediate family members–may result in loss of employment. With an increasing privatization of the health care services the women worker is forced to shoulder the extra financial burden in times of illness or injury. Thus, she has to meet these expenses by either spending her savings, borrowing from money lenders or selling or mortgaging her assets. As a result, the woman suffers reduction in her income and savings and a simultaneous rise in interest expenses.

The reduction in assets eventually leads to a depletion of her income, borrowing and consequent indebtedness, thus trapping her inexorably in the vicious circle of poverty. A strong body is the only capital that a women worker has.

4. Old Age

An old women worker who has no support and is totally dependent on the others for survival is very vulnerable. Widowhood further adds to her vulnerability. Social security for has her many facets. Income security is only one aspect – she is often forced to work for long hours even when her age does not permit. Old age not only means loss or diminution of her income, it also means loss of her health and rise in the cost of medical care.

Solutions to the Social Security

Child Care

Child care needs to be made the responsibility not only of the woman worker, but also of the family and of the state. All labour legislation should include provision of crèche where there are 10 or more workers, irrespective of the gender of the worker so that whether the worker is a mother or a father, the child can be brought into the crèche. The Integrated Child Development Services (ICDS), is the best known government programme which aims at the total development of young children.

A flexible, autonomous child care fund could be also created. This fund can be drawn to provide child care facilities to all women regardless of income, number of children or other consideration. The fund would be at the state/national level, for administrative convenience and could have multiple sources of raising its income and enjoying autonomy action. A statutory scheme for the implementation of maternity entitlements which would cover all women, under an income criterion. The scheme would provide financial support for childbirth and child care and breast feeding in the first few months of the child's life. The funds would be multistoried including a combination of employer, employee and state contributions through cesses and community contributions. It could be linked with the maternal and child health provisions of the public health system.

Welfare Funds

Welfare funds have been very effective in reaching social security to workers without a clear employer-employee relationship. One major short coming of the existing funds is that they are not so effective for women workers. Women workers are generally in 'weak' sectors like coir, where the fund collection is low. Even when funds exist, the needs of women worker, like maternity benefit, is given low priority. The funds could be made sensitive to the needs of the women workers each existing and future fund should have maternity benefit and child care as one of its activities. Each fund should have women workers on their boards at the decision making position, the structure should be changed to make them more decentralized and more efficient. The structure of the welfare fund could be remodeled so that they are autonomous, decentralized, multi financed and with considerable size of benefits.

A pension scheme with in the existing provident fund Act can be devised for women workers in the unorganized sector which would provide them coverage for old age, disability and widowhood. Different schemes with different rate for different categories of women workers in the unorganized sector could be formulated.

Health Insurance

Health insurance is a major need for workers. It is found that health expenses are the largest major source of debt. At present, women workers, especially in the unorganized sector have no access to any form of health insurance such as the ESIS scheme. (Employees State Insurance Scheme) It is necessary to promote forms of insurance for these workers. There are a number of successful micro insurance schemes which could be up scaled.

The greatest problem facing the actual management of social security systems for unorganized workers is the contentious issue of the collection of finance. The collection of contributions must be timely, time-bound and transparent workers, employers and government-all need to contribute. Each should have clear information about who is contributing what. Joint and participatory management of fund collection, and managing of the fund itself must be undertaken. Amount of funds to be collected should be jointly decided. Accordingly, information should be provided clearly to potential contributions. Fund collection mechanisms should be simple, decentralized and accountable to a local multipartite committee. Periodic but regular review of fund collection and management must be undertaken.

Need for Organizing

In India we have treated social security in the unorganized sector as the obligation of the government where the various government departments are the providers, and the workers and citizens are the 'beneficiaries' or the receivers. This breeds a lack of accountability and inefficiency within the system. However, it has been found that where the workers have been able to organize the system becomes more accountable. It is also found that organized workers begin to crate their own social security systems in which governments can contribute. Further more, participatory and accountable systems also lead to further organizing. We therefore, need to have social security systems, which lead to greater organizing among the unorganized workers. We need to promote membership based organizations which are controlled and managed by the women workers themselves. These can include trade unions, co-operatives, producers associations, etc.

It has been found that certain types of social security systems do promote organizing. In particular, studies of welfare boards have shown that workers tend to organize themselves in order to draw benefits from the boards and also make the boards more effective. Moreover, women workers tend to organize better when they receive child care facilities and other issues relating to child care.

Conclusion

Organizing the women in the unorganized sector and provision of social security are closely linked. From the above stated matters it is clear that the development of social security in India is reasonably good for industrial employees especially to women workers. Finally, it is high time for brining reforms in our outdated social security policies for unorganized sectors. This will give sustainability to basic social security for all in unorganized sector and India would also be able to protect basic human rights of its citizens.

References

Ramnath Sharma, *"Labour Problems Social Security and Welfare"*, A Rajhans Publication, Meerut, pp. 295-310, 1996.

National Commission on Self-employed women and women in the informal sector, Shramshakti, New Delhi, Government of India, pp. 99-102, 1988.

Subrahmanaya R.K.A., *"The unorganized sector: work security and social protection"*, Sage Publication, New Delhi, pp. 29-40, 2000.

8

Globalization and Female Labour Force in Farm Sector

D. Kumar and A. Saleem Batcha

India is primarily an agricultural country. Agriculture forms the backbone of the Indian economy. Nearly 70% of the people in India depend on agriculture for their living. It is the largest and the most important sector in India 50% of the national product constitutes agricultural outputs. In the last few decades, agriculture occupies a place of pride. Being the largest industry in the country, agriculture is the source of livelihood for over 75% of population in the country.

Women play a vital role in rural economy of India. Female constitutes nearly half of the total rural population. The size of the female population in India indicates the potential strength of women in total human resources in the country. Agriculture is the major economic activity for rural women.

Females provide a largest part of unpaid family labour in agriculture and the proportion of women and children in the labour force tends to be higher than in other sectors. The number of women engaged in agriculture is always at high rate. The daily work schedule of the rural women is very demanding and arduous. The day for her starts in the early hours of the morning and she is the last to retire to bed at night. It is estimated that during the peak period women works for about 8-9 hours national sample survey has shown that the percentage contribution of women in agriculture is more than men where as most of the day operations at farm are done by them. In agriculture the nature does the business and man is merely the manager. National Commission for Women reported (1994) that there is exploitation of women agricultural workers and discrimination in wage inspite of the hard work done by them.

This does affect their motivation to engage in different types of income generating activities. It is in this context that the involvement of women in production oriented training and extension programming not only as beneficiaries but also as change agents assumes great significance.

Women as wives and mothers have a considerable part in decision making in the farm and the home. Decision-making is important because much of success of farming depends upon how well the family makes decision. The average number of days that women agricultural labourer get employment in a year is 138 days as compared to 193 days for men. The incidence of unemployment is almost twice of high for female agricultural labourers as for male agricultural labourers. According to the agricultural survey, women are unemployed for 124 days in a year as against men's 75 days of unemployment due to want of work. In India as per 2001 census work participation rate is 39.2% for both men and women taken together. 51.9% for men and 25.7% only for women out of the total female population of 49.8 million, only 25.7% (127.0 million) are female workers. Among the rural female population of 359.8 million, only 31.0% (111.5 million) are female workers.

Changes in the agricultural labour force and its composition are largely influenced by the female component of labour force, therefore it becomes necessary to look at the trends in female labour force are not only more stable. Changes in female rates in the rural areas cannot be explained in similar terms, female participation rates are in general, lower than in the rural areas that in the urban areas. The urban rates shows relatively stable, but the rural rates are unstable and are sensitive to definitions mainly rice and millet growing states and lower in the wheat growing states. Among the agricultural labourers female workers have a relatively larger share that the male workers. It has been reported that women workers in self-employment household activities trend to be under reported and under estimated. Much of the productive work that women do (as in dairying or winnowing rice or grinding flour or storage of gain) is not clearly differentiated from domestic work. On the other hand working for wages outside the household does not suffer from this misclassification, male activities, whether productive or otherwise, do not suffer on this count because a male is expected to be engaged in income generating activities.

The existing structure of women's participation in India's agriculture, as summarized by Unni.

- The functioning of rural market and female labour participation within it are dynamic process influenced by the broad macro process and structural factors.
- Women's participation in the work is dependent on the economic/social status of the households to which they belong and the position of the households in the rural hierarchy.
- In better-endowed households women work to increase households incomes. Women wage or salaried workers and to incomes directly. While women family workers do so indirectly by reducing wage costs.
- Poor households use female participation in the work force as a strategy for survival to maintain their total households real incomes.
- From the employer's point of view, female labour forms a large reserve of cheap docile labour.
- The household strategies of surplus extraction and survival are to large extent, conditioned by the structure and the level of demand.
- The following are the common features of Female Workers in India's agriculture.
- Female agricultural labourers are belonging to the age group between 20 to 60. The reasons are, they are the only wage earners.
- 70% of female agricultural labourers are SC and ST.
- Most of the female workers are uneducated and illiterate.

- Higher percentages of the female workers are living in the improper sanitation condition.
- Family income depends upon the number of working members in their family. There is a significant correlation between size of the family and their income.
- Due to the poor wage income they don't have surplus to save. Wage income only equates the consumption expenditure of the family.
- To meet their social obligation they borrow from moneylenders at high rate of interest.
- Nature of the female labourers works are difficult and important one in the agricultural operations. Such as transplanting, weeding, harvesting, seedling, winnowing. These works are so technical and time consuming one, which lends to health hazards to the workers.
- Since agriculture is a seasonal one, during lean season, only few go for non-farm work but others are kept ideal because they do not know about the non-farm work.
- The only major discrimination is wage between male and female.
- The nature of the work only decides the working hours per day especially in the female works.
- From the above discussion the following suggestions are recommended.
- To improve the efficiency and employment opportunity it is suggested that literacy level should be improved.
- Female workers make use of government programmes for their development. Besides, this programme should be familiar by the government to the rural mass.
- During lean period many supplementary economic programmes could be introduced by the rural development agencies, NGO's and government organizations.
- Effective legal measures should be taken to remove wage discrimination between male and female.
- Female workers themselves form union in order to get their problems settled through the collective bargaining power. To have the union an urgent policy must be enacted by the government through labour welfare ministry at both state and central level.

- To have the social security in par with organized sector works, the government must take the insurance scheme at the village level with low premium amount.
- To enhance the asset position of the female workers assistance may be provided to labourers to develop poultry, sheep rearing, milk animals. These compensate the family consumption expenditure.
- All obstacles to the total participation of women must be removed to ensure that they find themselves on equal terms with men in all aspects of life, social, economic, political and cultural. Growth in Indian agriculture needs to be matched with feminization of agriculture for an overall development of rural economy. Appropriate strategy has to be made to extend the benefits to transfer of technology process to the women, which will help in modernization of agriculture.

References

Economics Survey 1999-2000.

Jeemol Unni, *"Women's participation in Indian Agriculture"*, IJAE Vol. XLIV.

Muthuraja.C, *Women's employment in India's Problems and Prospects*, Peninsular Economist.

9

Unorganized Labour Force in India during the Globalization Era

R. Albert Christopher Dhas and M. Helen Mary Jacqueline

The term 'unorganized labour' has been defined as those workers who have not been able to organise themselves in pursuit of their common interests due to certain constraints like casual nature of employment, ignorance and illiteracy, small and scattered size of establishments, etc. Indian economy is characterised by the existence of high level of informal or unorganized sector. It has been estimated that the workers in the unorganized sector constitute about 80 per cent of the country's total work force and they comprise of subsistence farmers, agricultural workers, fisherfolk, dairy workers and those working in traditional and small manufacturing and service activities.

The overall objective of this paper is to examine the impact of globalization on the unorganized labour force in India. However, the specific objectives are (a) to highlight the major characteristics of unorganized labour, (b) to analyse the broad trends in the growth pattern of non-agricultural enterprises and its employment scenario and (b) to examine the impact of globalization and economic reforms on the unorganized workers in India.

The discussion on this paper is organized in the following manner. In section 1, the extent of unorganized labour and the important characteristics of the unorganized labour in India are discussed. In section 2, the trends in non-agricultural enterprises and their employment scenario are discussed. In section 3, the impact of globalization and economic reforms on the unorganized labour is analysed. The last section summarises the main findings.

Section - 1: Characteristics of Unorganized Labour in India

As per the 2001 census, the total work force in our country is 402 million, of which 313 million are main workers and 89 million are marginal workers. Out of the 313 million main workers, about 285 million is in the unorganised sector, accounting 91 per cent (Government of India, Economic Survey:2002-03).

Ministry of Labour has categorised this unorganized labour force under four groups in terms of occupation, nature of employment, specially distressed categories and service categories. In terms of occupation, it included small and marginal farmers, landless agricultural labourers, share croppers, fishermen and those engaged in animal husbandry, beedi rolling, labeling and packing, building and construction workers, leather workers, weavers, artisans, salt workers, workers in brick kilns and stone quarries, workers in saw mills, oil mills etc. In terms of nature of employment, they are attached agricultural labourers, bonded labourers, migrant workers, contract and casual labourers. Toddy tappers, scavengers, carriers of head loads, drivers of animal driven vehicles, loaders and unloaders, belong to the specially distressed category while midwives, domestic workers, fishermen and women, barbers, vegetable and fruit vendors, newspaper vendors etc. come under the service category. In addition to the above categories, there exists a large section of urorganised labour force such as cobblers, hamals, handicraft artisans, handloom weavers, lady tailors, physically handicapped self-employed persons, rikshaw pullers/ auto drivers, sericulture workers, carpenters, leather and tannery workers, powerloom workers and urban poor.

The extent of unorganised workers is significantly high among agricultural workers, building and other construction workers, and among home based workers. But, the availability of statistical information on its intensity and accuracy vary significantly.

Agricultural workers constitute the largest segment of workers in the unorganised sector and their number according to 1991 Census was 74.6 million. In addition, out of 110 million cultivators, about 50 per cent belong to the category of small and marginal farmers. Many small and marginal farmers, because of their small and uneconomical holdings and low yield, also work on the land of others and hence qualify as agricultural labourers. Further a significant number, about 6 millions, are engaged in rearing livestock, forestry, fishery, orchard and allied activities.

Construction workers constitute the second largest category of workers in the unorganised sector. According to the NSSO estimates, there are about 8.5 million workers engaged in building and other construction works. The construction industry covers a vast field of activity in the civil, mechanical, electrical and public health areas processes. A large number of multinational, national and local companies employ lakhs of such workers. More over, a large number of self employed individuals are engaged in actual construction works and allied activities like white washing, painting, plumbing and fixing of mechanical or electrical fixtures etc.

Home Based Workers are those who are engaged in the production of goods or services for an employed or contractor in an arrangement whereby the work is carried out at the place of the worker's own choice, often the worker's own home. In India, there is no authentic data on home based workers. Official data sources such as Census of India do not recognise these workers as an independent category but have included them in the broad category of those working in house-hold industries. Home based workers are mainly engaged in beedi rolling, garment making, agarbati making, gem cutting, preparation of food items like papad, pickle, etc., handloom, lace and chikan work etc. The beedi rolling industry, which is generally family based, employs about 45 lakh workers out of which 90 per cent are home based workers.

The major characteristics of unorganised workers could be listed as below:

- The unorganised labour is overwhelming in terms of its number range and therefore, they omnipresent throughout India.

- As the unorganised sector suffers from cycles of excessive seasonality of employment, majority of the unorganised workers do not have stable and durable avenues of employment. Even those who appear to be visibly employed are not gainfully and substantially employed, indicating the existence of disguised unemployment.
- The workplace is scattered and fragmented. The workers do the same kind of job(s) in different habitations and may not work and live together in compact geographical areas.
- There is no formal employer-employee relationship between small and marginal farmers, share croppers and agricultural labourers as they work together in situations which may be marginally favourable to one category but may be broadly described as identical.
- In rural areas, the unorganised labour force is highly stratified on caste and community considerations. In urban areas while such considerations are much less, it cannot be said that it is altogether absent as the bulk of the unorganised workers in urban areas are basically migrant workers from rural are
- Workers in the unorganised sector are usually subject to a lot of fads, taboos, and outmoded social customs like child marriage, excessive spending on ceremonial festivities etc. which lead to indebtedness and bondage.
- The unorganised workers are subject to exploitation significantly by the rest of the society. The unorganised workers receive poor working conditions, especially wages much below that in the formal sector, even for closely comparable jobs i.e., where labour productivities are no different. The work status is of inferior quality of work and inferior terms of employment, both remuneration and employment.
- Primitive production technologies and feudal production relations are rampant in the unorganised sector, and they do not permit or encourage the workmen to imbibe and assimilate higher technologies and better production relations. Large scale ignorance and illiteracy and limited exposure to the goings on in the outside world are also responsible for such poor absorption.

- The unorganised workers do not receive sufficient attention from the trade unions.

With this background understanding on the characteristics of the unorganized labour force, the trends in the informal or unorganized non-agricultural enterprises of India from the employment perspective are analysed in the next section.

Section – 2: Trends in Non-Agricultural Enterprises in India

As Indian economy is agriculture-based, its development has been also agri and agro-oriented. In both rural and urban sectors, the developments in the non-agricultural enterprises provide a fillip to the growth in agriculture through its forward and backward linkages. It also absorbs the additional labour forces that are added to the total work force every year and the workers pushed into the unorganised sector from the organised sector. Therefore, the growing importance of non-agricultural sector is an inevitable effect of the process of development in India.

The data on unorganized enterprises are available from Economic Censuses. The first Economic Census was conducted in 1977, covering non-agricultural establishments (employing at least one hired worker on a fairly regular basis). However, a fairly comparable data is available from the second Census (1980) onwards as it covered both agricultural and non-agricultural enterprises of Own Account and establishments. Hence, in order to understand the changing dimensions of non-agricultural enterprises, the data from the Economic Censuses 1980. 1990 and 1998 are analysed (see Table 1).

In terms of absolute numbers, there has been a steady increase in the total number of Non-Agricultural Enterprises and the total employment in it. The number of NAEs has increased from 167 lakhs to 291 lakhs between the years1980 and 1998, recording an increase of about 75 per cent. The total number of employment in the NAEs also showed an increase from 503 lakhs to 738 lakhs during the same period, recording an increase of 47 per cent. It could be seen that the increase in employment is much lower than that of the number of enterprises, indicating the low labour absorption capacity of NAEs.

Table 1: Trends in Non-Agricultural Enterprises (NAEs) in India (1980-98)

Particulars	*Numbers / Percentages*			*Growth Rates (%)*	
	1980	*1990*	*1998*	*1980-90*	*1990-98*
Total Number of Non-Agricultural Enterprises (in lakhs)	167.2	221.9	290.9	3.27	2.20
Total Employment in Non-Agri-cultural Enterprises (in Lakhs)	503.1	656.8	738.3	3.05	1.55
Share of NAEs to the Total Enterprises (in %)	92.03	90.55	88.32		
Share of Rural NAEs to the Total NAEs (in %)	58.27	55.37	53.70		
Share of NAEs workers to the Total Workers in Enterprises (in %)	94.62	93.32	91.57		
Number of Workers per NAEs	3.01	2.96	2.83		

Source: Economic Census: 1998.

In terms of growth rates, a differential pattern of change could be observed between the eighties and the nineties. Both the number of NAEs and employment are at the higher order of growth during the eighties compared to that of nineties, indicating a deceleration of NAEs in India, in recent years. While the number of NAEs recorded an annual growth rate of 3.27 per cent during the eighties, it declined to 2.2 percent during the nineties. The similar decline in the growth rate of employment from 3.05 per cent to 1.55 per cent during the respective periods is also observed.

The relative role played by the Non-Agricultural Enterprises compared to that of Agricultural Enterprises and its changes are revealed by the trends in the share of NAEs to the Total Enterprises, share of employment and the workers per enterprise. The share of NAEs to the Total Enterprises has declined from 92 per cent to 88 per cent between 1980 and 1998. Almost similar decline in the share of workers of NAEs to the total employment (95 to 92 per cent) is also observed during the period under reference. In fact, the share of Rural NAEs to the total NAEs has also shown a marginal decline (from 58 per cent to 54 per cent). Above all, the number of workers per enterprise has shown a steady decline from 3.01 persons to 2.96 persons between 1980 and 1990 and further to 2.83 by 1998. This trend revealed the falling trend in the labour absorption of non-agricultural enterprises. Altogether, the above discussion revealed that the role of NAEs have been declining from the employment perspective in the recent past.

In this context, it is worth analyzing the realized and possible impact of globalisation and economic reforms on the unorganized sector, which is attempted in section 3.

Section – 3 : Globalization, Economic Reforms and Unorganized Workers

The impact of globalization and economic reforms on employment in general is said to be divergent. In fact, unemployment and disguised unemployment are the normal feature of Indian economy. There is heavy dependency on unorganised sector by the labour force for their employment, income and livelihood. In such a situation, the economic policies towards delinking budgetary support to the public sector enterprises and reducing labour absorption in public sector as part of the globalisation strategy leads to adverse effect on employment situation in India. The growth of employment from the Seventies is given in Table 2.

Table 2: Growth of Employment in India

Period	*Growth rate of overall employment*	*Growth rate of employment in the organised sector (%)*		
		Public	***Private***	***Total***
1972-73 to 77-78	2.75	---	---	2.45
1977-78 to 1983	2.36	2.99	1.41	2.48
1983 to 1987-88	1.77	2.17	0.43	1.38
1987-88 to 1993-94	2.37	1.00	1.18	1.05
1993-94 to 1999-2000	1.07	(-)0.03	1.87	0.53

Source: Economic Survey 1998-99 and Planning Commission, 10th Five year Plan, Vol. 1.

It can be seen that the growth rate of organised sector employment maintained its declining trend from the period 1977-88 to 1999-2000. The growth rate of public sector employment declined sharply and this trend continues up to the present. From 1997, the public sector employment grew negatively (Economic Survey: 2002-2003). When the labour absorption in the organised sector declines during the period of reforms, it would naturally push the additional labour force to the unorganised sector leading to further swelling of unorganised workers. The situation gets worsen if pruning or retrenchment activities by the public sector are taken into consideration. Taking into account the backlog of unemployment and overall magnitude of additional employment to be generated, there lies a major challenge for the country. In the context of declining growth rate in employment generation in organised sector and no scope for creating additional jobs, the additional labour force have to find work on self-employed or remain casual workers.

As a large number of labour force is pushed into the unorganised category of workers, the excess labour supply creates disequilibrium or imbalance in the labour market that leads to several adjustments in the unorganised labour economy. The surplus or excess labour supply into the unorganised category leads to partial or casual employment at low wages and with out job or social security of any kind (Rao and Rao: 1994). Unni (2001), based on the study conducted in Ahemedabad highlighted the differential benefit between a regular and casual employee. It revealed that the casual labourers are highly exploited in terms of assurance of employment, contract procedures, paid leave, PF/pension, medical and other benefit and notice for termination.

Another significant impact of globalisation on the unorganised workers is the jobless growth promoted by the new technological changes and structural shifts in the global economy in favour of the so-called new economy. Though a country like India needs a labour intensive technology at least in the unorganised sector to accommodate the job-seeking labour force, the process of globalisation and liberalisation sets on a shift towards capital-intensive technology. Needless to say that in order to meet competition and to increase productive efficiency, firms are forced to modernise their operations involving machinaries, capital and high technologies. The choice of labour intensive technology becomes obsolete.

The immediate and direct consequence of the shift in the industrial technology is the replacement of unskilled personnel with skilled people (Rao and Rao: 1994, Wood: 1997). Under the new production environment, the nature of work changes and that warrants skilled workers. Taking into account the basic qualifications and nature of an Indian unorganised worker, it is difficult to visualise the effort and time needed to shift an unskilled person into a skilled worker. Till then, the inefficiency would continue even in the new production environment.

Section-4: Summary and Conclusion

The foregoing analysis revealed that the impact of globalisation and economic reforms on the unorganised workers in India is more of warning signals. The unorganised workers would expand further due to globalisation. Under the present deprived conditions of unorganised sector, this would lead to imbalance in the labour market leading to more supply of labour, low wages and low level of income. This process of change was getting reflected in the trends in non-agricultural enterprises sector. This situation would affect the social and economic conditions of the unorganised working population. The unorganised workers will be in the highly disadvantageous position as there would be a shift in the technology from labour to capital intensive and use of unskilled to skilled workers. On the whole, the evidences available indicate more of negative implications of globalisation on the unorganized sector and the unorganized labour force.

To conclude, it can be argued that the benefits of globalisation and economic reforms on the Indian economy would get shattered and nullified, if the negative impacts on the unorganised workers are not settled or neutralised. Hence, along with globalisation and restructuring the economy, concerted efforts should be initiated to restructure the unorganised workers towards their benefit so that they would also benefit in that process on the one hand, and on the other, contribute towards the success of globalisation.

References

Alternative Survey Group, Alternative Economic Survey: 1991-1998, Rainbow Publishers Limited, Delhi, 1998.

————————————————, Alternative Economic Survey: 1998-2000, Rainbow Publishers Limited, Delhi, 2000.

Chakraborty, Debashis and Prabalkar, De, *"Economic Reform and the Emerging Trends in Employment"*, The Indian Economic Association 84th Conference Volume, Vellore, 2001.

Dalip S.Swamy, *"The World Bank and Globalisation of the Indian Economy"* in George K.K, Sankaran Nair, V and Jose Jacob, Economics, Development and the Quest for Alternatives, Concept Publishing Company, New Delhi, 1997.

Das, Bhagirath Lal, *An Introduction to the WTO Agreements,* Eartheorm Books Pvt Ltd, Chennai, 1998.

Das, Keshab *"The Unorganised Sector" in Alternative Survey Group*, Alternative Economic Survey: 1991-1998, Rainbow Publishers Limited, Delhi, 1998.

Debroy, Bibek and P.D Kaushik, *Reforming the Labour Market*, Academic Foundation, New Delhi, 2005.

Dhas A.C and H.M.Jacqueline (2005): "Globalisation, Economic Reforms and Unorganised Labourforce in India" in Jugale V.B (2005) World Trade Organisation and Indian Economic Reforms Vol.2, Serials Publications, New Delhi.

Dutt Ruddar, *"Economic Liberalisation and its Implications for Employment in India"*, The Indian Economic Association 84th Conference Volume, Vellore, 2001.

Government of India, *Economic Survey* 1998-99, 1999-2000, 2000-01, 2001-02, 2002-03.

Governemt of India, Planning Commission, *Tenth Five Year Plan*, 2002-2007, Vol.1.

Government of India, Ministry of Labour, *Annual Report* 2000-2001.

Irani Dutta Medhi, *"Employment Scenario in Organised and Unorganised Sectors of India in the Liberalisation Period"*, The Indian Economic Association, 84th Conference Volume, Vellore 2001.

Rao K.V and Rao M.K, *"Restructuring Indian Economy and Its Impact on Labour"* in Rao M.K Growth of Urban Informal Sector and Economic Development, Volume 1, (Edited) Kanishka Publishers Distributors, Delhi, 1994.

Shridhar Pandy and J.S. Tiwari, *"Economic Liberalisation and Employment in India"*, The Indian Economic Association 84th Conference Volume, Vellore, 2001.

Uchikawa, Shuji, *"Labour Market and Institution in India: 1990s and Beyond"*, Manohar, New Delhi, 2003.

Unni, Jeemol, *"Gender and Informality in Labour Market in South Asia"*, Economic and Political Weekly, Vol. 36 (26), 2001.

Wood, Adrian, *"How Trade Hurt Unskilled Workers"* in Borkakoti J.and Milner C., International Trade and Labour Markets, Macmillan Press Ltd, London, 1997.

10

Training of Handloom Weavers in Value added Production

R. Seerangarajan and K. Karnan

Indian Textile industry is more vibrant today contributing to the economic growth of India. Textile Industry contributed 4% to the country's GDP, 14% to industrial production and 8% to indirect tax revenue. The total clothing production in India was 49462 million square metres in 2005-06 an export was at Rs 75620 crores. At present textile industry accounts for direct employment of 35 million workers and indirect employment to about 45 million workers.

With the above back drop, handloom sector accounted for 6263 million square metres with a share of 12.8% only. But this sector provides employment to about 10 million weavers across the country in rural areas next to Agriculture. This handloom sector has to be protected in order to support millions of rural work force engaged in hand weaving to arrest migration of weavers to urban areas in search of alternate employment. In an effort to retain the weavers in handlooms weaving, it is inevitable to increase their earnings thro' better marketing of their products. The marketing of handloom goods depend on several factors like quality, higher value addition, attractive colours and proper advertising. Thus, value addition has a greater role in enhancing the marketing of handloom goods. Often the weavers have neither been exposed to any kind of awareness programmes making their lives more vulnerable to economic forces like globalisation and liberalization.

What is value addition?

'Value addition' is defined as the process of enhancing the value of a product or services thro' appropriate techniques and methodologies in order to attract more customers' Value of a product or service may include factors like level of performance, capability appeal, aesthetics, colours, ornamentation, styles and finally-may be, the cost.

Value addition is done by improving the existing product or modifying the charactertics. Value addition should not be aimed at the final product level alone. It needs to be ensured along the entire value chain right form the stage of raw material. Though we have improved our cotton quality and yarn quality tremendously in the recent past, still there is a mis-match in the quality parameters and the final woven handloom goods produced in the country and the requirements of the customers. Hand weaving and processing of handloom goods are the weak links in our value chain due to primitive technology adopted by the weavers and processing houses. Such a situation has compelled some of our garment producers to import fabric. It is necessary to improve the value distortions on priority. Technology upgradation of the handloom and modernization of work practices thro' training will ensure the desired quality in the value chain. This was realised by planners and Government departments in 1990 and the concept of value addition got its right importance, because the decentralized sector in weaving and processing took over the reins which they still continue to hold. Hand weaving tools are very primitive in nature and technological up gradations are found to be very low affecting the productivity of the operations.

If any improvements in terms of technology tools are implemented it may be very scattered and their share is very minimal. The reasons may be;

1. Lack of adequate awareness about the improved tools,
2. Inability of the weavers to invest any money in the tools,
3. Inadequacy of space in the house or workshed,
4. Lack of governmental intervention,
5. Absence of training in handling the improved tools etc.

In the light of the above reasons, it is necessary to impart training to the handloom weavers in, (i) Creating adequate awareness about value addition methodologies, (ii)Handling of improved technology tools,(iii) Practicing new methods of surface ornamentation techniques on handloom goods.

Why Training?

Training is a learning experience in that it seeks a relatively permanent change in an individual that will improve his or her ability to perform on the job. Typically, say training can involve the changing of skills, knowledge, attitudes, or social behavior. It may mean changing what employees know, how they work, their attitudes toward their work, or their interactions with their co-workers or their supervisor.

Training Needs and Priorities

What training should include, and look at how one can assess whether there is a need for training. This could be determined by answering four questions:

1. What are the unit's goals
2. What tasks must be completed to achieve these goals
3. What behaviors are necessary for each job incumbent tc complete his or her assigned tasks
4. What deficiencies, if any, do incumbents have in the skills, knowledge, or attitudes required performing the necessary behaviours? These questions demonstrate the close link between human resource planning and determination of training needs.

Training will be judged by its contribution to performance where performance is a function of skills, abilities, motivation, and the opportunity to perform. Managers must compare the value received from the increase in performance that can be attributed to training with the costs incurred in that training.

Training Methods

On-the-Job Training

The most widely used methods of training take place on the job. This can be attributed to the simplicity of such methods and the impression that they are less costly to operate. On-the–job training places the employees in an actual work situation and makes them appear to be immediately productive. It is learning by doing. For jobs that either are difficult to simulate or can be learned quickly by watching and doing, on-the-job training makes sense.

Off-the Job Training

Off-the job training covers a number of techniques-classroom lectures, films, demonstrations, case studies and other simulation exercises, and programmed instruction. The facilities needed for each of these techniques vary from a small makeshift classroom to an elaborate development center with large lecture halls, supplemented by small conference rooms with sophisticated audiovisual equipment, two-way mirrors, and all the frills.

Classroom lectures or Conferences.

1. Films
2. Simulation exercises
3. Experiential exercises
4. Computer modeling
5. Vestibule training

There is no training method that is right for all situations. A number of trade-offs must be made when actually making the choice of techniques and putting the program together – costs, time, and capacity of the trainer or trainees.

Value Added Handloom Textiles – Training Inputs

Quality Yarns

As stated earlier, value addition in handloom textiles could start from raw materials in hand weaving. Yarns form the basic raw materials for handlooms. Use of quality yarns that have better uniformity (U%), less number of thin, thick places per kilometre and less incidence of neps will be helpful in crafting high quality fabric 70% of the output quality of handloom fabrics depend on the quality of the yarns used. Only 30% - 40% of the quality will be added in weaving process. Thus, if weavers are trained in selecting quality raw materials, then the output quality is assured. Hence any weavers' training programme should spell out the quality parameters to be considered while purchasing the raw materials and the need for undertaking sampling tests. This will enable the societies to up grade the quality and there by winning the confidence of the customers.

The aesthetics and appearance of cotton handloom textiles could be enhanced thro' use of mercerized yarns. Mercerisation is the process of treating cotton yarns in strong alkaline solution having 54° Tw Strength of NaoH (24%) concentration for about 3 minutes with or without tension. This process makes the yarn cross section as round as possible. The bulky round yarn cross section enables the yarn to gain more lustre, strength and improve dye absorption characteristics. Hence, the training in yarn Mercerisation using hand yarn mercerizing machine will help to add value to the handloom textile.

Use the Fancy Yarns

Fancy yarns are special yarns that impart few special physical characteristics to the yarn surface. Fancy yarns may be either single or multi thread structures depending upon the construction requirements of the fabrics. Few examples are,

- Grandrelle yarn
- Spiral or cork screw yarn
- Curl or looped yarn
- Diamond (knotted) yarn
- Cloud yarn
- Knicker Bocker yarn
- Nub yarns
- Soft twisted yarns from air jet spinning dref spinning.

These yarns create fancy designs in the fabric and their application is mainly limited to weft way. Weavers must be given adequate orientation and awareness in using the above types of fancy yarns in handloom fabrics. These fancy yarns could attract customers and generate higher value to the fabrics weavers training will address to the areas like sourcing of fancy yarns, methods of using the yarns in weaving and marketing of such fancy yarn woven handloom textiles.

Surface Ornamentation of Hand Woven Textiles

Handloom textiles are generally woven with intrinsic motifs to appeal the customers. Enough advancement has taken place in producing extra warp figuring and extra weft figuring of motifs. These ornamentation techniques were in existence for centuries without any modification. Now ,fashions and styles are changing once in six months. And the traditional designs will not move in the market forcing huge stocks of handloom textiles. Hence, there is a need for introducing new methods of surface ornamentation techniques to hand woven textiles. The new methods may be,

- Embroidery
- Stone work
- Bead work
- Painting
- Lace work.

Embroidery was practiced during Mogul periods and later on, it could not sustain. This craft is practised in unstructured and fragmented style in various clusters known for embroidery shawls and other materials. In order to ensure long term growth and sustainability embroidery of the work it is necessary to upgrade the technological inputs and develop adequate platform for training the weavers and other artisans engaged in this type of trade. In training the methodlologies include standardization of the embroidery art for handloom textiles, dissemination of the best methods and documenting the same for future markets.

Hand embroidery techniques are cumbersome and pose drudgery to the operatives. Now –a- days mechanized embroidery, fashion maker or zig-zag machine or computerized- two head, four head, six head, twelve head and twenty four head automated embroidery machines are available. Use of such advanced tools in a cluster or by a group of handloom societies will help to add better value to their products and training in such areas will facilitate better earnings to the societies and the weavers.

Similarly, artistic bead work, stone work and exclusive craft based painting will be the areas of other surface ornamentation techniques for handloom textiles. Training the weavers in the above areas will definitely enhance the wage earning capacity of the weavers. The trainings should focus on choice of materials, quality of materials, profiling of designs and methods of undertaking the ornamentation work.

Conclusion

Training of weavers assumes greater importance in the globalised environment. Particularly training in 'Value addition' methodologies will definitely help to rejuvenate hand weaving activity and facilitate better earnings. Particularly trainings in design and design management will impart uniqueness to the handloom products in creating aesthetics to the buyers. Training in value added methodologies will provide a strong foundation in the livelihood process of the weavers. Such trainings will try to take advantage of the traditional skills of the handloom weavers and simultaneously seeks to reduce the labour costs. Globalisation has shown new dimensions in the economy of the handloom sector. This new light should be tapped to the advantage of the handlooms and enhance this social sector thro' appropriate training methodologies. Further frequent refresher trainings should be conducted to ensure that the changes in the textile environment are disseminated to the weavers in right mix continuously.

References

1. David A. Decenyo and Stephen P.Robbins, *Personnel / Human Resource Management*, Prentice Hall of India, IV Editor. New Delhi, 1998.
2. The Hindu. *Survey of Indian Industry*, Chennai. 2006.
3. Textiles committee, Textile care' July – Sept 2006, Mumbai, Design plus, News & View Volume: XXII; National, Institute of Design, Ahamedabad.

11

Empowering Rural Women in Unorganised Sector through - HLL Shakthi Projects

P. Poongodi

Globalisation can be a major force for prosperity only if it is backed by adequate national policies and conducive social and economic environment. Large groups of working women of India are in the rural and unorganised sectors. Socially the majority of Indian women are still tradition bound and are in a disadvantageous position. Since globalisation is opening up the Indian economy suddenly at a very high speed, without the required economic and social policies to provide the much required safety net, women who have been involved with production in the traditional ways, have to cope with numerous problems and yet try to avail of the opportunities which an open economy promises. The changing scenario will diversify the information needs of women at different levels.

Globalisation is a double edged process as far as women are concerned, as majority of women in India and other developing countries find themselves stripped off the benefit of social security, government subsidy protection of labour rights and than safety nets. There are possibilities for better education facilities and opportunities at the transnational sense which are very attractive to the privileged few. It is however necessary to understand that effective development requires full integration of women in the development process as agents of change as well as beneficiaries because Indian women can be utilized as development resources in many ways.

Problems Encountered by Indian Women

- Patriarchy and social pressures.
- Caste based discrimination and social restrictions
- Inadequate access to productive resources
- Poverty
- Insufficient advancement facilities
- Powerlessness

Possibilities and Opportunities

On the positive side globalisation has contributed to bring about welcome changes in the lives of women who have been able to avail of the opportunities, which have opened up in the various sectors of development. These are:

- Prospects of higher and quality education.
- Employment in technological and other advanced sectors, which have global bearing, has opened up for suitably qualified women.
- With changing attitude towards women, especially in the urban areas, Women enjoy more egalitarian set of gender relationship.
- Augmentation of women's movements through exposures at the International level will help bring about major changes in the economic, social and political lives of women.
- Reduction in gender inequalities will have positive effect on women's empowerment in the socio- economic context.
- Attitudinal changes towards women's role in the family due to good education, benefits of family planning and health care, child care, good job opportunities etc. will surely help in the development of more confident and healthy women.
- Positive approach to economic and cultural migration will facilitate women to be exposed to better prospects at the international level.

Steps to Cope with the Changing Scenario

It is seen that the situation facing the majority if Indian women is far from positive. However efforts are underway to circumvent many of these problems through governmental and the non-governmental programmes. Both the government and NGO's seem to be aware of the fact that the globalization process requires proper focus on rural development, education, health and child care and proper gainful employment for the underprivileged at the initial stages. Since poverty alleviation programmes are the main responsibilities of the Government, there are direct and sector wise schemes. Some of the important schemes are:

- Public Distribution system for food security
- Work security through various schemes
- Health schemes and services
- Child care schemes
- Credit schemes
- Insurance schemes

There are also sector wise schemes through Small Farmers Development Agency and other schemes of the Department of Agriculture, Schemes of the Dairy Development Boards in the dairy sector, Schemes of Forest Corporation in the forestry sector etc.

The main goal of the Department of Women and Child Development is to empower women and to bring them within the purview of the mainstream development process. Also the capacities and capabilities of women addressing their own development have been the main focus of important NGOs and women's organisations. Innovative approaches for poverty alleviation such as savings, credit, and asset creation for poor women have evolved in India as well as in other developing countries. These experiments have been able to organize and support women to:

- Strengthen their capacity to survive
- Mmeet there social needs
- Eenter into income generating activities
- Increase their savings
- Utilise the savings along with available credit
- Iimprove their socio-economic conditions and that of their families
- Sustain the process

NGOs such as Self Employed Women's Association (SEWA) in Ahmedabad, Working Women's Forum (WWF) in Madras, Centre for Women's Development Studies (CWDS), New Delhi etc have done commendable work in these directions. The Government departments have also given such experiments the necessary boost through the support for expansion in many ways.

The Role of Information in Rural Development Process

It is believed that the modern day phenomenon of Information and Communication Technology is the key to information flow for development. Especially in the Globalization and liberalization scenario, ICT can surely act as the major component in the developmental process.

In the World Development Report 2000-2001 it is observed that the spread of relevant information through technology will help in bridging the gaps between the information haves and the have nots. This will be a major step towards poverty reduction. India has seen a number of experiments to wire the rural sector to provide the right information to the right person at the right time and place.

In Rajasthan, the village named Neyla has the Information kiosk 'Rajnidhi' which is a project to use ICT especially the Internet to replace traditional form of governance with more open and responsive service delivery system. Gyandoot a prominent information facilitation programme in Madhya Pradesh has connected many villages through an intranet and has kiosks called Soochanalayas.

The M. S. Swaminathan Research Foundation have set up Knowledge Centres which give access to information on Government programmes well as information relevant to fishing. There is farmer bazaar. com in Punjab for marketing the rural produce. The Warna Wired Village Project of the Kolhapur and Sangli districts of Maharashtra is a joint venture of the Government organization NIC and the Maharashtra State.

Most of these projects disseminate information meant for the disadvantaged groups which includes:

- Government circulars/notifications regarding programmes of Assistance

- Leaflets released by NGOs about their programmes to spread awareness among the rural poor
- Public health bulletins especially for family planning, health and childcare etc.
- Some of these ICT based information system deal with wide ranging topics such as
- Agriculture produce market rates
- Copies of land records
- On line registration of applications
- On line public grievance filing
- Rural e-mail
- Village auction sites
- On line matrimonial sites
- Information pertaining to government programmes
- Career counselling service
- Technical expertise programmes regarding agriculture, animal husbandry, health, etc.
- Online application forms
- Weather information for the fishing community.

Some of these programs also use digital media clubbed with audio and video capabilities to give access to information to those who cannot read.

What Happens at the Ground Level?

All these commendable projects act as information supply agents which do not deal with information demands of special groups such as women.

The information disseminated through most of these programs still caters to the English educated middle class. However there are efforts and regional language facilities in many programs But the slant is still on the educated and literate few.

The information thus disseminated and is often not need based. Such information are also not professionally organized for proper access and dissemination in the ICT environment.

Information Needs of Women

Information needs of women in the new globalized environment are as diverse as the socio- economic scenario.

Treating women, as a monolithic group will over simplify their information needs. The information needs will also differ accordingly.

The urban educated women need information mainly pertaining to:

- Research
- Educational opportunities including prospects abroad
- Career advancement facilities
- Job/ employment prospects in India and abroad
- Matrimonial
- Fashion and market values
- Health and child care facilities which includes sexual and reproductory information
- Art and entertainment
- Social support system for working women
- Legal rights and provisions

Urban lower middle class women however will specially need information on :

- In -expensive educational facilities
- Career advancement and job opportunities in the city itself
- Matrimonial within the restrictions of caste and class
- Inexpensive health and childcare
- Inexpensive social support systems for working women
- Legal rights and provisions against social injustice, domestic violence, dowry system etc.

Information Needs of Women in the Rural Sector

Once again women have to be divided on the basis of economic and social positions in the rural society to understand their information needs. Elite women in the rural sector are mainly from the landed gentry's class or from the highly sophisticated politically important families. They are also usually from the upper castes.

Their information needs are akin to that of the urban elite women excepting for the fact that they often are passive viewers in the changing socio-economic scenario because they are bound by the upper caste traditions where patriarchy rules supreme. The rural educated middle class women are more prone to change.

They are in the process of gradually breaking the caste and class barriers and are working towards better education and economic independence. They are in urgent need of information regarding their new entitlements-

- Educational opportunities outside the village
- Job opportunities in both formal and informal sectors

Who Gives Information to Women?

There has been no research conducted in India on the information needs of Women, though this is a very vital aspect and a prerequisite for any developmental process. Women get information through various sources that are often not geared to their specific requirements.

- NGOs and the Government Departments generate information about women and prepare leaflets, indigenous newspapers, and small booklets etc. for distribution.
- The ICT based information systems give pertinent information concerning the rural sector activities but these are still general in nature. They however help women as well to a certain extent.
- Public libraries are a total failure at the rural sector because they are still traditional libraries dependent mainly on the print medium.
- Family members and friends are often the main source of information.
- The male members of the family who have better access to information source often share relevant information.

HLL's Initiative in Rural Development

Hindustan Lever Limited (HLL) and its constituent companies have been in India since 1931.Over these decades, while HLL has benefited from the developments in the country, it has contributed equally to these developments. HLL has consciously woven India's imperatives with the company's strategies and operations. The company's main contributions include developing and using relevant technologies, stimulating industrialization, boosting exports, adding value to agriculture and generating productive employment and income opportunities.

HLL has been proactively engaged in rural development since 1976 with the initiation of the Integrated Rural Development Programme in the Etawah district of Uttar Pradesh, in tandem with the company's dairy operations. This Programme now covers 500 villages in the district. Subsequently, the factories that HLL continued establishing in less-developed regions of the country have been engaged in similar programmes in adjacent villages.

These factory-centered activities mainly focus on the following issues:

1. Training Farmers and Animal Husbandry
2. Generating Alternative Income, health and hygiene
3. Infrastructure Development.
4. Change in the woman's status
5. Education of the children, especially the girl child
6. An Overall betterment in living standards

Learnings on Rural Development

The principal issue in rural development is to create income-generating opportunities for the rural population which is mutually beneficial to both $$the population for whom the programme is intended and for the company. HLL launched Project Shakti in the year 2001, for the purpose of integrating business interests with national interests.

The following table exhibits the participation of various States in Sakthi Projects with the numbers of Sakthi Entrepreneurs in the various Districts.

Empowering Women in Rural India

The objective of Project Shakti is to create income-generating capabilities for underprivileged rural women, by providing a sustainable micro enterprise opportunity, and to improve rural living standards through health and hygiene awareness.

The pioneering work carried out by Grameen Bank of Bangladesh, invites several institutions, NGOs and government bodies to work closely with Self Help Groups (SHGs) of rural women in villages across India over a period of five years.

Table – 1: Participation of Various States in Sakthi Projects

Sl. No.	*State*	*No. of Sakthi Entrepreneurs*	*No. of Districts*
1.	Tamilnadu	784	27
2.	Andharapradesh	2114	22
3.	Karnataka	1736	26
4.	Madhyapradesh	1442	41
5.	Gujarat	893	23
6.	Chattisgarh	482	15
7.	Maharastra	1661	33
8.	Orissa	928	22
9.	Punjab	660	17
10.	Rajasthan	976	32
11.	Uttarpardesh	3248	64
12.	West Bengal	530	14

Role of NGO's in Promoting Sakthi Projects

Shakti is working closely with the rural development departments of the state governments, as well as large number of NGO's across the geographies it currently operates in. There are about 231 NGO's are involved in Promoting Sakthi Projects. Marketing and Research Team (MART) is HLL's implementation partner on Shakti, helping HLL to identify prospective Shakti Entrepreneurs and to provide information to the needed entrepreneur and business training for the women at the initial stages.

Catalysing Prosperity in Indian Villages

The project offers a range of mass-market products to the SHGs, which are relevant to rural customers. HLL is investing significantly in resources that work with the women on the field and provide them with on-the-job training and support, Micro- credit and direct-to-home distribution in the rural markets. These are the key factor in ensuring the stabilization of their fledgling businesses.

Strategy

The most powerful aspect is to create a win-win partnership between HLL and the consumers.

Vision

HLL envisions the creation of 25,000 Shakti Entrepreneurs covering 100,000 villages, and touching the lives of 100 million rural people by the year 2005.

A key factor that has inhibited the development of rural India has been lack of access to critical information and services. Given India's large geography and weak infrastructure, it is often difficult to reach out to the rural areas.

'I-Shakti'

In order to impact both livelihood opportunities and living standards of rural communities 'i-Shakti' - an IT-based rural information service has been developed to provide information and services to meet rural needs in agriculture, education, vocational training, health and hygiene. The premise of the i-Shakti model is to provide need based demand driven information and services across a large variety of sectors that impact the daily livelihood opportunities and living standards of the village community.

The i-Shakti kiosk will be operated by the Shakti Entrepreneur by providing the need based information that improves the productivity of the rural community and unlock economic and social progress with the help of various institutions (both corporate and not-for-profit organizations) that are experts in agriculture, health, insurance, financial services and education.

'i-Shakti' kiosks have been set up in 8 villages in Andhra Pradesh, and have been functional since August 2003 which received an overwhelming response from the local populace. During the initial stage, the sarpanch, schoolteacher and doctor are invited to help the villagers. The kiosks remain open from 9 a.m. to 7 p.m., six days of the week. To enable access to the services, users have to register themselves first and obtain the unique registration number. An id card with the registration number is provided for use every time they visit the kiosk. The kiosks offer information chiefly in the form of audio-visuals in the following areas:

- Health and Hygiene
- E-Governance
- Education
- Agriculture
- Employment
- Legal services
- Veterinary services

The information provided in the above areas is collected from the best available resources. taking additional care to ensure that information, especially in areas like agriculture, is locally relevant and includes inputs from home-grown experts. These experts are also available on request, to help provide solutions to problems raised by users through a query mailing system.

System Running On Interactive Dialogue

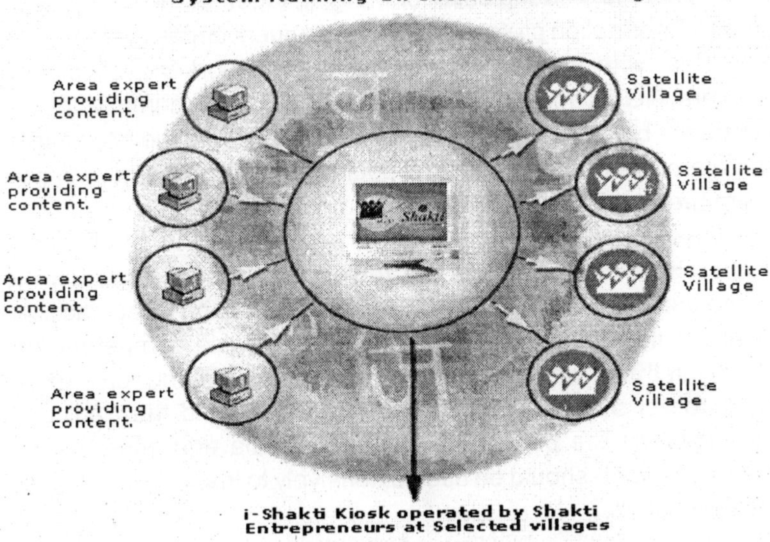

Provided by Unilever Corporate Research Team, United Kingdom

A farmer from the village can obtain a quick solution to a pest problem with his crops. People can also send queries on health and hygiene to a local doctor for a speedy response. Villagers can avail of discount coupons from the kiosk for medical treatment from doctors operating in local areas.

What is the Way Out?

Just as NGOs and the Government have come together to make poverty alleviation programmes successful through women centric initiatives in which poor women have been organized to circumvent the problems of liberal development processes. Once women make their decisions based on information relevant to them, their requirements will also be fulfilled as per their own terms. Presently someone else thinks for them and gauges their needs e.g. libraries and other information centres, media, educational/ Research institutions in the urban sector and the NGOs, government departments and recently the ICT managers in the rural sector prepare information capsules and disseminate for use.

There is a strong case for bringing together the expertise of library / information professionals, Government department officials who deal with women's problems, health workers, child care workers, NGOs and the ICT managers to envision communication centres in both urban and rural sectors to deal with the information requirements of urban and rural poor marginalized women, to give them the rightful opportunities for empowerment.

Relevant information has to be prepared in need based comprehensible formats in the regional languages to reach the unreached. ICT managers have to utilize audio and video, facilities to reach the illiterate women who are otherwise competent and worthy in their own fields of activities. Libraries in the rural sector have to act as communication centres and shed the traditional bias towards the print medium. Mass media and interpersonal communication should be used extensively to improve information dissemination.

Conclusion

It is only through full understanding of the plight of women in the Globalization process can the government, NGOs, decision makers and information managers prepare proper strategies to empower women and bring them into the mainstream developmental process. This is the greatest challenge, which confronts India and its women because globalization will stay but with half the population suffering under its yoke will only make it draconian and not a facilitator of progress. In this context, the role of HLL in upliftment of rural women is noteworthy. Such socially responsible efforts on the part of the corporate sectors and NGO's will certainly give a lending hand in Government measure in upliftment of the downtrodden.

After all, "FEW DROPS MAKE THE MIGHTY OCEAN"

References

Rajput, Pam,ed. *Globalisation and Women*. New Delhi; Ashish Publications, 1994.

Goswami,P.R. *Literacy, Information, and Governance in the Digital Era: An Indian Scenario,* Libr.Rev. 34; 2002; 255-270.

Siwal,B.R, *Structural Adjustment Macro Perspective*, Social Welfare - 45;1;1998;6-8 and 48.

Sood, A.D, *How to wire Rural India: Problems and Possibilities of Digital Development*, Economic and Political Weekly. 27; 2001; 4134-4141.

12

Changing Economic and Occupational Structure with Feminisation of Service Sector

Kishor Bhanushali

For almost four decades after independence, public sector was expected to play the role as an engine of train of economic growth. But towards the end of seventies, it was realized that public sector has failed severely as far as role assigned to it was concerned. Late Rajiv Gandhi, under its prime ministership has outlined new direction to the growth path of Indian economy. His intention was very clear when he said "the public sector has spread in to too many areas where it should not be". This was regarded as starting point of the private vs. public debate. Public sector was characterized as sector with low rate of return on investment, negative contribution to national savings, poor capacity utilization, over staffing and waste of public resources. At the same time Private sector was facing challenged in their growth path due to undue interference form the government. As a remedial measure Rajiv Gandhi suggested various measures such as improvement in production technology, fuller utilization of production capacity and greater role of private sector in economic progress. Major policy changes were introduced during that time with regard to industrial licensing, technological upgradation, export import policy, foreign equity participation, removal of controls and restrictions and rationalization and simplification of administrative regulations. All these measures were intended to boost private sector on growth path.

At this stage we will not go into the details of these policy measures and its impact on the economic growth process, but the fact remains that these measures fails to give desired results in terms of improvement in the performance of public sector, growth of private sector and overall economic growth. This was evident form the scenario prevailed in 1991. Public sector emerged as white elephants' from its position as 'navratnas', national income was growing at a rate called 'hindu rate of growth', private sector was not taking off on its growth path due to unwanted controls of 'license raj', inflation was at double digit. Coupled with this, growing fiscal deficit, increasing public debt and low level of foreign exchange reserves compelled the government to resort to IMF and World Bank for financial assistance to save the country from bankruptcy in international market. While providing loan these internationals agencies insisted that the government should take appropriate measures to put the economy of the country on rails. This was the second wave of new economic policy which was imposed conditions and not chosen conditions as first part of reform process. Accordingly Congress (I) Government under the chairmanship of Narshimha Rao and finance ministership of Dr. Manmohan Singh, soon after adoption of power on June 21, 1991, adopted number of policy measures to restore internal and external balance and confidence. Monetary policy was tightened with raising interest rates; rupee was devalued along with other measures to restore trade balance. To restore and control public sector deficit, measures to control expenditure and raising tax and non-tax revenues were initiated along with reduction in subsidies. A system of administered prices for public sector was also initiated. Industrial Policy Resolution of 1991 was also intended towards changing the regulatory framework which acts as a barrier to entry and growth of private sector and to provide more autonomy to industries. Industrial licensing was abolished for all industries except small list of industries related to security, strategic or environmental concerns and some industries producing luxury items with high component of imported inputs. The list of industries reserved for public sector was narrowed down by opening more areas for private sectors. MRTP Act restrictions were removed allowing companies to expand its operations without prior government approval. Criteria for foreign direct investment were liberalized for wide range of industries. To promote international integration of Indian industries, quantitative restrictions were removed in phased manner. The policy of disinvestment along with competition from private players was introduced to provide market discipline for public sector enterprises. The number of industries reserved for public sector was reduced from 17 to 8. The scheme of voluntary retirement was also introduced in public enterprises to reduce burden of surplus workers.

The objectives of all these reforms were manifold. Along with higher economic growth, reforms were intended to, change the structure of Indian economy, enlarge employment opportunities both for men and women, better performance of public sector, poverty reduction, reduction in regional disparities, growth of private sector etc. The performance of the economy on achievement of these objective largely depend on how fast the structure of the economy is adapting to reforms in globalised market.

After 14 years of reforms, its right time to evaluate the impact of reform on various sectors of the economy and various segments of the society. It will be feasible at this point of time to evaluate the changing industrial pattern in terms of contribution of different sectors to gross domestic product and employment of men and women. This will help us in identification of achievements and shortcoming of reform process based on which further strategy can be planned. This evaluation is focus of this paper. The Objective here is to identify the impact of reforms on economic growth along with changing sectoral contributions. At the same time paper also aims at highlighting emerging sectors in terms of employment, especially employment among women. Second section tries to capture the impact on economic growth and changing sectoral contribution. Third section aims at highlighting the changing employment pattern across sectors and male and female employment across different sectors. Final section summarises and conclude the paper.

Changing National Income Structure

One of the main expectations from reform was its positive impact on growth of national income. Reform measures were intended at providing momentum to economic growth. Table: 1 revealed the fact that reforms have contributed a lot in putting economy on sustained higher growth path. At the same time in post reform period the growth rate is stable as compared to pre reform period as seen in figure 1. Thus reforms succeeded in putting economy on sustained growth path. But the argument that reforms have contributed in increasing the growth rate of the economy do not sustain when we compare the difference between decadal growth rate pre and post reform. Growth rate remained same prior and post reform decades i.e. at 5.6 percent. GDP growth rate has gained momentum in post reform period especially after 1994-95, but recently there is downward trend in growth pattern. The root of changing pattern from instable to stable growth path lies in changing sectoral contribution. The stability in growth pattern is result of declining importance of agriculture in GDP. Seasonal nature of agriculture in India was responsible for fluctuations in national income year after year. In post reform period the share of agriculture in gross domestic product is reduced to little more than

Table: 1 - Annual GDP Growth Rate at Factor Cost (1993-94 prices)

Year	*GDP Growth at Factor Cost (at 1993-94 prices)*	*Year*	*GDP Growth at Factor Cost (at 1993-94 prices)*
1980 – 81	7.2	1990 – 91	5.6
1981 – 82	6.0	1991 - 92	1.3
1982 – 83	3.1	1992 – 93	5.1
1983 – 84	7.7	1993 – 94	5.9
1984 – 85	4.3	1994 – 95	7.3
1985 – 86	4.5	1995 – 96	7.3
1986 – 87	4.3	1996 – 97	7.8
1987 – 88	3.8	1997 – 98	4.8
1988 – 89	10.5	1998 – 99	6.5
1989 – 90	6.7	1999 – 00	6.1

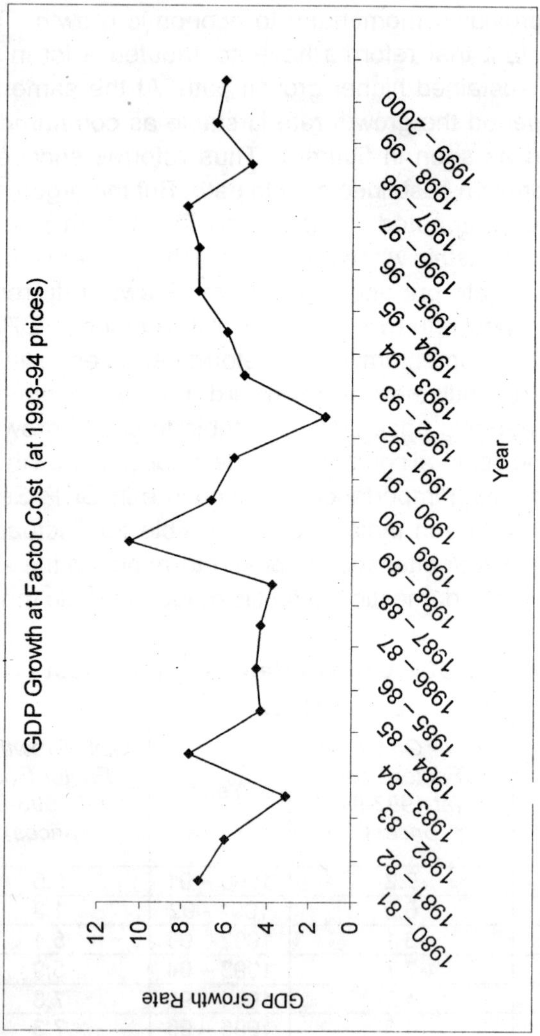
GDP Growth at Factor Cost (at 1993-94 prices)
GDP Growth Rate
12
10
8
6
4
2
0
1980 - 81
1981 - 82
1982 - 83
1983 - 84
1984 - 85
1985 - 86
1986 - 87
1987 - 88
1988 - 89
1989 - 90
1990 - 91
1991 - 92
1992 - 93
1993 - 94
1994 - 95
1995 - 96
1996 - 97
1997 - 98
1998 - 99
1999 - 2000
Year

Figure: 1

quarter from its high level of 32 percent in 1990-91. Secondly the service sector with almost independent of seasonality effect is emerging as a major contributor to GDP. This may provide stability to GDP along with putting economy on sustained growth path. One important fact them emerges about GDP growth rate is declining growth trend from its high level of 7.8 percent in 1996-97 to 4.4 percent in 2000-01. This downward trend is observed in GDP growth need adequate attention. (Figure 1)

The system of industrial licensing, which was considered to be major roadblock for industrial development, was dismantled under new economic reform. Under new system it was expected to have larger manufacturing base, but despite this major change in industrial policy the index of industrial production shows downward trend form 7.8 percent for the period 1981-81 to 1990-91 to 6.6 percent for the period 1993-94 to 2001-2002 (Table 2) Thus reforms have not contributed much in expanding manufacturing base of Indian economy.

Table: 2 - Annual Average Growth Rate of Industrial Production

Sector	*Annual Average Growth Rate (Percent)*	
	1981-82 to 1990-91	*1993-94 to 2001-02*
General Index	7.8	6.6
Manufacturing	7.6	7.0
Electricity	9.0	6.0
Mining and Quarrying	8.3	3.5

Source: RBI Handbook of Statistics on Indian Economy 2003-03.

The share of manufacturing sector in gross domestic product increased marginally from 16.6 percent in 1990-91 to 17.1 percent in 1999-2000 i.e. by 0.5 percent in post reform decades compared to increase by 2.8 percent increase in decade prior to reform i.e. 1980-81 to 1990-91) (Table 3). The contribution to GDP at factor cost by mining and quarrying declined in post reform period from 2.7 percent in 1990-91 to 2.3 percent in 1999-2000. The contribution by electricity, gas and water supply increased marginally in post reform period.

Table: 3 : Share of Gross Domestic Product by Industry of Origin (At 1993-94 prices)

Type of Industry	*Percentage Distribution*		
	1980-81	*1990-91*	*1999-2000*
Agriculture etc.	39.7	32.2	25.2
Mining and Quarrying etc.	2.1	2.7	2.3
Manufacturing	13.8	16.6	17.1
Electricity. Gas and Water Supply	1.7	2.3	2.5
Construction	6.1	5.5	5.1
Trade, Hotel and Restaurant	12.2	12.5	14.6
Transport, Storage and Communication	6.2	6.2	7.3
Finance, Insurance, Real Estate and Business Services	6.5	9.7	12.7
Community and Personal Services	11.7	12.2	13.2
Total Service Sector	36.6	40.6	47.9

Source: National Account Statistics of India (1950-51 to 2000-01) EPW Research Foundation 2002

Reducing contribution of agriculture along with marginal increase in the contribution of manufacturing sector only means increasing contribution of service sector to GDP. Service sector has emerged as major contributor to GDP. The contribution of service sector increased from 36.6 percent in 1980-81 to 40.6 percent in 1990-91 i.e. increase of 4 percent in decade prior to reform, in the post reform period the contribution of service sector increased form 40.6 percent in 1990-91 to 47.9 percent in 1999-2000 i.e. increased by 7.3 percent in post reform period.

Figure 2

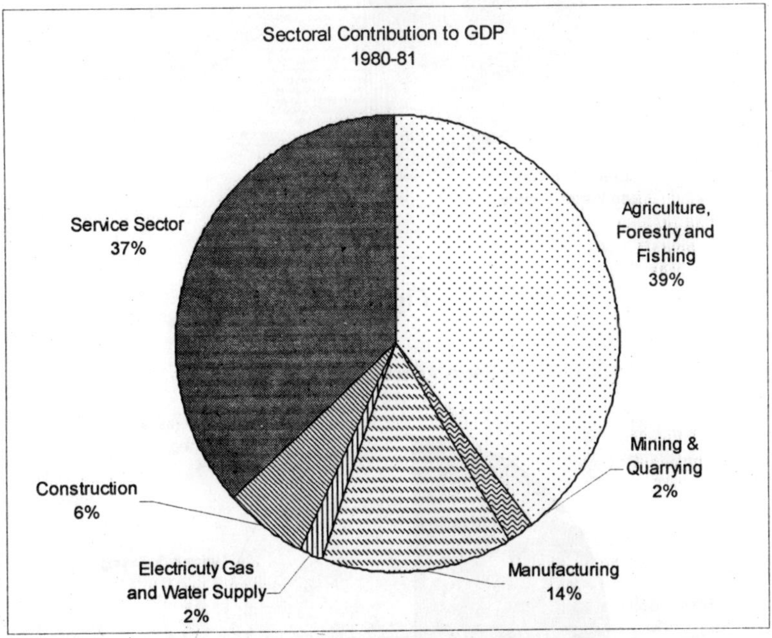

Within service sector, the contribution of trade, hotel and restaurant increased by 3 percent in post reform decade as compared to 1 percent in decade prior to reform. Similarly the contribution by other service including finance, insurance, real estate community and personal services also shows increasing contribution to GDP. Thus highest change is observed in service sector. The ratio of commodity sector to service sector which was around 1.73 in 1990-91 reduced to 1.02 in 1999-2000.

Figure 3

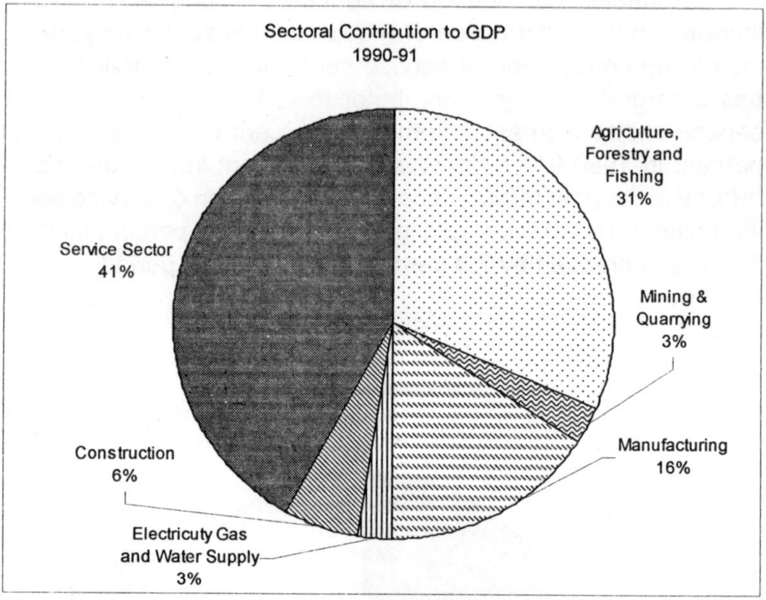

Figure 4

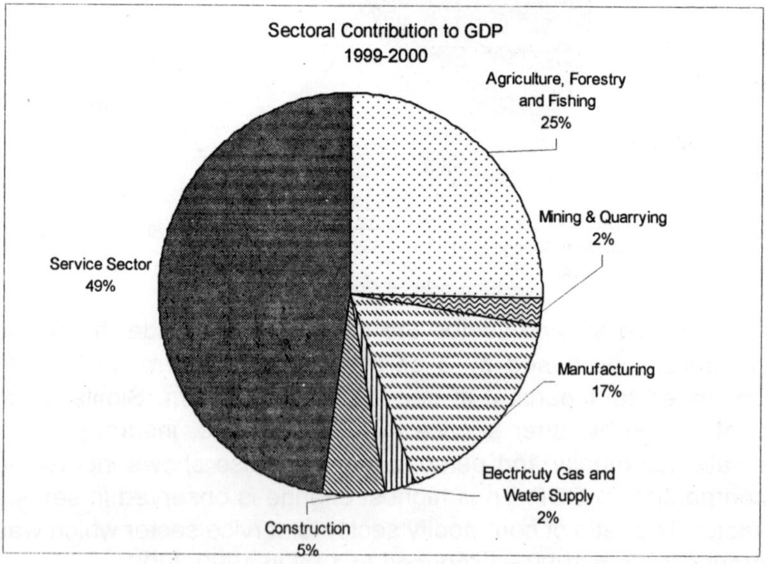

This structural change in composition of national income is result of reform process initiated after 1991 along with planning process initiated since 1951. Reforms have provided momentum to this structural transformation process.

In post reform period the service sector has growth at a faster rate as compared to agriculture and manufacturing sector. This is also evident form table 4 which shows compounded annual growth rate of various sectors for the period 1980-81 to 1990-91 and 1990-91 to 2000-01 and sectoral GDP growth rate at factor cost (Table 5). It is clearly evident that annual compounded growth rate of service sector increased form 6.7 percent (1980-81 to 1990-91) to 7.5 percent (1990-91to 2000-01).

Table: 4 : Compound Annual Growth of GDP by Economic Activity (% p.a. 1993-94 prices)

Sector	*1980-91 and 1990-91*	*1990-91 and 2000-01*
Agriculture, forestry & fishing	3.4	2.6
Mining and Quarrying	8.4	3.9
Manufacturing	7.6	5.9
Electricity , Gas and Water Supply	9.1	6.5
Construction	4.6	5.1
Trade, Hotel and Restaurants	5.9	7.2
Transport, Storage & Communication	5.6	8.0
Finance, Insurance and Real Estate	9.9	8.4
Community and Personal Services	6.1	6.7
Total Services	6.7	7.5
GDP at factor cost	5.6	5.6

Source: Computed from National Account Statistics of India, 1950-51 to 2000-01 EPW Research Foundation 2002.

Figure 5

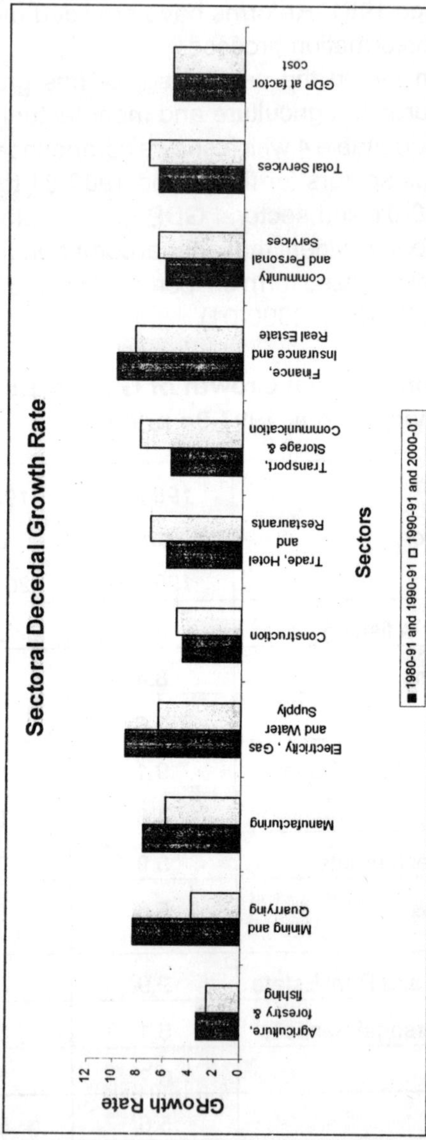
Sectoral Decedal Growth Rate
Growth Rate
0
2
4
6
8
10
12
Agriculture, forestry & fishing
Mining and Quarrying
Manufacturing
Electricity , Gas and Water Supply
Construction
Trade, Hotel and Restaurants
Transport, Storage & Communication
Finance, Insurance and Real Estate
Community and Personal Services
Total Services
GDP at factor cost
Sectors
■ 1980-91 and 1990-91 □ 1990-91 and 2000-01

The growth rate of agriculture sector declined for 3.4 percent in pre reform decade to 2.6 percent in post reform decade. Along with agriculture sector, mining and quarrying, electricity gas and water supply, construction also shows downward growth trend. In post reform period when commodity sector is showing negative growth trend service sector including trade, hotel, restaurant, transport, storage, communication, community and personal services shows positive trend. Among services downward trend is observed only in finance, insurance and real estate services. The increasing growth trend in service sector is also observed in annual average growth rate of various sectors (Table 5) (Figure 5)

Table: 5: Growth Rate of Real GDP at Factor Cost

Sector	*Average Annual Compound Growth Rate (%)*				
	1980-81 To 1990-91	*1990-91 To 1993-94*	*1992-93 To 1996-97*	*1993-94 To 2000-01*	*1990-91 To 2000-01*
All Sectors	5.5	4.2	7.1	6.3	6.1
Agriculture	3.4	3.0	4.0	2.9	3.2
Industry	6.6	3.1	9.4	6.6	6.5
Services	7.0	5.9	8.2	8.5	7.9

Source: "Impact of Economic Reforms on Economic Growth, Labour and Employment in Gujarat 2004" Mahatma Gandhi Labour Institute, Ahmedabad.

Employment Structure

As far as impact on economic growth and reform on employment is concerned, we have sufficient literature available to support the argument that growth pattern has an impact on employment structure across different sector. With economic growth the employment structure changes from agriculture to industry and form industry to service sector. There are large numbers of studies available regarding the impact of reform measures on employment structure. But most of the studies including Visaria and Minhas (1991), Deshpande (1992), Mundle (1992), Bhatacharya and Mitra (1993) And Kundu (1997) are pessimistic about prospectus of employment in post reform period because of the labour displacing production technologies used under compulsion of growing competition in the international market. Large number of studies concluded that reform have depressing impact on employment, especially in the labour surplus countries like India. D.P. Pal and P. K. Pal in "Structural Reforms Development and Employment Projections in India" observed that structural adjustment programmes is expectedly employment depressive in the short run, though in the long run it will be employment inducive. The overall economy has experienced lower employment growth rate in the post reform period than in the pre reform period.

Rao M (2000) stated that for globalize the Indian economy the government is following outward oriented economic policy which has tremendous effect on labour market. Immediate consequences of new economic policy of privatization are the negative impact on the labour. The growth of employment will be adversely affected and erosion in wages, saturation in wage employment and saturation in the employment in agriculture and informal sector. He further stated that in the context of declining growth rate in agriculture and industry, there will be no scope for creating additional jobs. This may create further erosion of employment opportunities in the years to come.

Outlining the employment strategy Ninth Plan mentioned: 'a primary objective of state policy should be to generate productive work opportunities in the growth process itself by concentrating in sectors, sub-sectors, and technologies which are more labour intensive and in regions characterized by higher rate of unemployment and under employment. The focus of employment strategies will be shifted towards creating conditions whereby employment opportunities should not only expand but also lead to significantly better living and working conditions upholding and dignity of labour'

Report of "Task Force on Employment Opportunities, 2001" established by the planning commission clearly shows the growth rate of employment is less than the growth rate of labour force indicating increase in the unemployment rate.

A study by A.R. Choudhary (2000) indicates that the share of public sector in total organized sector employment increased initially but decline after 1994 for 79.30 percent in 1994 to 70.72 percent in 1995 and further declined to 69.25 percent in 1997. As a counterpart the share of private sector in total organized sector employment declined initially but there after it increased from 20.70 percent in 1994 to 2928 percent in 1995 and further to 30.75 percent in 1997.This is due to leading role assigned to private sector in growth process under reform.

Ahulawalia (1999) in his book "India's Economic Reforms: An Appraisal" indicated that an important area untouched by reform so far is the labour market. He further states that rigidities in the labour market make it difficult for industries to undertake much needed restructuring.

Ruddar Datt (2001) in his detailed analysis of employment and unemployment situation during the pre and post reform period has observed that major problem of Indian economy is not open unemployment but under employment. There is an increase in unemployment especially in rural areas in post reform period. He further observed deceleration in growth of employment in primary sector, moderate improvement in growth of employment in secondary sector and deceleration of rate of growth in the tertiary sector during the post reform period.

The report of Task Force on Employment Opportunities, established by Planning Commission reveals the fact that Total annual employment growth rate declined from 2.04 percent for the period 1983-94 to 0.98 percent for the period 1994-2000 (Table 6). During the period 1994-2000, negative tendency was observed in the employment market with negative employment growth in agriculture (-0.34 percent), mining and quarrying (-2.85 percent) and Electricity, gas and water supply (-0.88 percent). Annual employment growth rate declined in manufacturing sectors from 2.14 percent for the period 1983-94 to 2.05 percent in 1994-2000. Among commodity sector only construction has emerged as

Table: 6 : Growth of Employment by Sectors (UPSS), India (1983-2000)

Industry	*Workers (Million)*			*Annual Growth Rate (%)*	
	1983	*1993-94*	*1999-00*	*1983-94*	*1994-00*
Agriculture	207.23	242.46	237.56	1.51	-0.34
Mining and Quarrying	1.76	2.70	2.27	4.16	-2.85
Manufacturing	34.03	42.50	48.01	2.14	2.05
Electricity , Gas and WS	0.85	1.35	1.28	4.50	-0.88
Construction	6.78	11.68	17.62	5.32	7.09
Trade	19.22	27.78	37.32	3.57	5.04
Transport, Storage & Communication	7.39	10.33	14.69	3.24	6.04
Financial Services	1.70	3.52	5.05	7.18	6.20
Community Social and Personal Services	23.80	32.13	33.20	2.90	0.55
Total Employment	302.76	374.45	397.00	2.04	0.98

Source: Report of 'Task Force on Employment Opportunities, 2001.

employment provider. As compared to commodity sector, service sector has emerged as major service provider with positive growth trend in trade, transport, storage and communication. Both these service sectors emerged as main employment hubs. The annual employment growth rate increased from 3.57 percent in 1983-1994 to 5.04 percent for the period 1994- 2000. The employment growth in transport, storage and communication also increased from 3.24 percent to 6.04 percent for corresponding period.

Thus sectoral change in employment shows service sector emerging as employment hub. Agriculture sector shows negative employment growth. Employment in manufacturing sector is increasing at vary low rate.

Within service sector on important trend which was observed to be emerging is feminisation of service sector with women outnumbered men in many service industries. In many cases the growth rate of female is higher than that of male. Hirway Indira (1999) while analyzing the changing pattern of female work force , shows that the trend of increasing participation of women workers in the tertiary sector has further gained momentum in the period from 1987- 88 to 1993-94. This trend is more pronounced in urban areas.

In their paper on 'Women and Work in Urban India: A Socio Economic Analysis', Rajeev Sharma & R. K. Sharma explored in detail the NSSO data and observed that labour force participation rates have gone up for all categories except for rural females, which remained unchanged and increase in male labour force participation rates both in rural and urban areas. They also concluded that the share of casual workers amongst the employed workers is higher in case of women as compared to men. The increase casualisation has been higher among the males in urban areas as compared to females.

S. Saklhivel & B.B. Bahtacharya (2002) also mentioned 'the factor that characterized the process of feminisation in advanced countries and other industrially developing countries is indeed missing in India context. But there is an unmistakable trend which reflects feminisation process where it is observed that both rural and urban India are witnessing increased rate of female work population.

Table: 7: Labour Force Participation Rates

Status	*Number of Persons in the Labour Force Per 1000 Persons*									
	Rural					*Urban*				
	Male		*Female*		*Sex Ratio of Labour Force*	*Male*		*Female*		*Sex Ratio of Labour Force*
	1993-94	*1999-00*	*1993-94*	*1999-00*		*1993-94*	*1999-00*	*1993-94*	*1999-00*	
Usual – ps	549	533	237	235	422	538	539	132	126	241
Usual – all	561	540	330	302	536	543	542	165	147	249
CWS	547	531	276	236	474	538	539	152	138	234
CDS	534	515	232	220	410	532	528	132	123	213

Source: Sarvekshana October 2001 – March 2002, 87th Issue.

Table: 8 - Distributions of Usually Employed Persons by Broad Industry Division per 1000 Persons

Industry	*1993-94*				*1999-00*			
	Male		*Female*		*Male*		*Female*	
	Rural	*Urban*	*Rural*	*Urban*	*Rural*	*Urban*	*Rural*	*Urban*
Agriculture	741	90	862	247	714	66	854	177
Mining and Quarrying	7	13	4	6	6	9	3	4
Manufacturing	70	235	70	241	73	224	76	240
Electricity, Water etc.	3	12	-	3	2	8	-	2
Construction	32	69	9	41	45	87	11	48
Trade, Hotel and Restaurants	55	219	21	100	68	394	20	169
Transport, Storage and Communication	22	97	1	13	32	104	1	18
Services	70	264	34	350	61	210	37	342

Source: Sarvekshana Vol. XXV No 2&3 , 87th issue.

Using NSS data Neetha N. (2001) also shows trend towards feminisation and marginalisation of labour force. She observed that women seem to concentrate increasingly in agriculture, and other low paid, les skilled occupations in the manufacturing and service sector.

The sex ratio i.e. number of female per 1000 males, of the labour force both in urban and rural India revealed the fact that female were outnumbered male (Table 7). The labour force participation rate according to usual, current weekly and current daily status by National Sample Survey also support this fact. However when the usual status of all workers is followed, there were relatively more female in the labour force. This was more so in rural areas than in urban areas. This reflects the feature of female being engaged in subsidiary economic activities was more common in rural areas than in urban areas.

Distribution usually employed persons by broad industrial categories (Table 8) indicates the fact that during 1999-2000, in rural India among all usually employed about 71 percent of males and 85 percent of female were engaged in agriculture sector. Urban female service sector accounted for the highest proportion of 34 percent of total usually employed followed y manufacturing 24 percent and agriculture 18 percent. The proportion of urban female employed in agriculture sector fall by about 14 percent and manufacturing sector by 6 percent with significant rise of about 8 percent in service sector. Trade, hotel and restaurants which accounted for about 10 percent of the employed urban women between 1983 to 1993-94 engaged as many as 17 percent of them during 1999-2000. Sectoral distribution of male and female across industries (Table 9) also shows the trend towards feminisation of service sector. The proportion of female in service sector increased from 27.6 percent in 1987-88 to34.5 percent in 1993-94 before declining marginally to 34.2 percent in 1999-2000. While the proportion of male engaged in service sector increased marginally from 25.3 percent to 26.1 percent and then declined to 21.0 percent for corresponding period. This reflects growing feminisation of service sector.

Further distribution of female worker across different industrial division and groups also reflect support the argument

Table: 9 - Industrial Distribution of Workers (in Terms of Usual Status) in Urban India by Sex

Workers	*NSSO Rounds & Years*				
	32nd	*38th*	*43rd*	*50th*	*55th*
Males	*1977-78*	*1983*	*1987-88*	*1993-94*	*1999-00*
1. Agriculture	10.6	10.3	9.1	9	6.6
2. Mining & quarrying	0.9	1.3	1.3	1.3	0.9
3. Manufacturing	27.5	27	25.9	23.6	22.4
4. Electricity, Gas & Water	1.1	1.1	1.2	1.2	0.8
5. Construction	4.2	5.2	5.9	7	8.7
6. Trade	23.6	20.2	21.7	22	29.4
7. Transport & Storage	9.8	9.9	9.6	9.8	10.4
8. Services	24.3	25	25.3	26.1	21.0
Females					
1. Agriculture	31.9	32	30.5	24.8	17.7
2. Mining & quarrying	0.5	0.8	0.7	0.6	0.4
3. Manufacturing	29.6	27.1	26.9	24.3	24.0
4. Electricity, Gas & Water	0.1		0.2	0.3	0.2
5. Construction	2.2	3.3	3.5	4.1	4.8
6. Trade	8.7	9	9.9	10.1	16.9
7. Transport & Storage	1	1	0.7	1.3	1.8
8. Services	26	26.2	27.6	34.5	34.2
All	**100**	**100**	**100**	**100**	**100**

Source :Various Rounds of NSSO.

Table: 10 - Industrial Distribution of Female Workforce: All India

Industry Division/ Group	*1993 – 1994 (%)*	*1999- 2000 (%)*
Agriculture, Forestry & Fishing	77.4	74.9
Crop Production & Plantation	66.6	64.3
Livestock	9.7	9.0
Agricultural Services	0.6	1.2
Logging, forestry and Fishing	0.4	0.5
Mining & Quarrying	0.4	0.3
Mfg.& repair services	9.5	10.2
Food Product	1.1	1.1
Beverages and Tobacco	2.5	3.0
Textile & Products	3.0	2.8
Wood, products & Furniture	0.9	0.9
Leather, for and products	0.1	0.1
Non metallic mineral products	0.7	0.7
Metal product & parts	0.0	0.1
Repair Services	0.0	0.0
Electricity, Gas and Water	0.0	0.0
Construction	1.4	1.7
Trade, hotels and restaurants	3.2	4.3
Retail Trade	2.6	3.4
Hotels and restaurants	0.5	0.7
Transport, Storage & Communication	0.3	0.4
Finance, insurance, real estate & business services	0.4	0.4
Community, social and personal services	7.5	7.9
Public admn.& Defense	1.0	0.9
Education & Research	1.9	2.7
Medical & health	0.5	0.7
Community Services	0.1	0.2
Personal services	3.6	3.2
Total Workforce	100	100

Source: Computed from Sundaram (2001), Economic and Political Weekly- August 11, 2001.

that service sector is becoming more and more feminised (Table 10). The percentage of women engaged in agriculture declined form 77.4 percent in 1993-94 to 74.9 percent in 1999-2000. But the women engaged in agricultural services increased from 0.6 percent to 1.2 percent. Percentage of female engaged in services such as retail trade, transport, storage, communication finance, real estate, and business services, and also community and social services increased over the period from 1993-94 to 1999-2000. This reflect the pattern that female getting more and more concentrated in service sector

Summary and Conclusions

The pattern of economic growth has changed after 1992-93 form fluctuating slow growth to stable high growth. The reasons for this change are changing sectoral contribution. The share of service sector is increasing with reducing contribution of agriculture. Service sector is growing at a rate faster than growth in other sectors. Service sector is emerging as major employment provider with positive employment growth when employment growth in other sectors is negative or declining. Service sector is emerging as employment hub for women as compared to male. Many reasons can be cited for increasing women participation in labour force. Women participation is increasing due to increasing education among women, new employment opportunities in industrial sector, increasing migration to urban areas and falling real incomes of household forcing women to enter the labour market (Jeemol Unni 2001). Service sector being more informal proved good opportunities for women to work part time basis or even from their home. Secondly, increasing global competitions which force the industries to follow the policy of cost cutting by employing more female as compared to male. Service sector being more competitive, the pressure for cost cutting is more forcing more and more employment of women. Fourthly, in countries like India income of the female is considered to be secondary income, so female work even at lower salaries to supplement family income. But along with work life female have to perform their household duties also. So female prefer to go for occupations with flexible timing which is more convenient in service sector as compared to manufacturing sector. Fifthly, industrialist also taking the benefit of this household behavior to use it as cost cutting measure and to increase their competitive strength prefers to recruit more female. Sixthly, the increased employment of female workers is primarily the result of the expansion of the industrial sector followed by growing service sector. Service sector is growing at a rate faster than manufacturing sector attracting more women employment. Seventhly, with changing technology and computerization many jobs are becoming less laborious and can be performed by female which was not possible in earlier times. The jobs in service sectors are less laborious as compared to agriculture and manufacturing. This attracts more women in service sector.

References

Neetha, N., *Feminisation and Marginalisation: Revelations of NSS 55th Round*, Labour and Development, December 2001

Paul Jacob, *Magnitude of the Women Work Force in India: An Appraisal of the NSS Estimates and Methods*, Sarvekshana, April-September 2001

Gupta K.R., *Liberalisation and Globalisation of Indian Economy* in Liberalisation and Globalisation of Indian Economy, Ed. K. R. Gupta, Atlantic Publishers & Distributors, 1997.

Ramanjaneyulu, M, *Pros and Cons of Indian Economic Liberalisation* in Liberalisation and Globalisation of Indian Economy, Ed. K.R. Gupta, Atlantic Publishers and Distributors, 1997.

Sen R.K., *Globalisation and Indian Economic Thinking in the Past and their Relevance in the Present and Future*, Indian Economic Journal, Vo. 51, No. 2, 2003-04.

Choubey, S.K., & Pendse, N.G., *Structural Adjustment and Employment in India* in Liberalisation and Globalisation of Indian Economy, Ed. K. R. Gupta, Atlantic Publishers and Distributors, 1997.

Mukherji R, *Globalisation and Labour* in Liberalisation and Globalisation of Indian Economy, Ed. K. R. Gupta, Atlantic Publishers and Distributors, 1997

Sharma Rajeev & Sharma R.K., *Women and Work in Urban India: A Socio-economic Analysis*, Labour and Development, Dec. 2000.

Sundaram, *Employment and Poverty in India in 1990s: Further Results from NSS 55th Round*, Employment and Unemployment, Economic and Political Weekly, August 11, 2001

National Accounts Statistics of India 1950-51 to 2000-01, EPW Research Foundation, July 2002.

Sarvekshana, Vol. XXV, No. 2&3, 87th Issue, October 2001 – March 2002.

Sakthivel S & Bhattacharya B.B, *Labour and Development*, December 2002.

Ruddar Datt and Sundaram K.P.M., *Indian Economy*. S. Chand & Company Ltd, New Delhi, 2004

Impact of Economic Reforms on Economic Growth, *Labour and Employment in Gujarat*, Mahatma Gandhi labour Institute, Ahmedabad, 2004.

Atherya V., *Gender and Survival in the Decade of Reforms: What does Census 2001 Reveal?*, Indian Economic Journal, Vol.50, No. 2, October- December -2002-03

Handbook of Statistics on Indian Economy, Reserve Bank of India, 2002-03.

Choudhary A.P., *Economic reforms and Employment*, Economic Reforms and Employment, Ed. P.D. Hajela & M. P. Goswami, 2000

Ghose A. K., *Current Issues of Employment Policy in India*, Indian Journal of Labour Economics, Vol.44, No. 3, September 4-10, 1999

Ruddar Datt, *Liberalisation and its Impact on Employment*, Economic Liberalisation and its Implications for Employment, Paper presented at the annual conference on Indian Economic Association, Deep & Deep Pub. Pvt. Ltd., New Delhi, December 2001

Report of Task Force on Employment Opportunities, Planning Commission of India

D. P. Pal & P. K. Pal, *Structural Reforms, development and Employment Projections in India*, Economic Reforms and Employment, Ed. P.D. Hajela & M.P. Goshwami, Deep & Deep Pub. Pvt. Ltd, New Delhi, 2000

Hirway Indira, *Economic Reforms and Women's Work*, Gender and Employment in India, Ed. T.S.Papola & Alakh N. Sharma, Vikash Pub. House Pvt. Ltd, 1999

Unni Jeemol, *Gender and Informality in Labour markets in South Asia*, Economic and Political Weekly, June 30 – July 6, 2001

13

Unorganised Labour – The Plight of Bidi Workers

C. Swaminathan and G. Barani

The unorganised labour sector in India is known for its substantial contribution to the GDP and also for its rudimentary and often unsafe process, low wages for workers, exploitation and in many a trade even bonded labour. This is so not in India but also in Pakistan, Bangladesh, Afghanistan and several other labour intensive countries.

Table – 1: Employment in various sectors during 1999-2000

Sector	*No. of employees (in crores)*
Organised	2.8
Unorganised	
Agriculture	23.7
Construction	1.7
Manufacturing	4.1
Trade & Transport	3.7
Total	**36.9**

Source: NSS Survey 2000.

The term "unorganised labour" has been defined as those workers who have not been able to organize themselves in pursuit of their common interests due to certain constraints like nature of employment, ignorance, illiteracy, small and scattered size of establishments, etc...

Categories of Workers

The unorganised labour can be categorized under the following heads:

Occupation: Fishermen, Bidi rollers, construction, handloom weavers, brick kilns, stone quarries, etc.

Nature of employment: Attached agricultural labours, bonded labour, migrant workers, contract and casual labours, etc...

Specially distressed categories: Scavengers, head load carriers, loaders, unloaders, etc...

Service categories: Midwives, domestic workers, barbers, vegetable, fruit and newspaper vendors, etc...

Problems of Unorganised Labour

- suffer from excessive seasonality
- lack of stable employment
- low legislative protection
- no formal employer, employee relationship
- primitive production technologies
- illiteracy and ignorance
- low status
- poor payments and subsequent indebtedness

Various Acts applicable to workers in this sector:

- Payment of Wages Act, 1936
- Employee State Insurance Act, 1948
- Plantation labour Act, 1951
- Maternity Benefits Act, 1961
- Payment of Gratuity Act, 1972
- Personal Injuries Act, 1963
- Cigar Workers Act, 1966
- Beedi Workers Welfare fund Act, 1976
- Interstate Migrant Workman Act, 1979
- Equal Remuneration Act, 1946

The number of unorganised labour has increased over the past two decades, while the proportion of the organized work force is decreasing. In the name of increasing Foreign Direct Investment, lands have been allotted; tax holidays and other concessions have been provided by the government thus driving out the self employed vendors on the road side. So is the impact of such measures on agricultural subsidies, public distribution, monsoon allowances, etc...

Table – 2: Growth rate of Employment in organised sector (in percent)

Year	*Public sector sector*	*Private organized*	*Total*
1995	0.11	1.63	0.55
1996	(-) 0.19	5.62	1.21
1997	0.67	2.04	1.09
1998	(-) 0.09	1.72	0.46
1999	0.00	0.11	0.04

Source: Planning Commission.

In the era of Globalization, right to life has become the central issue not only for the unorganised sector workers, but more so with the organised workers. Since the retrenchments are invisible and no compensation is provided. Due to globalization, closures and large scale retrenchments are taking place. Contract and apprentice systems have also increased in the organised sector. The table above vividly depicts the constant fall in employment in the organised sector in which the public sector falls on the worst side. Thanks to privatization.

Due to rural unemployment and no alternatives in the urban areas, people are driven to penury. Central and state Governments have to take urgent steps to stop the domination of foreign companies and loss of employment and livelihood of workers.

Labour and Employment

Employment generation to meet the backlog of unemployed and new additions to the labour force is a challenging task. The increasing diversification of the economy together with acceleration in economic growth in the recent past has resulted in lower employment intensity. This may be more than compensated by new opportunities in the service sector which would also be in the organised sector which remains unreported.

Home based Worker

A major category of unorganised workers is home based workers. Home based workers are those who are engaged in the production of goods and services for an employer or contractor in an arrangement whereby the work is carried out at a place of workers own choice, often the workers own home.

The issues and problems of home based workers are very complex because of the absence of master servant relationship. Though there is no official source of data on home based workers, an estimate says that over three crore workers are in the home based segment of which 45 lakhs are employed in Bidi rolling.

Historical Trends in Bidi production in India

Bidi production in India began in the early 1900's and it grew tremendously to become a major source of employment. However, 1980's set a decline in the trend. As early as 1931, the Royal Commission of labour described the working conditions of bidi rollers in factories as exploitative and unhygienic and from the enactment of factories act, 1948, the factories began closing down and work becoming home based. According to Government figures, there had been a decline in production of bidis from 2885 crores in 1998 to 781 crores in 1999.3

Employment in Tobacco Industry

Over 90% of the employment in the tobacco industry in India is in bidi manufacture. According to Government estimates, bidi rolling employs nearly 4.45 million people of whom 65% are women and 15-25% are children. According to the Government of India, as of April 1999, there were estimated 43,99,644 bidi workers out of which only 35,85,018 had ID cards.4

According to National Sample Survey (NSS), three fourths of the total employment in the tobacco industry is in bidi manufacture. Amongst the women in the tobacco industry, 91% are employed in the manufacture of bidi's. The total numbers of women/girls in the bidi industry constitute three fourths of the total bidi work force. The official estimates of women in the bidi manufacture vary from 2.2 to 4 millions.

Reliable estimates are difficult to obtain because 40% of them are home-based workers who make bidis. Large number of home-based workers are mostly under reported to the authorities and only a small fraction of them have been issued identity by the employers.5

Victims of Exploitation

Mostly home-based, these workers face problems of exploitation by the contractors, who often refuse to grant them the legally compulsory ID cards, rejection of their major proportion of work, inadequate raw materials, health problems, poor payment and such. About 10% of the bidis rolled by worker are arbitrarily taken away as standard deduction by the contractor to replace defective bidi actually rejected. Thus, the workers lose an average of 20-25% of their daily wages.

Contractors remove or change names of bidi workers from their register every two months depriving workers of their legally stipulated benefits. Neither women nor children are mentioned in the register, but are considered helping hands to a male worker who is registered.

A study entitled "Hands that roll bidi" was conducted by self employed women association of West Bengal. It revealed that though the state wage rate is Rs.39 for 1000 bidis, many rollers are paid actually Rs.35.30, as contractors reject bidis that lack quality and do not confirm to specifications. The study also revealed that most workers are unaware of their legal rights and of the bidi workers welfare schemes, and that there is an urgent need to create awareness among them.

Most of the women roll 300-800 bidis per day, and face the problem of receiving substandard raw materials. The decline in availability of bidi work has not affected the incomes of the majority of the households due to various strategies adopted by women bidi workers.6 The unionization has helped the women workers improve their lot. There is limited occupational diversification among women than men. On an average, each household has Rs.36,706 of income and about 36% of the households live below the poverty line and the income from bidi rolling is important for the poorest.

Health Ailments

The conditions of the workers in the bidi industry all over the country are deplorable and reports have highlighted the miserable lot of bidi workers in the specific areas of Maharashtra, Karnataka, and West Bengal.

Major health problems associated with bidi making are respiratory ailments, burning eyes, conjunctivitis, occupational dermatitis, green tobacco sickness, irregular menstruation, miscarriages, significant neo-natal deaths, chromosomal anomalies resulting in an abnormal child, accumulation of anesthetic gases causing spontaneous abortions and accumulation in milk affecting neo natal children's eyes and skin.7

Other major problems faced by bidi workers are perpetual poverty, very low wages, no wage bargaining system, no access to entitlements, benefits and gratuity, delayed payments, illiteracy, hidden child labour, constant exposure tobacco dust, postular pains and induration of the hands.

Alternate Employment

Almost all of the studies aimed at identifying alternate employment suggested the women to learn new skills. Some of the skill areas included watershed management, lift irrigation, forest management, dairying, horticulture, fisheries, tailoring, and artisinal work.8

The women are not in a position to accept that there is a need to think in terms of alternatives. This would be a major stumbling block for any development efforts in this regard. In order to enable the women to undertake these alternatives, a multi-pronged long term strategy is needed. They may be formation and consolidation of SHG's, building a collective of NGO's, interface between people institutions and policy change through lobbying and advocacy.

Government Interventions

The Government of India has begun to formulate policies and laws to address the problems of women and children in the work environment. A special cell within the Ministry of Labour seeks to improve working conditions, wages and skills of women. Under the equal remuneration Act, state committees' advice to Central Government on Women's employment.

The enactment of bidi and cigar workers act in 1996 was intended to regularize the conditions of work and ensure the payment of minimum wages. The bidi barons were to shift bidi rolling to home-based system, where the laws could easily be avoided. When a part of its liberalization programme in 1994-95, the Central Government halved the excise tax on cigarettes of length less than 60 mm. several large cigarette companies began producing mini cigarettes. As a result women workers wages have been further reduced on the premise of reduced sale of bidis.9

In 1977, the Government of India extended the provisions of the Employees Provident fund Act to bidi workers including home-based workers. The bidi workers welfare fund has been beneficial to those who hold ID cards/pass book. The size of the fund is observed to be too small to meet the needs of all the workers.

The Government laws for minimum wages and benefits, like paid holidays and health care, do not reach a large proportion of workers, as individuals and do not view a family as a unit of production. Thus the informal workers like other family members and children are not benefited.

The Final Word

The trend of growing disorganization together with the industry's propensity to shift to other states have reduced the bargaining power of bidi workers. Consequently, they continue to be a group of neglected workers whose conditions remain miserable. This may be minimized by implementing a uniform regional wage policy in all the state legislation directed to ameliorate their pathetic conditions and they have not been honestly or effectively implemented in order to enhance the quality of life of, it is essential to intervene at a techno social plain.10

A futuristic perspective therefore can also be traced based on the strengths of collaborative efforts from SHG's families of workers, owners co-operatives. This is crucial for ensuring a systematic change that could be brought about in the existing level of inequity, exploitative relationship among the owner, middlemen and unorganised work force who are at the receiving end a tangible change that could be visualized out of such collaborative in a series of incremental as well as adaptative changes in the production relations, working and living conditions.

References

The Hindu, Chennai edition, 11th May 2005, http://www.hindu.com/2005/05/11 stories/accessed on 01-07-05.

Truimph of Labour, 20th Jan'06. http:Indiabudget.nic.in/es 2000-01/chapter 1002.pdf.

International Labour office, Making ends meet, Bidi workers in India today- a study of four states, 151 pages, Geneva.

Aghi MB. *Exploiting women and children-India's bidi industry*. Life line-volume 6, October 2001, 8-10.

Sudharshan.R. and Kaur.R, *The tobacco industry and women's employment: Old concerns and new Imperatives*, Indian Journal of Labour economics, 42, 1999, 675-685.

Rajasekhar.D and Shreedhar.G – *Identifying alternative employment and income opportunities for women bidi workers*, reports submitted to ILD, New Delhi, February 2001, 33 pages.

The Plight of Indian Women workers, http://ehp.niehs.nih.gor/docs/1996/104-3/ focus India. Html accessed on 26th Jan, 2006.

Chauhany. *History and struggles of bidi workers in India*, AITUC, New Delhi, November 2001, 114 pages.

Srinivasalu.K, *Impact of liberalization on bidi workers*, Economic and Political Weekly, March 15, 1997, pp. 515-517.

Mitra.J, Sethi.G, *Proceedings of the brainstorming on Techno social integration* held at TERI on 7th May, 2005.

14

The Issue of Child Labour and Poverty Alleviation Programs: Way Out For Elimination of Child Labour in Globalization Era

A. Abdul Rahman

Child labour continues as a mass phenomenon, though it has been considered one of the important issues in political and academic discourses in India for last two decades. Not withstanding varying forms of interventions to deal this complex social issue, the problem is elusive and remains as major problem in rural areas. Legal and other interventions in India have mainly focused more on visible forms of child work in urban areas. However most of the working children in urban areas are immigrants from backward rural areas and according to various available estimates on the incidence of child labour, rural areas account for the largest chunk of child labourers.

In the above context, carried out a study using participatory methods to understand the issue of rural child labour. The main objective of this study is to understand the socio-economic conditions, causes, livelihood patterns and solutions to end child labour in rural areas. An effort has been made to explore possibilities of integrating child labour issues into ongoing rural development programmes. Therefore, appropriate policies may emerge and rural development programmes that will have child labour as one of the key priority issues of focus.

Magnitude of Child Labour in Dindigul District

Dindigul is one of the districts where the highest incidence of child labours in Tamilnadu. About 15 per cent of all child workers in the state were concentrated in Dindigul and its adjacent villages. Work participation rate of children (5-14) in Dindigul was 10 per cent while it was around 5 per cent for the state as whole. Work participation rate of children (5-14) in urban and rural areas is 14.1, 13.6 and 11.2 percent respectively. A survey conducted during mid 90s by NGOs estimated that there were 150,000 children in the age group of 5-14 in the workforce in Dindigul district.

Another important aspect of children in this district is the significant number of children who are neither in work nor in school. Though they are not categorized as child workers, these children are vulnerable to work related exploitation.

Incidence of Child Labour

The incidence of child labour is found to be high in Dindigul and its adjacent villages ranging from ten to sixteen percent. The proportion of children who are neither in school nor in work is also very high in these areas. Most of the villages are very backward where irrigation facilities literacy levels are relatively less. Incidence of out of school children and child labour is highest in M.Pudupatti village near Sithayan Kottai and it constituted nearly 47 per cent. This means one out of every two children in the age group of 5-14 are vulnerable to child work. Child labour in M.Pudupatti. Social profile of M.Pudupatti appeared to be heterogeneous.

On interviewing the map, it was revealed that backward community constitute 81 per cent of the total population. People belonging to other castes are very few. Among others, two households belong to other community who immigrated to this village two generations back from Karnataka. Rest of the other households are Muslims who are considered economically and socially backward compared to general Muslim community.

Child Labour Profile of M.Pudupatti appears quite disheartening. Out of 416 households, children in the age group of 5-14 were not present in 125 households. Of the remaining 291 households working children were found in 185 households. However, during the participatory sessions the villagers revealed that all children were vulnerable to child work. Even those who were going to school may drop out after five years of schooling and join some work either at home or for wages and those who attend school may also work after school hours.

Table – 1 : Social profile of M.Pudupatti

Community	*Number*	*% to Total*
Backward Castes	337	81.0
Scheduled Caste	71	17.0
Other caste	8	2.0
Total	**416**	**100**

There are in all 622 children in the age group of 5-14 in 291 households. Out of these 430 children are working children. The following Table – 2 provides the child labour situation in M.Pudupatti.

Table -2 :Child labour profile of M.Pudupatti Number of Children in the Age group of 5-14

Community	*Total*	*School going*	*%*	*Working at home*	*%*	*Working for wages*	*%*
Backward Castes	503	118	23	118	23	267	53
Scheduled Castes	117	73	62	3	3	41	35
Other Castes	2	1	50	-	-	1	50
Total	**622**	**192**	**31**	**121**	**19**	**309**	**50**

About 70 per cetn of all children in the age group of 5-14 are already in the workforce in this village. Majority of these children are working for wages with other than family members mainly in agriculture within the village. Most of them also migrate outside the village to other states along with their parents and work with them in construction, fish processing and so on. Those who are working at home do participate in their family farms (only one rain-fed crop in a year) and or involved in tending livestock, besides household work.

Causes of Child Labour

(a) Push Factors

Poverty and large size of families are the strongest negative forces. These were followed by lack of irrigation facilities and illiteracy of parents. During PRA the villagers explained that lack of rain and irrigation facility ensured low productivity of agriculture, in the face of use of HYV seeds. Lack of credit added to shortage of working capital for both on-farm and off-farm livelihoods. Thus those who owned lands faced unviable agriculture and those who were landless faced scarcity of capital to undertake off-farm activities. These amongst themselves ensured income poverty for a majority of the people.

Illiteracy of parents ensured that access to family welfare facilities are not sought and hence each household has large families. Illiteracy also ensured that people and irrational habits such that men/women do not resort to "family planning operation" as they believed it would lead to loss of strength. It is said that those who undergo family planning operation has to rest for at least a month or two and nobody can compensate the loss of income during this period. Thus large families for income poor households meant further misery.

(b) Pull Factors

The various push factors elaborated above is not uncommon in any village in Tamilnadu. But what makes leaving school is such a widespread phenomenon in these parts of the country is the presence of many pull factors that are quite unique to the villages in this part of Tamilnadu, namely, the attractive economic opportunities offered to children by these fireworks factories. Since the intricate tasks of manufacturing crackers and other fireworks require the nimble fingers of the children and women, fireworks factories go all out to attract these young children and women to work in their factories. This combined with lack of employment opportunities and gainful economic opportunities for men folk, contribute to the increasing feminization and juvenilization of labour in these parts of Tamilnadu.

The fact that formal schooling appears irrelevant and uninviting assumes more glares in the context of what these factories could offer as incentives. In fact these factories thrive exactly because they offer all that the schools refuse – freedom, flexiblility, immediate reward for hard work, comradeship, play fullness so on and so forth. Ironically all these incentives overshadow the long-term damages that these toxic materials that these children and women have to dabble with would cause to their minds and bodies in the long run.

Many of the children we talked with value going to work more than going to school. In fact on the part of the children themselves going to school is treated as the fate befallen the unlucky and miserable mortals. "The privileged ones go to work and earn", they say. This is because the school system does not reward and work and skillful display of learning abilities. They teachers hardly had taken cognizance of it. The parents are uneducated or illiterate enough to reward it and value it. But in the factories the reward is directly proportionate to hard work. The more skillful they are, better and more immediate the rewards would be. Some young girls and boys even mentioned as to how factories provide the space and opportunities where they could outshine not only their peers but even the experienced adults in the type of work they do in the factories. It is such a moral booster that they can beat the adults in their own game. School fails to provide opportunities to these kinds.

Over a period of time the child quickly graduates from childhood to adulthood both because the child discovers the skillful adult in it and also because the parents too begin to treat the child as a responsible and active contributor to the running of the family itself. Childhood turns out to be such a short-lived experience for these children. But they value it and found it well rewarding both psychologically and economically.

The flexibility of the factory system is another factor that attracts these children to value work in the factory more fulfilling than going to school. Here not only they have the freedom to shift their choice of factory at will, but even in the area they chose to work they can work in any number of days in a week and still return to work in a factory. Commuting to the factory is easy, even if it is far away from their village. The factory owners send in a cozy van to pick up and drop these kinds right at their doorsteps.

For the parents their wisdom and experience in handling factory system and the owners of it is far deeper and more extensive that that which is required to deal with educational system. Indeed, for a failing student the parents take much less responsibility and interest in putting the child back in school, because they see much less reward coming in return and also feel less self assured to deal with the teachers at school. In contrast, they take much more responsibility for their working children and take lot of effort to convince the factory owners to accept back in work. Thus the children feel more protected as workers than as students, who are on their own when it comes to negotiating with the formal school system. In other words the parents take more interest is returning a truant child labour to work, then returning a truant student to school. This heavily eases the burden on the children.

Where do the Children Work?

Given that there are so many push and pull factors operating for child labour and given the large number of children working as child labour, it was important to probe the sectors, which absorbed child labour.

About 40 people including a few females participated in the livelihood analysis. Initially the facilitator explained the purpose of the livelihood analysis and ensured participation of all who had gathered.

Though initially the process was a bit slow, latter it picked-up. A person who was able to read and write started the process. Each source of livelihood was written on a flash card, which can be easily read by any one in the group. While listing out the livelihoods a lot of discussion went on among the participants with regard to sources of livelihood and it was agreed to list only the major sources of livelihood. Nineteen such important sources of livelihoods were listed. And they were arranged in one column. Of these, certain occupations, the villagers explained, like vegetable vending, small business, cobbling, washing cloths, black smithy, hair cutting, buying and selling of dead animal's hides, pillcw and mattress making and toddy tapping, provided livelihood to a small group of people in the village. Those who were involved in these livelihoods got employment, though not full employment, all through the year.

What is the way out? Concluding Remarks

A large group of men and a few women participated while discussing the solutions for elimination of child labour. Initially the group felt that this issue has never been discussed among people and never even thought about. One of the important suggestions was to discuss this issue regularly in the gram panchayat and see how they can enroll all children in school.

The most important cause of child labour being poverty, the solution suggested by people is to improve irrigation facilities in the village and establishing small and cottage industries for providing year round employment. People felt that implementing the long pending irrigation canal scheme from Thungabadra river would solve the problem of irrigation and improve the agricultural base in the village. This may also lead to prevention of migration. Provision of free and compulsory education is also suggested as an important intervention. Since people can't afford education of their children it is suggested that free boarding schools should be opened in the vicinity of the village. Another important suggestion is to open early childcare centres in the village so that the girl children will be released from babysitting and they can attend schools. In order to tackle the problem of low rainfall people suggested developing social forestry in the area. Adult literacy programme is felt as essential for creation of awareness among adults about negative impact of child labour. Though large family size is identified as one of the causes of child labour, there is a myth among the people that family planning operations will disable a person to do hard work after family planning operation. There is a mental stigma among people on family planning. It is suggested that there is a need for educating people on health aspects and family welfare.

Improvement in institutional credit facilities would go a long way in releasing people from private moneylenders and traders. In turn it will save people from paying high rate of interests. This will also reduce the dependency of families on income of children.

In order to tackle the demand side factors, like preference of children to work in cottonseed fields, it is suggested that adults should replace children in such work. This will also pull away children from the economic incentives that they get from work. People's perception about solutions to end child labour is presented in picture.

Table - 3 : Villager's Perception on Solution for Ending Child Labour

Sl. No	*Problems*	*Solutions*
1.	Poverty	Improvement of irrigation Small & cottage industries Free and compulsory education
2.	Low rainfall	Social forestry
3.	Illiteracy of parents	Adult education programme
4.	Large family size	Health education Family planning
5.	Lack of irrigation facilities	Surface irrigation Implementing the spending irrigation scheme
6.	Not able to spend money on education	Free residential school
7.	Lack of land	Land to landless
8.	Baby sitting	Early child care centers to be opened
9.	No assistance from banks	Institutional credit facilities should improved
10.	Providing pocket money for working children by parents	Adults should replaced the children
11.	Children are preferred for cotton seed cultivation	Adults should replaced the children

K.Chidanandappa, H.Anjanaiah, H.Eeranna Pedda Hanumanthu, N.Narashimhulu, T.Narasanna, H.Griddaiah and others.

Solutions to End Child Labour

In Dindigul district there has already been some intervention in the form of National Child Labour Project. This scheme has provided special schools for working children with some economic incentives. However, this scheme has not touched even fringe of the problem of child labour. There is not much scope for addressing the supply side factors for child labour in the above scheme. Only rural development schemes can tackle the supply side factors. Unless supply side factors in a holistic way are dealt it is very difficult to move towards elimination of child labour.

An important supply side factor that needs to address is to stop at least migration of children from this village, as people migrate along with their families that leads to children dropping out of school and discontinue schooling. In order to stop migration or at least to prevent the whole family migrating, it is essential to improve the livelihood in the village. Improving the agricultural base can do this. People have been mentioning about a pending canal scheme and this has to be pursued. Secondly there is need for water shed management with people's participation. Motivation of people for such collective work is required. The suggested method of self-help group should be planned with the people and it should have a comprehensive agenda. These groups should be involved in improving the agricultural base in the village as also alternative means of livelihood taking into account locally available resources. There are number of stone quarries in and around the village. People have been forthcoming with the demand for establishing some stone crushing units. This is to be seriously considered, as there is scope for core activities under SGSY scheme.

15

Impact of Economic Reforms on Wages in Tamil Nadu Manufacturing Sector

R. Bagavathi Muthu, T. Indra and S.K. Sathya Prabha

The industrialization has a major role to play in the economic development of any country in the world. There is positive relationship between per capita income and share of manufacturing output. The gap in per capita income between developed and underdeveloped countries are largely reflected in the disparities in the concentration of industrial sector. The process of industrialization is associated with the development of skills of industrial workers and industrial management, which are beneficial to growth of productivity, production and employment.

New Industrial Policy

The government announced the new industrial policy on 24th July 1991. It provided a major thrust to the process of economic liberalization aimed at fastening the pace of the country's industrial and agricultural development. The major objectives of new industrial policy package will be to build on the gains already made, correct weakness that may have kept in maintaining a sustained growth in productivity and gainful employment and attain international competitiveness. The pursuit of these objectives will be tempered by the need to preserve the environment and ensure the efficient use of available resources. All sector of industry whether small, medium or large belonging to public, private, co-operative sector will be encouraged to grow and improve in their past performance.

Reason for Choice of Study

The reform process in India so far has concentrated at the central level, the reforms at the state level have been slow moving because of state level policy reforms. The major states can be divided into (i) Reform oriented states, (ii) Intermediate reformers and (iii) Lagging reformers. Tamilnadu is one of the industrial state in India. Indian trade union movement has its root in the good old industries in the state. Though collective bargaining and industrial relations in Tamil Nadu is admired, the industrial wages are much higher in Tamil Nadu. Thus Tamil Nadu has been selected for this study. Naturally the question arises what is the impact of new economic policy in Tamil Nadu manufacturing sector. So the study of the manufacturing sectors of Tamil Nadu during the pre and post reform periods is essential.

Significance of the Study

The availability of accurate statistical information on labour productivity, growth rate of output and wages are very essential for effective policy frame work. A successful and socially significant wage policy can we build up only the strong foundation of correct and meaningful data on various aspects of problem such as wage determine and wage levels.

Moreover earlier studies on wage productivity nexus in Indian industry based on aggregate manufacturing. However the present study makes for an attempt to find out the impact of economics reforms of wages of manufacturing sectors in Tamil Nadu. The present studies examine the wage rates and share of wages in manufacturing sectors of Tamil Nadu. And also to find out the nature of the relationship between employment and related variables. In this context the study is more significant.

Statement of the Problem

Tamil Nadu is reform oriented state and industrially forward state in India. The Government announced a new industrial policy on July 24, 1991. The major objectives of new industry policy are correct the weaknesses and maintain a sustained growth in productivity and gainful employment and attain international competitiveness. Naturally the question arises as; what the impact on new economic policy is on manufacturing sectors of Tamil Nadu. So present analyses the impact of reforms on manufacturing sectors of Tamil Nadu.

Objectives

1. To measure the wages rates for pre and post reform periods in manufacturing sectors of Tamil Nadu.
2. To study the share of wages in value added in the manufacturing sectors of Tamil Nadu at pre-reform and post reform periods.
3. To study the growth of employment in the pre and post reform period.

Methodology

The present study is disaggregate two digit industries based on the secondary data. The basic data for the present study recording gross value added, number of employees and total emoluments have been collected from the ASI report published by Central Statistical Organisation, Government of India for the study period 1979-80 to 1997-98. Wage rates calculator by the ratio of

Table – 1: Industries

Sl. No	*Industries*
1.	Manufacture of Food product
2.	Manufacture of Beverages, Tobacco and related products
3.	Manufacture of Cotton Textiles
4.	Manufacture of Wool, Silk, and Man-made Textile
5.	Manufacture of Jute
6.	Manufacture of Textile product
7.	Manufacture of Wood and wood products

(Contd.)

(Contd.)

Sl. No	*Industries*
8.	Manufacture of Paper and paper products
9.	Manufacture of Leather
10.	Manufacture of Chemical and chemical products
11.	Manufacture of Rubber and Plastic products
12.	Manufacture of Non-metallic mineral products
13.	Basic metal and Alloys
14.	Manufacture of Metal products
15.	Manufacture of Non-Electrical Machinery and parts
16.	Manufacture of Transport equipment and parts
17.	Other Manufacturing industries
18.	Electricity

real value of total emoluments to the number of employees. Real value added is calculated by the ratio of cross value added to the WPI and multiplied by 100. Annual growth rate is calćulated for employment, wage rate, labour productivity and real value added.

Table – 2: Annual Growth rate for Employment

Industry	*Overall (1979-80 to 1997-98)*	*Pre reform (199-80 to 1990-91)*	*Post reform (1991-92 to 1997-98)*
1.	1.186772	-0.38131	3.677579
2.	1.720307	2.700043	0.140765
3.	2.998978	1.479971	5.385844
4.	-0.10837	-2.46924	3.014665
5.	64.66382	102.295	14.05246
6.	12.85347	10.35907	17.75229
7.	-0.41566	-1.00768	-0.54472
8.	3.163929	1.980965	4.332004
9.	5.950176	8.589768	1.366555
10.	93.99798	159.7932	-9.39454
11.	4.22457	3.26671	4.76186
12.	2.578264	2.493087	1.366152
13.	2.877591	-0.29388	6.415272
14.	2.380481	0.475499	3.40345
15.	3.40352	2.349338	3.40345
16.	2.447568	2.724067	0.077009
17.	7.550335	6.430678	7.959843
18.	0.9808	1.750693	-2.66035

From the table 2 it is observed that the annual growth rate of employment has been increased during the study period. In the post reform period employment has been increased more than ten industries among the eighteen manufacturing industries in Tamil Nadu which has been taken for the present study. Among the industries of positive impact, some industries like manufactured of food product, cotton textiles, paper & paper product, basic metal and alloys industries and metal product show significant increase in the growth rate of employment.

Table – 3 : Annual Growth rate for Wage Rate

Industry	*Overall (1979-80 to 1997-98)*	*Pre reform (199-80 to 1990-91)*	*Post reform (1991-92 to 1997-98)*
1.	5.773608	7.396824	3.222839
2.	5.460593	4.760944	6.56004
3.	1.221856	2.539593	-0.84887
4.	4.932354	5.231309	4.462568
5.	3.038192	4.079921	1.401188
6.	4.368694	3.557786	5.642978
7.	4.912995	5.530864	3.942057
8.	2.523751	3.318525	1.274822
9.	1.649735	1.128164	2.469347
10.	85.15981	66.58847	114.3433
11.	1.174582	0.886711	1.62695
12.	-3.81124	-4.21379	-3.17866
13.	2.666671	3.809045	0.768655
14.	2.940562	2.866436	3.057046
15.	2.373873	2.69789	1.864703
16.	3.300407	3.758057	2.581241
17.	-1.49348	7.402133	-15.4723
18.	32.90867	6.991163	73.63617

The table 3 shows the annual growth rate of wage rate in the manufacturing sectors of Tamil Nadu. From the table only seven of the eighteen industries have the positive impact due to the reforms of growth rate of wage rate. It is found that the annual growth rate is not increased in the post reform period as compare to the pre-reform period. So it can be inferred that the impact of economic reforms has resulted in declaration of wage rate in the manufacturing sectors in Tamil Nadu.

Table – 4 : Annual Growth rate of share of wages in value added

Industry	*Overall (1979-80 to 1997-98)*	*Pre reform (199-80 to 1990-91)*	*Post reform (1991-92 to 1997-98)*
1.	0.261353	0.295055	0.291222
2.	0.269977	0.348736	0.340507
3.	0.428702	0.562808	0.558953
4.	0.472342	0.650363	0.6476
5.	-0.79742	-0.57724	-0.65001
6.	0.332888	0.624847	0.61291
7.	0.580511	0.553404	0.626981
8.	0.314239	0.338557	0.272553
9.	0.349364	0.376669	0.302554
10.	0.242873	0.243303	0.242135
11.	0.005622	0.006939	0.003365
12.	7.147172	9.589508	2.96031
13.	0.372222	0.401457	0.322104
14.	0.387262	0.421322	0.328873
15.	1.07411	0.375473	0.28236
16.	0.467466	0.500532	0.41078
17.	0.306342	0.333011	0.260623
18.	0.347054	0.398434	0.258975

Table 4 shows the annual growth rate of share of wages in value added in the manufacturing sectors of Tamil Nadu. From the table it is clear that the share of wages in value added is falling in almost all the industries except manufacture of wood & wood product industry. That is the share of wages in all the industries have been decreased in the post reform period as compare to the pre reform period. It can be said that the economic reforms has led to decrease in the share of wages in value added during the post reform period because in the post reform period the intensity of capital in almost all the industries have resulted in the falling of wages in value added.

Table – 5 : Annual Growth rate of real value added

Industry	*Overall (1979-80 to 1997-98)*	*Pre reform (199-80 to 1990-91)*	*Post reform (1991-92 to 1997-98)*
1.	9.325162	10.11077	8.090641
2.	28.98497	23.16426	38.1318
3.	6.661035	7.506288	5.33278
4.	16.69584	8.61304	29.39737
5.	-145.197	-242.366	7.498493
6.	20.90926	18.59899	24.53969
7.	7.410252	10.96392	1.825918
8.	11.72578	12.56014	10.41463
9.	10.01898	12.58295	5.989881
10.	5.68377	8.356869	1.483185
11.	24.35191	37.25015	4.08324
12.	10.63457	13.83721	5.601853
13.	10.49332	6.692503	16.46604
14.	7.459491	6.405796	9.115297
15.	7.132623	7.680487	6.271694
16.	7.297369	10.69389	1.95998
17.	14.88183	20.16786	6.575226
18.	8.921242	9.008053	8.784825

For this study value added has been used for measuring output. The money value of total output in deflated by the whole sale price index output in order to set real value of output. Table 5 shows the growth rate of real value added in Tamil Nadu manufacturing sector. It is observed that annual growth rate of real value added Tamilnadu manufacturing sectors has been increased only in seven industries namely manufacture of food products, manufacture of beverages, tobacco and related products, manufacture of wool products, manufacture of jute products, manufacture of textiles, manufacture of basic metal and alloy products and manufacture of non electrical machinery, in post reform period. Expect these seven industries there is a negative impact of economic reforms on the real value added of other manufacturing sector in Tamil Nadu.

Conclusion

From the above analysis the following, the revealed results are pointed below.

- The growth rate of employment during the post reform period is increased more than in ten industries among eighteen industries. So there is a positive impact of globalization with the employment.
- There are only seven industries which have the positive impact on annual growth rate of wages. So it can be concluded that the impact of economic reforms has resulted in declaration of wage rate in the manufacturing sectors in Tamil Nadu.
- From the study it is very clear that the share of wages in value added is falling in almost all the industries except wood and wood products industry. This is because due to the intensity of capital in almost all the industries this fall in share of wages have occurred.
- Real value added is increased only in seven industries during post reform period. There is a negative impact of globalization in other industries.

References

Francis Chrunilam, *Industrial Economics-Indian Perspective*, Himalaya Publishing House, Bombay, 1990.

Goldar.B.N., *Productivity Growth in Indian Industries*, Allied Publishers Private Limited, New Delhi, 1986.

Ruddar Datt and K.P.M.Sundaram, *Indian Economy*, S.Chand and Company Ltd, New Delhi, 2005.

Balakrishnan.P, Pushpangadan.K. and Suresh Babu.M., *"Trade Liberalization and Productivity Growth in Manufacturing"*, Economic and Political Weekly, October 7, 2000.

Chiranjib Neogi and Ghosh, *"Impact of Liberalization on Performance of Indian Industries: A Firm Level Study"*, Economic and Political Weekly, vol.28, 1998.

16

Impact of Globalisation on Labourers in SSI

M. Soundarapandian and A. Chandraprabha

In a very fast changing world, there is a very strong need for technology transfer if we have to survive in the competitive world in an era of globalization which has already dawned. By accepting the membership of the World Trade ORganisation (WTO), India is under obligation to bring down its tariffs in line with the mandate of the WTO. This shall, it is hoped, facilitate the process of technology transfer and create a new environment for the absorption of modern technologies.

A Brief Review of Strikes and Lockouts

A Review of the data pertaining to industrial disputes, number of workers involved and number of man days lost during the last 40 years (1961 to 2000 reveals that the entire period can be sub-divided into three sub-periods (i) 1961-75, the period before emergency, (ii) 1975-90, the period following emergency, and (iii) 1991 and thereafter, the period beginning with new economic reforms.

(i) During 1969 to 1975: The number of man days lost due to strikes varied in the range of 60 to 84 per cent of the total man days lost, while that of lockouts ranged between 16 to

40 per cent. Obviously labour organised strikes to press for a better deal in the fruits of industrial productivity in the form of higher wages, dearness allowances, protection against retrenchment and lay-offs and improvement in the terms and conditions of work

(ii) 1975 to 1990 – the second phase: The year 1975 marks a watershed in industrial relations. This was the year of emergency declared by Mrs.Indira Gandhi. The authoritarian forces unleashed by the Congress (I) Government were able to ruthlessly muzzle the voice of the working classes. Consequently, this gave rise to employers militancy and this was reflected in the sharp increase in man days lost due to lockouts to 9.9 million in 1976 as against only 2.8 million man days lost due to strikes. In relative terms, lockout which is the kind of punishment inflicted on the labouring class accounted for as high as 78 per cent of the total man days lost, and the share of strikes touched a record low level of 22 per cent.

(iii) 1991 to 2000 – the third phase of new economic reforms: The Congress (I) Government led by Mr.Narasimha Rao announced the New Economic Policy which marks another watershed in favour of the private sector. Emboldened by New Economic Reforms, the employers pleaded for flexibility in labour policy in the name of boosting efficiency and productivity. The arm of the state supported the industrialists and big business. This had a natural effect of increasing employer's militancy. By 1993, the share of lockouts in man days lost jumped to 72.3 per cent. It was of the order of 68 per cent in 1994 and about 65 per cent in 1995.

There is no doubt that total man days lost has shown a decline from 31.26 million in 1992 to 20.29 million in 1996 and 14.92 million in 1997, but a greater share of this decline in mandays lost has been contributed due to strikes from 15.13 million in 1992 to 5.0 million in 1997 as against it, the man days lost due to lockout indicated a relatively slower decline from 16.13 million in 1992 to 10.68 million in 1997. However, mandays lost due to lockout again increased to 16.80 million in 2000 as against 11.96 million due to strikes. The new economic reforms have also increased employer's militancy and this is reflected in the sharp increase in the share of lockouts.

New Economic Reforms and Labour Relations

New economic reforms are emphasizing liberalization and globalization of the economy. This implies greater reliance on the market forces both within and outside the economy so that we promote efficiency and productivity leading to competitive capability in the world economy.

Table – 1 : Employment in Organised (Public and Private Sector) (in lakhs)

Year	*Union*	*State*	*Quasi*	*Local*	*Public*	*Private*	*Organ-isation*
1991	34.10	71.12	62.22	23.13	190.57	76.76	267.3
1992	34.28	71.90	63.93	21.98	192.10	78.46	270.6
1993	33.83	72.93	64.90	21.60	193.26	78.51	271.8
1994	33.92	73.37	65.14	22.02	94.45	79.30	273.8
1995	33.95	73.55	65.20	21.97	194.66	80.59	275.3
1996	33.66	74.14	64.58	21.92	194.29	85.12	279.4
1997	32.95	74.85	65.35	22.44	195.59	86.86	282.5
1998	32.53	74.58	64.61	22.46	194.18	87.48	281.7
1999	33.13	74.58	63.85	22.59	194.15	86.98	281.1

Source: Reserve Bank of India, Handbook of Statistics on Indian Economy 1999.

Industry has, therefore, started restructuring, downsizing and reducing overheads with a view to cost reduction. All these efforts at restructuring and downsizing imply loss of jobs. Obviously, new economic reforms are leading to a process of jobless growth.

The basic problem with all attempts at economic reforms is not to treat labour as an asset, but as a mere instrument, which can be dispensed with when in the judgement of the employer, it is no longer useful. This is a very mechanical view of labour, which is presented by trade unions on the one hand, and judiciary on the other. For the employer, it is an attempt at cost reduction, but for the employee; it is the loss of job. In developed countries, where social security systems have been extensively developed, the process of downsizing is much less painful, because the worker can atleast get some unemployment dole and thus is not deprived of a basic minimum essential for livelihood, hut in an underdeveloped country, this restructuring and downsizing leading to retrenchment or closure results in depriving the workers of their livelihood.

Full employment is the primary objective of our macro economic policy and the 11 five year plan documents stressed the need for full employment. But the strategies followed by various Indian governments appear to be counter productive. In areas like productivity, profitability, efficiency, the results of economic reforms are mixed but in the sphere of employment, it is really adverse. The productivity gains achieved 3.2 percent had not passed on to the working class. The workers received only 1.2 per cent of the productivity gains.

Impact of Globalization on SSI

The impact of the policy regime of RIEs may be discussed as follows:

1. Rural and small-scale industrial enterprises were not clearly distinguished.
2. The problem of industrialization of backward areas was recognized, but its linkages were not properly considered
3. Setting up of six separate promotional Boards did not contribute to evolution of an integrated regional micro-level approach to RIEs.
4. Constitutionally, rural industries form a part of the domain of the State Government. But the Union Government tended to assume large responsibilities and by and large, a uniform (or regionally non-differentiated) all India approach. Financially, weak states with badly any regional max/level planning failed to attract such industries.

5. There were badly any systematic and sustained attempt to forge, renew and strengthen the linkages between agriculture and industry either in the pre-green revolution approach or in the green revolution approach.
6. The problems arising from excessively small and non-viable size of rural settlements (which provided abode to nearly 24 percent of the population) were not responded to

In a nutshell, if was not recognized that a) while all RIEs (Rural Industrial Enterprises) are small, all of them are not rural; b) that household industries may exist in urban/metropolitan areas too (urban informal sector); c) that the capital and resource cost of a unit of output, and employment, intersectoral linkages, utilization of conventional and easily imparted skills, generation of surpluses, etc., in the rural cottage units are generally different from those seen in the small modern industries segment; and d) hat non-traditional, non-household industries may be found in rural areas buy they are unlikely to be very common and that at the present stage of Indian development, rural industrialization has to proceed in terms of small-scale RIEs, with strong forward and backward linkages the rural sector, though they need not necessarily follow small commodity production, organizational pattern, and have to experiment with new organizational models.

Generally speaking, RIEs have received attention as they provide some answers to the special needs of late-industrializing countries. However, they need regeneration (more urgently for the sick or problem RIEs) and growth in order to bring about dispersal of industries so that over and unbalanced urbanization can be checked and rural development especially targeted on the poor and the marginalized can be accelerated, for a time bound, structural impact.

Policy Thrusts

The major elements of the policy regime relating to RIEs are the following:

1. Encouragement for creation of domestic capacity to produce intermediate and capital goods, mainly through import-substitution in conditions of highly protected markets.

2. Increased role of the public sector in basic and heavy industries, requiring large, risky and slow-maturing investments and new, imported technologies.
3. Large and growing role for a controlled regulated and liberally helped private sector in modern industries, mainly consumer goods (at least initially) with an announced but flexible demarcation of spheres between the public and private sector.
4. Liberal and multifaceted aid for large and medium industries in the private sector within the framework of the Industrial Development Regulation Act, with special ancient on spatial dispersal in favour of backward regions.
5. Initiation of number of regulatory, promotional and preferential measures to support the growth of village and small industries, (VSIs) basically on social grounds like employment, dispersal and decentralization.

The VSI programme was originally a part of the community Development Programme (CD). In some CD blocks, special emphasis was given to the performance of cottage and village industries. In keeping with the prevalent centralized approach, some central level organization like KVIC, coir Board, Silk Board, Handicrafts Board, etc., were set up. Later on, some special financial help and subsidized credit were also made available the concept of "tiny sector" was introduced. District Industries centres (DICs), meant for single – roof services followed. Programmes like IRDP, TRYSEM and ISB too were designed for the rural non-fane sector. The village industries were treated on par with the SSIs.

Economic Reforms Labour and Employment

Positive Feature of Recommendations

NCL has made certain important and in some cases, certain path breaking recommendations in the interests of labour in the context of review of labour laws. Important among them are:

1. NCL recommends a specific provision in the Trade Union Act to enable workers in the unorganised sector to form trade unions and get them registered. It has recommended a waiver of the condition of employer-employee relationship and also of 10 per cent membership in the establishment.

This is a path-breaking recommendation which can pave the way for bringing into the fold of the labour movement 92 per cent of the workers in the unorganised sector.

2. The Commission has recommended the use of check-off system to determine the negotiating agent in an establishment. Moreover, the Commission by fixing 66 per cent membership for entitlement as negotiating agent has not favoured the principle of simple majority but has opted for two-third majority.
3. The Commission has recommended a three-tier system of Lok Adalats, Labours Courts and Labour Relations Commissions while Lok Adalats and Labour Relations Commission has been empowered to deal with both individual problems and problems of collecting bargaining when bilateral negotiations are unable to reach a settlement.
4. The Commission has also recommended 'strike ballot' as an essential condition before giving the call for a strike. This is intended to infuse greater democreatization in functioning of the trade union movement with regard to vital decisions. The rank and file should not be taken for granted and they should not be hustled into accepting decisions taken by the leadership. In this sense, strike ballot should form a part of the decision-making before launching a strike.
5. Another recommendation which is in vital labour interest is: Against permanent jobs, casual or temporary workers should not be employed for more than 2 years.
6. The Commission has guaranteed 8.33% bonus for all employees when it states that every employer should pay each worker one month's bonus before an appropriate festival.
7. The Commission's categorical view that no exemption from labour laws should be allowed to export promotion zones or special economic zone, is another evidence of its sincerity about implementation of labour laws.

Issues for Further Debate and Deliberation

There are certain recommendation which are either vague or which require further debate and deliberation. It would be desirable to take up certain issues.

1. Definition of the Term 'Worker'

The Commission has recommended that the Government may lay down a list of such highly paid jobs in the high wage islands like those of air pilots who may be declared as non-workers or alternately fix a cutoff limit of remuneration which is substantially high enough, such as Rs.25,000 p.m. beyond which employees will not be treated as ordinary workers.

Fixing a cut-off of Rs.25,000 can open a Pandora's box because a very large number of supervisory and managerial personnel are drawing less than Rs.25,000 per month. All these categories will put pressure on the Government to be included in the category of workers to avail of the benefit of labour laws. At present, during 1998-99, out of a total of 8.59 million persons employed in industry in India, 6.36 million (74 per cent) are classified as workers, 1.0 million (11.6%) belong to supervisory and managerial staff and 1.22 million (14.2 per cent) are other employees. The Commission has left the issue vague. There is a need to arrive at a specific definition of the term 'worker'.

2. Binding Nature of Settlement with a Negotiating Agent

The Commission has explicitly stated in its report: "A settlement entered into with a negotiating agent must be binding on all workers". The basic aim of this recommendation is that once the negotiating agent with either over 66 per cent representation or a composite negotiating agent constituted from major trade unions enters into an agreement, such an agreement must be binding on all workers.

3. Check-off System to be Limited to Establishments Employing 300 more Persons

The Commission states: "Though the check-off system will be preferred in the case of establishments employing less than 300 persons too, the mode to identifying the negotiating agent in these establishments may be determined by the LRCs.

4. Worker's Participation in Management to be Applicable for Establishments Employing 300 or more Workers

The Commission is of the view that workers' participation in management should be made applicable to all establishments employing 300 or more workers. This is welcome. But the question which needs an answer is: Why should establishments employing less than 300 workers is left out? If the functioning of an establishment and its productivity has to be enhanced, then workers; participation can be used as an effective instrument for the purpose.

5. Lockouts and Strikes Treated Par

The approach of the commission to treat strikes and lockouts at par is basically unjustified. The Commission, however, recommends "that an illegal strike or illegal lockout should attract

Table – 4 : Workers involved and Mandays lost in Strikes and Lockouts in India during 1991-2000

Year	Workers involved in (000's)		Mandays lost (in million)		Mandays lost per worker	
	Strikes	Lockouts	Strikes	Lockouts	Strikes	Lockouts
1991	872	470	12.43	14.00	14.3	29.8
1992	767	485	15.13	16.13	19.7	33.3
1993	672	282	5.61	14.69	8.3	52.1
1994	626	220	6.65	14.33	10.6	65.1
1995	683	307	5.72	10.57	8.4	34.4
1996	609	331	7.82	12.47	12.8	37.8
1997	637	344	6.31	10.68	9.9	31.0
1998	801	488	9.35	12.71	11.7	26.0
1999 (P)	1099	212	10.62	16.16	9.7	76.2
2000(P)	1044	11.96	11.96	16.80	11.5	44.9
1991 to 2000	7810	3513	91.60 (39.8)	138.54 (60.2)	11.7	39.4
2001(P) Jan-sept	138	148	2.49	10.76	18.0	72.7

Note: figures in brackets give the percentage share of strikes and lockouts in madays lost.

Source: compiled and computed from labour Bureau, Shimla as reported in Ministry of Labour, Annual Report (2001-02)

P=Provisional

similar penalties. A worker who goes on an illegal strike should lose three days; wages for every day of illegal strike, and the management must pay the worker wages equivalent to three days; wages per day for the duration of an illegal lockout. The union which leads an illegal strike must be derecognized and debarred from applying for registration for a period of two or three years.

6. Lay-offs and Retrenchment

The Commission, therefore, has recommended more rationalized system by grating higher compensation in case of running concerns than in the case of sick units.

7. Denial of the Right to Strike in the Public Sector

The principal motivation for this recommendation is to restrict hardship to the people since these services affect the entire population of the country.

8. Sole vs. Composite Negotiating Agent

They may not accept a decision to which they are not a party, but find it very difficult to oppose an agreement which, by and large, would satisfy a majority of workers. Consequently, it would be more pragmatic to adopt a composite negotiating agent in all cases and let different trade unions to exert their pressure at the negotiating table to hammer out the settlement.

Conclusion

The Report of National Commission on Labour is internally inconsistent. This would leave near 60 per cent of labour force employed in industry to face 'hire and fire' with the changing structure of market demand. The question of proving 'reasonable cause' does not arise. In this sense, the NCL Report suffers from logical inconsistency.

References

Syed Vazith Hussain, *"Small Scale Industries in the New Millenium"*, Sarup & Sons, New Delhi.

Ruddar Datt, *"Economic Reforms, Labour and Employment"*, Deep & Deep Publications, New Delhi.

Report, The National Commission on Labour, Vol. I, Part-I, 2002.

17

Labour and Employment Issues under Globalized Era

N. Mukundan and S. Thiyagarajan

At present time, there is an euphoria in the international business community about a new phenomenon euphemistically called "globalization". Globalisation has become a buzz word. It is a popular term in the lexicon of bureaucrats, consultants, journalists and policy analysts. The term 'globalisation' is widely used but seldom defined in precise terms. Different people use the word for different aspects and its consequences. Antagonists of globalization tend to protest against different aspects viz. market interaction, consumer culture, unfair trade, environmental impact of modernization, dehumanization due to technology, effects of mass media, dominance of market etc. In brief globalization is a process with several dimensions such as social, political, economic, environmental, cultural and religious all of which affect each of us.

From an economist's perspective globalization is transnationalization of production and capital, standardization of consumer tastes, legitimization of global capitalism through transportation, creation of international institutions. In brief it facilitates to border less world market.

Labour Issues under Globalization

1. Globalization has resulted in human right violations for millions of workers (particularly women workers) peasants

and farmers and indigenous communities. The result has been massive unemployment.

2. Globalization has also endangered or accentuated the process of the casualisation of labour and the informal of labour. (Employers are increasingly resorting to employment of workers on part and short term contracts).

3. Globalization with its demand for "flexible" labour has resulted in the "feminization of labour", the point is that the overwhelming majority of female labour in the south is concentrated in low wage industries such as textiles and food wear production. Workers in such industries are not only inadequately protected as regards health and safety but they also do not only inadequately protected as regards health and safety but they also do not enjoy security of employment in view of the tendency of such investors to move offshore to cut costs.

4. The impact of globalization on traditional cottage industries has also adversely affected women workers. Cheap imports have resulted in the closure of number of such industries in India and Pakistan and retrenchment of their largely women workers.

5. Globalization has by intensifying the tendencies towards uneven development within countries and within regions intensified the development of the phenomenon of migrant workers. Such workers (especially those who are national frontiers) are subject to a whole range of human right violations, discrimination, protection of low wages and physical and (in the case of women) sexual abuse.

6. Globalization poses a serious threat to the right of livelihood of million of traditional farmers in the developing countries as the hitherto protected agriculture sector of the south in compliance with the requirements of the GATT final Act. It is also feared that patenting of seeds by multinationals such as Gargill will result traditional farmers being displaced.

Employment Issues under Globalization

The New Economic Policy in India even now poses a threat to the aggravation of overall unemployment level. The reason

Table – 1 : Total Employment and Organized Sector Employment

Sector	*Employment (million)*				*Growth rate (% per annum)*	
	1983	*1988*	*1994*	*1999-00*	*1983-94*	*1994-2000*
Total population	718.21	790.00	895.05	1004.10	2.12	1.93
Total labour force	308.64	3.49	381.94	406.05	2.05	1.03
Total employment organized sector	302.75	324.29	374.45	397.00	2.04	0.98
Employment	24.01	25.71	27.37	28.11	1.20	2.53
Public sector	16.46	18.32	19.44	19.41	1.52	-0.03
Private sector	7.55	7.39	7.93	8.70	0.45	1:87

Note: 1. The Total employment figures are on Usual Status (UPSS) base.

1. The organized sector employment figures are as reported in the Employment Market Information System of Ministry of Labour and pertain to 31st March 1983, 1988, 1994 and 1999.
2. The rate of growth of total employment and organize sector employment are compound rates of growth.

behind this is the use of modern technology which is labour displacing. And also the recent trend towards rise to a new phenomenon of 'jobless growth'. Jobless growth implies an overall acceleration in the growth rate of GDP in the economy which is not accompanied by a commensurate expansion of employment opportunities. It was witnessed the post reform period in India.

The rate of growth of employment was of the order of 2.39% during 1983-1990. During 1990-91 – 1997-8-98, It was 0.06% in organized sector and 1.1% unorganized sector. Added to this, the closure of sick industrial units. Because of global competition most of the companies want to reduce costs and competitive. Since, 1992 many Indian companies have resorted to downsizing by introducing Voluntary Retirement Schemes (VRS).

Trends in Employment and Unemployment rates Industrial Distribution of Total Workforce

1. Overall employment is estimated to have grown at around 1.01 per cent, per annum in 1990s compared to 1.5 per cent per annum in 1980s.
2. The number of unemployed in 1997 was more than the number employed in organized sector.
3. About 7 per cent to 8 per cent of the workforce is protected under organized sector whereas 92 per cent to 93 per cent is unprotected under unorganized.
4. There is a trend in growth of casual labour in the total workforce (the number of casual workers has gone up substantially from 27.7 per cent to 33.2 per cent).

Trends in Rural Employment

The proportion of casual labourers in the rural workforce has registered significant increase from 22.0 per cent between 1972-73 to 1997-98.

The trends in rural employment have been similar to those for the whole economy. Growth in rural employment has decelerated sharply from 1.87 per cent per annum during 1973-74 to only 0.66 per cent per annum during 1993-94 to 1999-2000.

Agricultural employment also decelerated the most from 1.44 percent per annum during 1973-74 to 1993-94 to 0.19 per cent per annum 1993-94 to 1999-2000. Estimate of Emplyment and Unemployment made by the N.S.S Organization for 1999-2000.

The estimates on employment and unemployment have been made on the basis of Current Daily Status (CDS), the following conclusions are drawn.

In spite of the higher growth in GDP over the period between 1983-84 to 1993-94 and 1993-94 to 1999-2000 from 5.2 per cent to 6.7% per annum the employment growth declined from 2.7 per cent to 1.07 per cent per annum. As a result the number of unemployed has increased from 20/13 million in 1993-94 to 26.58 million in 1999-2000.

Inter-state unemployment rates are also showing increasing regional disparity in the year 1993-94. The incidence of unemployment has been highest in Kerala for both males and females. The states of Assam, Orissa, Sikkim and West Bengal in the Eastern Region and Haryana and Punjab in the Northern Region recorded unemployment rates which exceeded all India rates. (Kerala of 20.97 per cent and lowest in Himachal Pradesh of 2.96 per cent).

Special Group Report on Targeting ten million employment opportunities per year under the chairmanship of S.P.Gupta mentioned that the raising unemployment is primarily an outcome of a declining job creating capacity of growth observed. Since 1993-1994 the employment growth fell to 1.07% per annum (between 1993-94 and 1999-2000) from 2.7% per annum in the past (between 1983 and 1993-1994) in spite of acceleration in GDP growth from 5.2% between 1983 and 1993-94 to 6.7% between 1993-94 and 1999-2000.

Tenth Plan Projections

1. The estimates of unemployed for the year 2001-02 have been given around 3.85 million person. When the unemployment rate went up around 9.21 per cent.
2. It also provides the estimates of addition to labour force over the Tenth plan period as 35.29 million person.
3. The Approach Paper recommends providing employment opportunities to all the additions in the labour force over the 5 years of the Tenth plan.

Thus, over the Tenth plan we have to deal with the problem of creating job opportunities against a potential job demand of more than 70.14 million person years.

The Main Recommendations made by Report of the Task force Employment Opportunities 2001

- Accelerating the rate of growth of GDP with particular emphasis on sectors likely to ensure the spread of income to the low income segments of the labour force.
- Pursing appropriating sectoral policies in individual sectors which are particularly important for employment for employment generation. These sector level policies must be broadly consistent with the overall objectives of acceleration GDP growth.
- Implement focused special Programmes for creating additional employment and enhancing income generation from existing activities aimed at helping vulnerable groups that may not be sufficiently benefited by the more general growth promoting policies.
- Pursuing suitable policies focused and skill development which would upgrade the quality of the labour force and make it capable of supporting a growth process which generates high quality jobs.
- Ensuring that the policy and legal environment governing the labor market encourages labour absorption especially in organized sector.

The Report of the Task Force has Evoked General Criticism

- A review of industrial relations in the perform decade (1981-90) reveals that as against 402.1 million mandays lost during the decade (1981-90) the number of mandays lost declined to 210 million during 1991-2000. But more mandays have been lost in lockouts than in strikes.
- A large number of workers have lost their jobs as a result of VRS retrenchment and colours both in the organized and the unorganized sector. The exact number is not available.

A Few other General Observations on Matters about the Industrial Relations Scenario

- It is increasingly noticed that trade unions do not normally give a call for strike because they are afraid that a strike may lead to the closure of the unit.
- Service sector workers feel that they have become outsiders and are becoming increasingly disinterested in trade union activities.
- There is a trend to evolve major disputes through negotiations at bipartite level, the nature of disputes or demands is changing.
- The attitude of the government especially of the central government towards workers and employers seems to have undergone a change, now permissions for closures, retrenchment were easily granted.

Conclusion

Globalization of market economy has spread all over the world in the last decade of 20th century after the collapse of socialist planned economy. It arrived in India through the backdoor of economic reforms as the Indian ruling elite had already mesmerized by the superiority and glitter of west. It had all the trappings of a 'white angel' as a result, affecting collective bargaining power and imperativiuous to human development. (Evidence of growth over the past 56 years in India as well as in other parts of the world reveals that there is no automatic link between growth and human development). M.A. Oommen stresses the need to search for alternative development paradigms. In his opinion, the dominant technological paradigm of development that dominates global capitalism has to be challenged from developing economy. Therefore, any New Development paradigm should work towards with humanistic approach.

18

Child Labour in Two-Wheeler Workshops in Tirunelveli

A. Selva Kumar and G. Karunanithi

Tirunelveli is very popular for good education. Here, Palayamkottai is called as Oxford of South India. But, unfortunately the possibility of employment of Child Labour in unorganized sector exists. Though child labour is a comprehensive term, this paper has specially examined the child labour in Two-wheeler workshops. Nearly, 520 Two-wheeler workshops are in Tirunelveli Corporation area. In these areas about 1600 boys, upto the age of 14 years are working. A great number of two-wheeler workshops are located at Tirunelveli Junction, Tirunelveli Town, Pettai, Palayamkottai, Melapalayam, Maharaja Nagar, Sankar Nagar, NGO 'A' & 'B' Colony, Perumalpuram, Thiyagaraja Nagar and KTC Nagar. In Two-wheeler workshops, children work under adverse conditions where,

(i) Proper ventilation at the work site is not there;
(ii) There are not proper toilets and if they are their, these are not cleaned properly,
(iii) The lighting is not sufficient;
(iv) Most of the work is carried out an the road side, so working children are exposed to health hazards;

(v) The working has are very !ong;

(vi) They pick up bad habits such as tobacco chewing, smoking from their guides and many of them become alcoholics and drug addicts subsequently;

(vii) Sometimes they are exploited sexually;

(viii) They are often beaten for doing anything wrong and as such always work under fear psychosis.

Above, all they are said co as wages with which they can have just two square meals. They lack nourishment and thus their overall development and growth is affected. Therefore the present study aims at finding the socio-economic problems of child labour in unorganized sector is two-wheeler workshops.

Objectives

(a) To study the earnings and work load on working children in two-wheeler workshops;

(b) To identify types of problems faced by working children;

(c) Opinions for willing and not willing to be the working children.

Methodology

The study was based on primary data and undertaken in two-wheeler workshops. Of the automobile workshops, only two-wheeler workshops were taken in Tirunelveli Corporation area. Convenient sampling technique was used to take sample of 100 working children from the study area. Survey method was used to collect the data from working children with the help of Interview-Schedule.

To identify the problem related to child, employers, Government officials, like, factory inspector and labour inspector, parents/guardians of children, NCLP Director, social workers, and NGO's were contacted and interviewed.

Work Load and Earnings

A child labour in two-wheeler workshops rises around 6 a.m. He finishes activities, like toilet, bathing, cleaning etc. from 6.00 a.m. to 7 a.m. At 7 a.m. He has a breakfast of left over rice or black coffee and packs lunch. Around 8 a.m. he leaves home for the work place. At 8.30 a.m. he starts performing the different activities like repairing, denting, puncuring etc. and continues, to work upto 1.30 p.m. He has lunch break from 1.30 to 2.00 p.m. At 2.00 p.m. he again starts working and continues to work upto 8 p.m. Around 4.00 p.m. he has tea. He comes back home around 9.00 p.m. At 9.30 p.m. he has dinner and sleeps. It is concluded that daily work life of children begins of 6 in the moving and ends at 9.30 p.m. This hectic schedule deprives the children from the enjoyment of their childhood.

At this tender age a boy works nearly 12 hrs. in a two-wheeler workshops. But he learns only Rs.500-750 per month as salary/ wage. His learning are supplement to the family income. But, some of the children have no wages.

Problems

It gives socio-economic and psychological problems of working children in two-wheeler workshops. Problems faced by child workers are, not able to studies, unfavourable working conditions, deprived of entertainment, undue scolding or ill treatment, underfed, to work beyond capacity, no fixed working hours, unpaid, exertions or fatigue, and constant threat of looking the job.

The data reveals that, of the total respondents 38 per cent are felt exertions and fatigue due to overload of work, 34 per cent are unable to study, 11 per cent are complaining of unfavourable working conditions, 9 per cent are deprived of entertainment 8 per cent are faced the problem of no fixed working hours.

Willing and Not Willing

The parents compel their children to undertake this work at a tender age of 8 or 9. A great majority of the child workers in the study area do not like do to this work. Whereas, only 16 per cent of them like do the work to supplement family income.

An attempt was made to know the reasons given by the child workers for not willing this work. A large majority (63 per cent) of the children are not willing the work because this work has prevented them from pursuing their study; about one-forth (26 per cent) of them are not willing the work because it is a painful work; one-tenth (11 per cent) of them are not willing the work because it is under payment and prevented from playing with others. This clearly shows that, the child workers do the work out of compulsion by their parents.

A boy of 13 years, working in a two-wheeler workshop in Tirunelveli Junction explains his plight as follows:

My parents are basically agricultural workers and absolutely unfamiliar to this work. But, they forced me to work due to severe financial crisis in our family. Though, I was demoted to the Vth standard. I had no other option but to resort to this work. I have two younger sisters and one brother. My father is under employed. My mother is sick. We have no adequate income to run the family. So, I have to earn money to supplement my family income. I am very much interested in studies. Unfortunately, my parents prevented me from going to school. Now I want to study at least in the high school level. Would you help me sir, to continue my studies? If you do so, I will never forget you in my life time.

Recommendations

(a) Enacting a stringent Act relating to compulsory primary education is an effective measure to put an end to this problem. In addition to this, the primary schools across the country should be provided with infrastructural facilities.

(b) Poverty eradication and employment generation programmes of the Government should be implemented with a spirit of commitment and dedication to eliminate poverty.

(c) An appropriate implementation of structure and strategies for the effective enforcement of legal measures for eliminating super exploitation of child labour must be discussed.

(d) That should be formulation of strategies for eradication of child labour. These strategies should be based on literacy level, income level and education level of working children.

Finally it is concluded that this problem is a multi-dimensional one and hence combined efforts of the Government, Non-governmental Organisations, Media and Public participation alone can solve the problem and help to establish a child labour free society in the coming generation.

19

Globalization and the Opportunities for Indian Labour

D. Gopalsamy

Labour and the New Economy

Globalisation involves changes in the structure of national economies, consumption patterns and product and factor price relatives. Accordingly, impact upon different groups of people differently. The pattern of global employment is shift from manufacturing to service or from the production of material goods to production of intangibles.

The emerging service sector activities in the new economy – some of which education, advertising, research and development, and accounting – demand high levels of knowledge and skills from workers. Even the traditional manufacturing activities are increasingly becoming service based, requiring ever more of workers soft skills. All the ways it is going to forwards the creation of "new knowledge for the making the goals. It is true that knowledge. The critical factor of production in the new economy, resides in the brain of the workers.

Employment Situation in India During the Era of Globalisation

The employment situation in India has worsened in the era of globalization. The rate of growth of employment which was the order of 2.04 per cent per year during 1983-94 declined to a low level of 0.98 percent during the period 1994-2000. This was largely the consequence of a negative growth rate of employment in agriculture which absorbed about 65 percent of total employed workers as also a sharp decline in community, social and personal service to 0.55 percent during 1994-2000 as against 2.90 percent during 1983-94.

Table : 1- Growth of Employment by sectors in India

Sectors	*1983-93*	*1994-2000*
Agriculture	1.51	-0.34
Mining & Quarrying	4.16	-2.84
Manufacturing	2.14	2.05
Electricity, gas & Water supply	4.50	-0.88
Construction	5.32	7.09
Trade	3.57	5.04
Transport, storage and communication	3.24	6.04
Financial services	7.18	6.20
Community & personal service	2.90	0.55
Total	2.04	0.98

Source: Govt. of India, Planning Commission.

This was largely the consequence of neglect of agriculture and shedding the load of excess employment in the public sector by imposing a continuous ban on recruitment and not filling up even the positions vacated by retirement of public sector employers.

Opportunities for Indian Labour in Software and ITES Industris

From the 1990, India's software industry has been growing at phenomenally fast rates, starting of course, from a low base. Between 1992-93 and 2000-01, software production in India grew at an average annual rate of approximately 50 percent. A rate more than three times faster than the growth of the country's whole economy.

Table -2: Total revenue in IT and ITES (Information Technology Enabled Services) industries in India.

Year	*Total revenue in US dollar*	*Share in India's GDP (%)*
1997-98	5	1.2
1998-99	6	1.5
1999-00	8.2	1.9
2000-01	12.1	2.7
2001-02	13.4	2.9
2002-03	16.1	3.2
2003-04	21.5	3.5
2004-05	28.2	4.1

The combined revenue from information technology and ITES industries in India increased from US$ 5 billion in 1997-98 to US$28.2 billion in 2004-05 a growth of 464 percent over a seven year period. As a share of India's gross domestic product (GDP). The combined revenue to the country from IT and ITES industries moved up from 1.2 percent in 1997-98 to 4.1 percent in 2004-05.

India's recent success in software industry owe largely to its vast pool of English speaking engineers whose wages are much lower than wages of similarly qualified people in developed countries and their skill levels quite high.

Employment Potential of Information Technology

Information technology has opened large avenue for educated youth in the country. It is estimated that one segment of IT industry. i.e. computers-both hardware and software. Computer engineers and system analysts are having a million jobs at present. In this sense, IT industry has great future in expanding employment opportunities.

Knowledge – Intensive Industries and Entrepreneurship

India's becoming a favoured destination for outsourcing of highly skilled, knowledge – intensive activities as well. Global technology companies like IBM, Motorola and Google have setup several research and development centres in many Indian cities.

The Reasons for Globalisation and Overall Improvement in the Quality of Jobs

1. With liberalization, expansion of trades would have to be based on comparative advantage and with India's advantage in labour based exports, such an expansion would lead to increase in employment.
2. The increase in employments will be significantly larger with faster economic growth expected to result from economic reform and liberalization which constitute essential elements of globalization.
3. The larger inflow of foreign investment will further strengthen employment growth both directly and indirectly through its contribution to economic growth.
4. Expansion of employment and consequent tightening of the labour market should result in improvement in the quality of employment interms of earnings as well as conditions of work and employment.
5. The globalised production system with supply chains and technological linkages is expected to provide greater possibility and observance of minimum labour standards.

Suggestions

1. In India, to meet the challenges from the emerging knowledge economy, it is important that domestic investment in research and development is stepped up.
2. India should first provide "work for all" and being a society in transition, should proceed to achieve "Decent work for All" as its ultimate objective.
3. Right to work as basic human right. For this purpose, a new model of development recouncilling GDP growth and employment growth should be developed.
4. The Government should provide financial facilities to weaker sections for the improvement of IT knowledge.

Conclusion

In sum, the new economy promises expanding opportunities for educated seditions of Indian labour. However, converting these early signals of progress in to wide spread and participatory development in the country requires, first, strong interventionalist policies by the Indian government, most importantly in education and social development.

SECTION – B

WOMEN AND AGRICULTURAL LABOURERS

20

Women Workforce in Rural Development

D. Kumar and M. Perumal

The need to promote and enhance women's participation on an equal basis with men in the social, economic and political process of rural development and share fully the improved conditions of life in rural areas, was reiterated and elaborated in the recommendations of the World Conference on Agrarian Reform and Rural Development (WCARRD, 1979) the Conference of non-aligned and other developing countries on the role of women in development. The WCARRD also observed that the situation of rural women has now been identified as one of the critical manifestations of the growing imbalances, which constitutes a threat not merely to the development of the female population but to the socio- economic progress of the nations themselves. The maximization of food production, the need to contain human misery, malnutrition and hunger that interferes with the productivity and growth and above all the need to reduce the rate of population growth are all linked up with better understanding of the situation of women.

Since, the largest section of women in the world love in rural areas and the majority of them are engaged in agricultural production, processing and distribution of products, the issue of rural women's participation in development, he manner in which their position and roles are being affected by the process of change, call for a far more critical analysis and understanding than they have received in the past development strategies.

NIRD and FAO's Report about Women Workforce

The National Institute of Rural Development and F.A.O. Workshop on the Integration of Women in Agriculture and Rural Development (1980) observed that there is an urgent need to expand knowledge and statistical data on all aspects of the rural poor, particularly with regard to women's role in rural activities and to disseminate this information in order to promote greater awareness of women's role in rural activities and to disseminate this information in order to promote greater awareness of women's role in society. Studies in this field have not shown much concern. In order to include women as a component in the mainstream of developments, it is essential to know as to what exactly she is doing now, where she needs help and where she can contribute to the development. It is, therefore of paramount importance to study the work roles of a rural woman so that the concerned organisation might have a better extension and rural service strategy to orient programmes to achieve the best results.

'Women' is the mother of race. Nehru once said, "To awaken people it is the women who must be awakened. Once she is on move the family moves, the village moves, the nation moves".

In 1974 study on "Women Towards Equality" was conducted by the Government of India. The study made it clear the intention and plans of the Government to improve the conditions of Indian women not only in the field of education, health, nutrition but also to the need of participation of women in the over all development of the society. It also recognised the potential of women who have always worked hard and relentlessly alongside the menfolk to fulfill the several roles assigned to them by tradition as well as economic throughout the ages has been underestimated. In order to release women's potential for fuller participation in productive and decision making process, there is need not only for a sharing of parental responsibilities but also for institutional provisions which would benefit women's participation in decision making. Tradition idealizes her role as a mother, and as a housewife.

Planning Commission's Report

The Five year plans which where formulated after the publication of the report have attempted to impart new thrust and direction to women's development through series of varying programmes, schemes and action plans administered. However, without economic independence women cannot achieve equality.

While women including rural women cannot be seen as a homogeneous group any where, this is especially true of developing societies like India where the caste and the class factors stratify women like men into different social layers. As a result of this fact their participation in development would differ according to their status in the socio-economic fabric.

This study has been taken up with a view to find out rural women's own perceptions of the effects of development programmes such as IRDP, Indira Awas Yojana, JRY,EAS etc. and their role in the development process. Secondly, but not secondary the actual functioning of Government programmes and the lacunae in policy formulation and implementation.

Rural Development Programmes and Women Workforce

It in fact is a peculiar situation that in spite of the extensive workload carried out by rural women their participation in the rural development programmes is overlooked. Their contribution to agricultural production has not been less than that of men. Both men and women share the pre-harvest and post-harvest manual –cum-technological operation almost equally. Unfortunately the policy makers, development planners and implementers have failed to reflect peoples' own perceptions of their need and aspirations in the strategies and programmes intended for their development. It has been realised that while examining the causes of failure of certain programmes, the intended beneficiaries in no way saw the programmes as being related to their needs. This is even more true in the case of rural women whose point of view seem to have never been taken into account. The problem of being statistically overlooked and neglected is further compounded by the urban middle class men who dominate policy planning and implementation. But as we all know any development strategy which neglects the need for enhancing the role of women cannot lead to comprehensive socio-economic development more in the rural areas.

The lives of the rural women is very closely linked with forests. In recent times the fact of deforestation has caused them much hardships. They have to travel long distances on foot to collect fuel, fodder and other raw materials for their requirements. The Government's afforestation policies have in no way helped rural poor, particularly women, in fulfilling their basic needs of fuel and fodder.

Traditionally, women have been systematically kept out of the core productive activity like wielding the plough or the potters' wheel while they are required to do all the ancillary activity which require hard, back breaking labour. Instead of countering this, modern day development efforts seem to enhance it or perpetuate this in different ways. While there is a growing recognition of inclusion of women in agricultural extension programmes not a single agricultural extension programme for women has been undertaken. The only programmes that have regularly been conducted are limited to housekeeping and child care.

The Report of the committee on the Status of Indian Women has some alarming findings to convey that the forces of development, modernisation and urbanization had tended to drive women backwards, to put matters in reverse gear; that there was no homogeneity in the concept of the " the Indian Women", since the geography, size and diversity of conditions in the country gave a variety to the status of its women; that the existence of several religions in the country with different set of personal law for each, touching a whole range of aspects affecting women, like marriage, divorce, succession etc. cannot be overlooked. All these factors highlight extraordinary challenges that we face in the task improving the status of our women.

Conclusion

The 73rd Amendment Act, 1992 has provided one third reservation for women including those belonging to SCs and STs. As a result of this provision that would be about 11 lakhs of women who have become members and chairpersons of Panchayats.

Among them about 2.5.lakhs would be women belonging to SCs and STs categories. Studies reveal that most of these women are not aware of the basics of decentralized governance, planning and development. Awareness and psychological empowerment of these women are indispensable for building confidence among them and for acquiring necessary knowledge and skill to play their role effectively at gross-root level.

References

Agarwal, Bina; *In Employment – The Status of Women*, Seminar, No. 165, May 1973.

Agarwal, Dipti and Indu Grover, *Women in Politics and Governance*, Social Welfare, No.12, Vol. 45, March 1999.

Ahmed, M. Ariz; *Empowerment of Women: Self – help Groups at Gossaigaon Assam*, Kurukshetra, No.7, Vol. 47, April, 1999.

Bardhan, Kalpana; *Women's Work, Welfare and Status: Forces of Tradition and Change in India*, Economic and Political Weekly, No.50, Vol.XX, December, 1985.

Jeffery, Roger, Patrica Jefferey and Andrew Lyen; *Taking Dung – Work Seriously – Women's Work and Rural Development in North India*, Economic and Political Weekly, No.7, Vol. XXIV, April, 1989.

21

Problems of Agricultural Labourers of Manakkarai Village of Tuticorin District

S. Lakshmi Ganapathy and D. Kathiravan

"It is one of the Primary objects of the five year plans to ensure fuller opportunities for work and better living to all sections of the rural community and particular, to assist agricultural labourers and backward classes to come up to the level of the rest". - III Five Year Plan

Agricultural Labourers

Agricultural labourers are the people who are come under the following four categories.

1. Landless labourers who work in farms.
2. Landless labourers who are personally independent but work for others.
3. Small farmers who have small size of lands and
4. Farmers who have economic holding but who have one or more of their children and dependants working for other agriculturists.

Agricultural Labourers in India

According to the Second Agricultural Labour Enquiry (1960), Agricultural labour family constituted nearly 25 % of the total rural families. Among these families 85% of the rural workers are casual labourers.

One estimate revealed that agricultural labourers predominantly belong to the scheduled castes, scheduled tribes and other backward classes. It also revealed that 75% to 80% of all agricultural labourers belong to the scheduled castes.

According to the National Commission on Rural Labour (1991) the total Agricultural labourers households were 33.3 million. The Census of India (1991) revealed that the total number of agricultural labourers was 74.6 million in 1991.

Data about the wages paid to agricultural labourers reveals that the agricultural labourers do not receive notified minimum wages except in certain parts of the country like Kerala, Punjab, Haryana and Western U.P. Wherever agricultural labourers are unorganized and thus have weak bargaining power, the gap between actual wage paid and the minimum wage fixed by the government is large.

Problem of Rural Poverty

Poverty can be defined as a social phenomenon in which a section of the society is unable to fulfil even its basic necessities of life. On the basis of National Sample Survery (NSS) (38th round), the World Bank Report calculated the percentage of rural poverty in India was 46%. 64% of the agricultural labourers were below the poverty line in the year 1983. The following table explains the nature of poverty in India.

Table : 1 – Poverty in India

Year	*No. of Poor (in million)*		
	Rural	*Urban*	*Total*
1951 – 55	170.6	28.1	198.7
1961 – 65	183.0	38.6	221.6
1971 – 75	252.2	54.6	306.8
1976 – 83	246.0	58.1	304.1
1991 – 92	249.5	73.3	322.8

Source : Gaurav Datt (1996), Poverty in India.

Agriculture and Poverty

India is an agricultural dominant country depends on the agricultural productivity. Nearly 25% of the GDP of India is received from agricultural sector. But the living condition of the rural agriculturists is not in a satisfactory level. Table–1, explains the increasing trend in the rural poverty. i.e. 170.6 million in the year 1951 and 249.5 million in the year 1991. According to the 55th round survey by NSSO the poverty is declined from 36% to 26.1%. The rural poverty is declined from 37.3% to 27.1%. But the total number of poverty hidden people is 260 million people.

Importance (or) Need for the Study

"Rural economy is the backbone of Indian economy". This is the statement of our Father of Nation. But the rural community is still living a missarable life. Many plans were executed to minimize rural poverty. But the declining rate of rural poverty is not at all in an encouraging level.

Many measures were taken by both the central and state governments to solve the agricultural labour problems. Many laws were implemented. But what is the result? Is the standard of living of agricultural labourers increased? Is the problems faced by agricultural labourers solved? It is a small effort to find the problems of agricultural labourers and to identify the ways and means to reduce the problems faced by the agricultural labourers.

Profile of the Study Area

Manakkarai, the study area is a village. It belongs to Tuticorin District of Tamil Nadu. The Taluk head Quarter of this village is Srivaigundam. The total population of this village is 2837 (2001). Among this 1320 males and 1517 females. The literacy rate of this village is 42%. 90% of the population is belonged to agricultural sector. Nearly 50% of the population is agricultural labourers. There is one primary health center and one primary school in this village. It gets irrigation facility from river Thamirabarani.

Problems of Agricultural Labourers in Manakkarai Village

To get a better result the investigators selected only 30 respondents by random sampling method. A questionnaire was used and direct interviews were also done by the investigators. After the analysation of the collected data, the following important findings were picked up.

1. *Size of the family*

Though the government has taken so many measures to control the population, the size of the family in the study area is big. The following table shows it clearly.

Table – 2 : - Size of the Family

Size of the Family	*No. of Families*	*%*
Below 3	6	20
4-6	10	32.33
Above 6	14	46.66
Total	**30**	**100**

From the above table it is clear that the size of the family in the study area is generally big.

2. *Unemployment*

Unemployment is the biggest problem of the study area. Only one or two persons are getting employment and others in the families are unemployed. Therefore the income source of the family is limited and causes many financial problems. The following table explains the unemployment level of the study.

Table : 3 – Unemployment Level

Size of Unemployment	*No. of families*	*%*
Below 2	16	53.33
3 – 4	8	26.66
Above 4	6	20.00
Total	**30**	**100**

3. Days of employment

Indian agriculture is monsoon based. The study area is belonged to North East Monsoon area. Therefore, there is a possibility of employment for four or five months per year. But at the same time the days of employment are also limited because of various reasons. The following table shows the days of employment particulars.

Table – 4 : Days of employment

No. of days	*No. of families*	%
Below 2 days	18	60.00
3 – 5 days	7	23.33
More than 6 days	5	16.67
Total	**30**	**100**

From table 4 it was understood that the maximum number of agricultural labourers in this area are getting employment for few days only.

4. Social Cost

In the expenditure side, expenditure on religious functions is the largest and it leads to borrowing also. Nearly 50% of the population borrowed an average amount of Rs.5000/- for the car festival expenditure. For this they pay 3% interest rate per month. It is the most important burden of the agricultural labourers of the study area which affects their standard of living and push them into the vicious circle of poverty.

Suggestions to Solve the Problems

On the basis of the findings, the investigators want to suggest the following remedial measures to reduce the problems of agricultural labourers.

- Steps must be taken to bring awareness among to rural people about the benefits of small family by conducting awareness camps and Literacy drive.
- The governments (both Center and State) should implement self – help group programme in an effective manner in the rural areas to reduce rural unemployment. The self – Help group programme can be used as a self – employment generator.
- Proper Training and Education must be given to the agricultural labourers in Crop rotation and intensive cultivation system.
- The available co-perative bank should function effectively to meet the financial needs of the agricultural labourers. !t can reduce the problem of agricultural labourers in indigenous borrowings.
- The Government should watch the implementation of minimum wage policy in an effective manner.

Conclusion

India as a developing country has some fundamental problems. Problems of agricultural labourers are also such type and it can be controlled through the remedial measures suggested here. Have your eyes on poor agricultural labourers and protect them from rural exploitation.

22

Problems of Agricultural Labourers in Madurai District

S. David Amirtha Rajan and
P. Gnana Soundari

India is a nation of agriculture, facing a lot of problems during the failure of monsoon. There are lots of evidences in the history. At the time introduction of industry in India by then British Government, the skilled agricultural labours were used in textile industry and other type of industry. This caused a set back in their life style and lead an immoral life. Later the same conditions have been continuing in their life. Whenever or wherever, there is a failure of rain or season, the ultimate sufferers are agricultural labours. Last few years, it could be seen in some states in India like Andhra Pradesh, Orissa and so on. In these areas, they were in poverty and thereby sold their kidney for their survival. On the other side, because of their illiteracy, they are usually cheated by money lenders. As a whole problems are common in their day to day life of agricultural labourers in India. The same is seen among labourers in Madurai district. Therefore, in this context an attempt is made to study on "Problems of Agricultural labourers in Madurai District." This study is developed on the basis of the following objectives.

1. To study the social problems of the respondents.
2. To analyse the working problems of the respondents.
3. To assess the economic problems of the respondents.

Women constitute nearly half of the world population, receive two-thirds of the world's income and own less than a hundredth of the world's property. In India, 90 percent of women are employed in the unorganized sector, without fair wages and occupational amenities. Domestic women labourers get a paltry sum for the unpleasant work they perform. Some of them are exploited economically as well as physically.

With the growth of industrialization and urbanization, landless labourers, in the absence of assured source of employment in rural areas, migrate to urban areas in search of employment. In urban areas, women are generally employed in informal sectors like weaving, handicraft, tailoring, sale of fish and construction activities.

Unorganised women labourers are outside the reach of most laws which seek to protect labourers, security and living conditions. They are exposed to various exploitations and discriminations.

Indian women, constituting nearly half of the total population, play a crucial role in the domestic sphere and also in the rural field, particularly in the agricultural sector. Yet, our traditional attitude is to treat women as second-class citizens. This is so in spite of the fact that women have proved their mettle in every walk of life. Their contribution is not given due credit. According to an ILO estimate, the value of unpaid household work constitutes 25 to 39 percent of the GNP.

The largest number of working women in India is engaged in farming operations either as cultivators or as agricultural labourers. They take up a wide variety of activities like sowing of seeds, transplanting, weeding, harvesting, preparation of compost and manure pits, application of manures, storage of seeds and food grains. An active farm woman spends eight to nine hours on the farm during the peak agricultural season.

The First Agricultural Labour Committee (1950-51) defined agricultural labourers as 'those people who are engaged in raising crops on payment of wages'. The Second ALC (1955-57) enlarged the definition of agricultural labourer to include 'those who are engaged in other agricultural occupations like dairy farming, horticulture, raising of livestock, bees, poultry etc'. According to the National Commission on Labour (NCL), 'an agricultural labourer is one, who is basically unskilled and unorganized and has little for his livelihood other than personal labour'. Thus persons whose main source of income is wage employment fall in this category. It consists of two sub-categories.

- Permanent Labour (PL) attached to a cultivating household, and
- Casual labour (CL)

'Permanent (or) attached labourers (AL) generally work on annual (or) seasonal basis and they work on some sort of contract. Their wages are determined by traditional methods. On the other hand temporary (or) casual labourers are engaged only during peak periods for work. Their employment is temporary and they are paid at the market rate. They are not attached to any landlord.

Causes of Poor Economic Condition of Agricultural Labourers

The following are the important reasons for the low wages and poor economic conditions of agricultural labourers.

Low Social Activity – Most agricultural workers belong to the depressed classes which have been neglected for ages. The low caste and depressed classes have been socially handicapped and they never have courage to assert themselves. They are like dumb-driven cattle.

Unorganized – Agricultural workers are mostly illiterate and ignorant, and live in scattered villages. Hence, they could not be organized into unions. In urban areas workers could generally organize themselves and it was convenient for political parties to take interest in trade union activity. This is difficult in case of farm labour.

Seasonal Employment – The agricultural workers find employment continuously for about 197 days in a year and for the rest of the year they are idle. Apart from underemployment there is also unemployment. In rural areas unemployment and underemployment are two important factors responsible for low income and consequently low economic position of the agricultural workers in India.

Paucity of Non-agricultural Jobs – Paucity of non-agricultural occupations in villages is another important factor for the low wages and poor economic conditions of the farm labourers. For one thing the growing pressure of population is increasingly felt in rural areas and the number of landless agricultural labourers is steadily increasing. The absence of occupations in rural areas and lack of inter-regional mobility have also been responsible for worsening the pressure of population on land.

Rural Indebtedness – Agricultural labourer is heavily indebted. Normally the farm labourers borrow from the landowners under whom they work. Since they have no security or guarantee in the form of wealth to offer, they pledge themselves to the money lenders and rich landlords and become bonded labourers in many areas. Naturally they are forced to accept low wages.

The Structure and Composition of the Unorganised Sector

The unorganized workers include people involved in agriculture, and agriculture – related work, forest workers, fisher folk, construction labourers, workers employed in small scale / ancillary units in the informal sector of industry, domestic workers, anganwadi workers, casual / contract labourers, home-based workers and self-employed workers.

Women labour in the informal sector is an important segment on the labour force. According to an estimate of the National Commission on Self-Employment of Women (NCSEW), 94 percent of the total female work force operates in the unorganized sector.

They do arduous work as wage earners, piece-rate workers, casual labour and paid family labour. The coverage of labour laws has not benefited these women workers in many areas of wages, working conditions, maternity benefits and social security.

According to the 1981 census, nearly 90 percent of women work in the unorganized sector, which does not offer fair wages and decent terms of work. Nor is there any opportunity to improve the earning potential. There is no supportive services like crèches, fuel and water. In the sphere of farm family labour, women's contribution is immense, but no effort has been made to estimate this.

According to the 1991 census, about 81 percent of female workers are employed in agriculture as labourers or cultivators, constituting 87 percent of the women work force in rural areas and 17.5 percent in urban areas.

The NCSEW has highlighted that the unprotected workers are those who are all outside the purview of the organized sector. Sometimes the unorganized sector is divided into institutionalized unorganized sector (IUS) and non-institutionalized unorganized sector (NIUS). Agriculture, agro-based industries, construction work, small industrial units like beedi making, domestic matches, tailoring, garment units, food processing units and other registered units of small scale business are included in the NIUS. These units are supposed to provide regular employment and minimum wages to its workers but, unfortunately, they fail to effectively implement it. And these issues are not uncommon to the domestic workers, sweepers, scavengers, vendors, hawkers and the self-employed.

Women labour is an important segment of the total workforce in India. According to the census of 2001, more than 90 percent of the working women are engaged as wage labourers in the unorganized sector. The women labourers particularly the rural women, suffer from social disabilities and are prone to continuous exploitation. Their living conditions are poor and their earnings are very low and are not sufficient for their subsistence.

Hence it is necessary to study the problems of agricultural labourers. The study was conducted in five villages of Madurai district. This district was selected in view of the availability of agricultural women labourers. The five villages are Chekkanoorani, Karumathur, Kuppanampatti, Matharai and Poochipatti, 10 samples from each village are selected and required data have been collected during the period 15th January to 31st January 2006.

The collected data have been analysed and following are the findings of the study.

The majority i.e 64 percent of the women labourers are in the age group of 20-39 years. It shows that the women are forced to share the family responsibilities at a young age. This may be the reason for their lack of awareness about their rights and privileges.

84 percent of them are married. It reveals that Indian women are allowed to work outside home after their marriage because they belong to poor families.

Regarding educational status, 70 percent were illiterates.

Caste plays a major role in the social stratification in Indian rural society and it is more so in rural areas. Among the respondents 72 percent is from the scheduled caste.

74 percent of the family members are also involved in agriculture and allied activities.

90 percent of the women labourers are working within the village.

94 percent of the women used to go on foot to work only 6 percent use public transport when they were outside their village.

The reasons for choosing their present occupation were non-availability of any other work (60 percent) and availability of this work within the village (50 per cent). This shows that they do not want to depend only upon agriculture but they want to find some employment opportunities to support their family income and hence they have no other alternative except to agree to choose any employment available.

The majority of the agricultural labourers (78 per cent) and 60 per cent of the non-farm labourers reported to work for 10-20 days in a month. They are unemployed for the remaining 10 days in a month. This shows that the labourers search for alternative work for their unemployed days.

In case of subsidiary occupations, 80 per cent of the agricultural and 68 per cent of the non-agricultural labourers got work for less than 10 days in a month. This shows that the women labourers should have subsidiary occupations like rearing of milch animal, doing petty business and other work in rural areas. The government should implement employment oriented development programmes, especially skill development and development of entrepreneurial skill. This will enhance their income.

In the study villages, the male (88 per cent) labourers got Rs.26-90 per day as his wage depending upon the nature of his work. For women (92 per cent), the wage rate was Rs.25. Group-wise, the female (18 per cent) got Rs.26-50 from the underdeveloped villages because of non-farm work. Therefore, to increase the income of women labourers, the government should give training in non-farm activities and steps must be taken to enforce minimum wages and equal remuneration for equal work.

The majority (84 per cent) or the women labourers received daily wages. This shows the temporary nature of the work. More number of (23 per cent) women labourers got their wages weekly because these labourers used to work mainly in mills.

Nearly 30 per cent of the women labourers face problems in getting their wages after work. The major types of problems are overtime work without any additional wages (54 per cent), delay in payment of wages (23 per cent), have to wait for a longer time to receive wages (10 per cent) and the demand for commission by the agents and contractors (10 per cent). These types of exploitation are more among the agricultural labourers because of its unorganized nature and basically they are illiterates lacking in skill and so they have low bargaining power.

Only 11 per cent of the women labourers enjoy some facilities like day care centre, first aid facilities, rest room, toilet, canteen and crèche in their workspot. This shows that the workers in the unorganized sector need to be given basic facilities in their workspot.

The majority of the women labourers (91 per cent) were not aware of the fixed working hours as per government rule. This may be because of their illiteracy and their negligence to know the rules and also there is nobody to educate them about this. Also, as this is an unorganized sector, no trade union involvement is seen and this may also be one of the reasons.

As for the maximum hours they work, the majority (64 per cent) used to work for 7-8 hours a day and nearly 16 per cent work 8-9 hours. Also more than three-fourths (34 per cent) of them work for more than 8 hours per day. This needs to be looked into and this may be due to their ignorance and hence, the employers try to exploit their labour.

It is really a sorry state of affairs that only eight women labourers out of the total were aware of the Minimum Wages Act. This necessitates to create awareness among the women labourers about the Minimum Wages Act and the various provisions and facilities for the labourers. The majority of the women labourers (89 per cent) receive their wages directly from their employers.

Conclusion

Despite more than five decades of interventions to raise the status of women since Independence, women in rural areas continue to be overwhelmed by economic and social barriers. Rural women throughout India, irrespective of caste or religion, continue to have a subordinate status both within the home and outside. Extent of awareness and access to education are prime determinants of rural women's status and role in the process of development. Limited awareness not only restricts economic options but affects their physical and social wellbeing. Lack of education and skill constrains rural women to work in spheres characterized by low skills and low pay. Women in rural areas have no access to formal credit, particularly because of their inability to provide guarantee in the form of assets. Moneylenders charge high interest rates and use unfair means like emotional and physical harassment to ensure repayment.

All the schemes launched by the government could not improve the living conditions and solve the problems of rural women's employment to the desired extent. Economic independence for rural women is the foundation of their rights, freedom and dignity. But the employment status of women in rural areas is far lower than that of men and the majority of women work in the unorganized sector. It is true that illiteracy and poverty marginalize the participation of women in gainful employment. The key to better employment is the participation of women in gainful employment. Education of women and diversification of employment opportunities supported by government projects promote women's employment. Women should be acquainted with the required skills and equip themselves with training in new trades for gainful employment. The easy accessibility of loans for self-employment has helped many women in improving their family income and gaining respect in the families.

References

Singh D.P., *"Women workers in unorganized sector"*, Deep and Deep Publication Pvt. Ltd, New Delhi, 2005.

Balakrishan A, *"Rural Landless Women labourers-problems and prospects"*, Kalpaz Publications, Delhi, 2005.

Economic Survey 2003-2004.

Dutt & Sundaram, *Indian Economy,* Sultan Chand & Sons, New Delhi, 2004.

23

Status of Women Labourers in Agricultural Sector-A Study

M. Soundarapandian and A. Inigo Antony Beaula

From time immemorial women have been working at homes, fields, factories and various work places, but still they are not recognized as workers in the economic sense of the term. The multiple roles played and productive inputs made by women in terms of work hours contributed or equivalent income generated in the family is neither attended nor recorded. There is greater involvement of women in various agricultural operations. The census of India estimated that 21 per cent of women participate in economic development. Women play a significant and crucial role in agricultural development and allied fields including crop production, livestock, horticulture and post harvest operations. (Kumar and Singh, 2002).

Women make almost half of the adult population. They constitute one third of the labour force but consume two-thirds of the world's working hours and yet earn only one tenth of the income (Chaudhary and Singh, 2003). The prosperity and growth of a nation depend on the status and development of its women. With this background, a study was conducted to assess the position of women labourers in the agricultural sectors of Dindigul District. The specific objectives of the study were delineated as follows.

1. To collect the information regarding the nature of work.
2. To find out the problems faced by women labourers in performing agricultural operations.

Dindigul Taluk consists of 4 different Blocks namely Dindigul, Reddiarchatram, Sanarpatty and Athoor. Dindigul Block had been selected for the study purpose. In Dindigul Block 3 revenue villages namely Mullipadi, Seelapadi and Balakrishnapuram had been selected. Because in this areas, 75% of the personnel needs are met from agriculture. These areas are agriculturally dominated area.

Twenty Five women respondents from each village had been selected for the study. Thus, 75 respondents had been selected and surveyed. Questions and needed particulars are asked through Direct personal interview method. All the selected respondents were agricultural labourers working in others fields for their wages.

Socio-Economic Conditions of Women Labourers

The socio-economic characteristics such as age, literacy, Religion, community, caste, family type, family size, wage level of the sample respondents give a clear picture of socio-economic status in the study villages.

Age-Wise Classification

In Dindigul town, 3 revenue villages namely, Balakrishnapuram, Mullipadi and Seelapadi had been selected and surveyed. In these 3 villages, 75 respondents had been interviewed. The Table 1 indicates that 10.67 per cent of the respondents come under the age group of 30 and below 30 and 33.33 per cent of the

Table 1: Age-Wise Classification

S. No.	*Age (in Years)*	*Number*	*Percentage*
1	30 and Below 30	8	10.67
2	31-45	25	33.33
3	46-60	26	34.67
4	61-75	16	21.33
	Total	**75**	**100.00**

Source : Computed from primary data.

respondents belong to the age group of 31-45. This table also shows that 34.67 per cent of the respondents fall in the age group of 46-60. Nearly 21.33 per cent of the respondents belong to the age group of 61-75. In these 3 revenue villages the respondents range from 30 to 75.

Literacy Wise Classification

This table reveals that 30.67 per cent (23 respondents) are illiterates and 69.33 per cent (52 respondents) have obtained the school level education.

Table 2 : Literacy Wise Classification

S. No.	*Literacy*	*Number*	*Percentage*
1	Illiterates	23	30.67
2	Primary	16	21.33
3	Middle	18	24.00
4	Hr. School	18	24.00
	Total	**75**	**100.00**

Source : Computed from primary data.

Community-Wise Classification

This table indicates that 5.33 per cent (4 respondents) belongs to the FC community. 55 respondents (73.33 per cent) belong to the BC Community. The number of respondents belong to the MBC Community and the SC Community are 15 respondents (20 per cent) and 1 respondent (1.33 per cent) respectively. It is inferred that most of the respondents (73.33 per cent) belong to

Table 3: Community-Wise Classification

S. No.	*Community*	*Number*	*Percentage*
1	Fc	4	5.33
2	Bc	55	73.33
3	Mbc	15	20.00
4	Sc	1	1.33
	Total	**75**	**100.00**

Source : Computed from primary data.

the BC Community. All the three revenue villages namely Balakrishnapuram, Mullipadi and Seelapadi are highly dominated by the BC Community.

Religion-Wise Classification

This table shows that 82.67 per cent (62 respondents) are the Hindus. 17.33 per cent (13 respondents) are the Christians. In these 3 selected revenue villages, most of the respondents belong to the Hindu religion.

Table 4: Religion-Wise Classification

S. No.	Religion	Number	Percentage
1	Hindu	62	82.67
2	Christian	13	17.33
	Total	**75**	**100.00**

Source : Computed from primary data.

Caste-Wise Classification

Out of the 75 respondents, 4 respondents (5.33 per cent) are the Brahmins and 19 respondents (25.33 per cent) are the Gownders and 23 respondents (30.67 per cent) are the Vanniars. The number of respondents belong to the Naidu and the Thevar Community is 21 (27.99 per cent) and 7 respondents (9.33 per cent) respectively. Only one respondent belongs to the Pallan caste. It is inferred that all the 3 revenue villages are highly dominated by Vanniar followed by Naidu and Gownder people. Amount these 3

Table 5 : Caste-Wise Classification

S. No.	Caste	Number	Percentage
1	Brahmin	4	5.33
2	Gownder	19	25.33
3	Vanniar	23	30.67
4	Naidu	21	27.99
5	Pallan	1	1.33
6	Thevar	7	9.33
	Total	**75**	**100.00**

Source : Computed from primary data.

revenue villages, Balakrishnapuram is dominated by Naidu people and Mullipadi is dominated by Vanniar people and Seelapadi is dominated by Gownder people.

Family-Status Wise Classification

Out of the 75 respondents, 50 respondents (66.67 per cent) are in a nuclear family and 5 respondents (33.33 per cent) are in a joint family.

Table 6 : Family-Status Wise Classification

S. No.	Family Status	Number	Percentage
1	Nuclear	50	66.67
2	Joint	25	33.33
	Total	**75**	**100.00**

Source : Computed from primary data.

Family-Size Wise Classification

This table reveals that 9 respondents (12 per cent) are having 2 members in their family. 28 respondents (37.33 per cent) belong to the family of 3-4 members. 38 respondents (50.67 per cent) are having 5 members or more than five in their families. It is inferred that most of the families in these 3 selective revenue villages, are having five or more than five members in their families.

Table 7 : Family-Size Wise Classification

S. No.	Family Size	Number	Percentage
1	1-2	9	12.00
2	3-4	28	37.33
3	5 and above	38	50.67
	Total	**75**	**100.00**

Source : Computed from primary data.

Wage Wise Classification

The wage distribution pattern depicted that the women agricultural labourers received very low wages per day which ranged between Rs. 30 and Rs. 60. A majority of the workers (32 per cent) received wages to th tune of Rs. 50-60 while 41.33 per cent of the workers received a meager wage of Rs. 30-40 only. Table clearly indicates that the women workers were exploited by paying less than their work.

Table 8 : Wage Wise Classification

S.No.	*Wage (in rupees)*	*Number*	*Percentage*
1	30-40	31	41.33
2	40-50	20	26.67
3	50-60	24	32
	Total	**75**	**100.00**

Source : Computed from primary data.

Results and Discussion

The highlights of the survey conducted in the selected study area were discussed in this section.

Women work for longer hours, doing heavy arduous and monotonous work. They take part in most of the farm field operations such as plantation activities, livestock management, fisheries, forestry and so on.

Table 9 : Duration of Work

S.No.	*Working Time*	*Number*	*Percentage*
1	6 a.m – 2 p.m	30	40
2	7 a.m – 3 p.m	13	17.33
3	8 a.m – 4 p.m	32	42.67
	Total	**75**	**100.00**

Source : Computed from primary data.

It is clear that majority (42.67 per cent) of the women workers reported that their working hours was 8 a.m – 4 p.m while about 40 per cent of the workers worked from 6 a.m – 2 p.m. Agriculture entails enormous of strenuous work by women.

Participation of Women Labourers in Agricultural Operations

Table 10 : Type of Work

S.No.	Activities	Number	Percentage
1	Sowing of seed	72	96
2	Harvesting	66	88
3	Transplanting	68	90.67
4.	Collecting harvested crop	70	93.33
5.	Threshing	68	90.67
6.	Fertilizer application	53	70.67
7.	Pesticide and weedicide application	58	77.33
8.	Transportation	45	60
9.	Drying	65	86.67
10.	Storage of seed and food grains	75	100

Source : Computed from primary data.

Women perform almost all types of agricultural operations like sowing, transplanting, weeding, fertilizer application, harvesting, threshing and storage of food grains. Large majority of women were involved in all agricultural operations for food grains. Storage of seed and food grains (100 per cent) sowing of seed (96 per cent), harvesting (88 per cent), transplanting (90.67 per cent), collecting harvested crop (93.33 per cent) and threshing (90.67 per cent). The study has shown that women's participation is least in fertilizer application (70.67 per cent) pesticide and weedicide application (77.33 per cent) and transportation (60 per cent). As a whole, women's involvement in agricultural operations was significant especially in post harvest operations.

Table 11 : Problems faced by the respondents

S.No.	Problems	Number	Percentage
1	Seasonal occupation	74	98.67
2	Inadequate rainfall	72	96
3	Low wages	75	100
4.	Heavy work	64	85.33
5.	Working time	58	77.33

Source : Computed from primary data.

The agricultural workers faced multivarious problems. Cent per cent of the women reported low wages as the major problem. The other problems were seasonal occupation (98.67 per cent), inadequate rainfall (96 per cent) heavy work (85.33 per cent) and working time (77.33 per cent).

Suggestions Given by the Respondents

The women workers suggested for higher wages (96 per cent) as they receive only very low wages ranging between Rs. 30 and Rs. 60 when compared to male respondents whose income ranges from Rs. 75 to Rs. 125. Agricultural occupation is only seasonal. During off season, women suggested to provide some training and skills regarding preparation of pickles, jams, masala powders, papad making and tailoring etc, so that they can earn their livelihood. They also requested to guide them in the area of Self Help Group (SHG's).

Table 12

S.No.	*Suggestions*	*Number*	*Percentage*
1	High Wages	72	96
2	Flexible Working time	60	80
3	Alternative job	55	77.33

Source : Computed from primary data.

Conclusion

The study has shown that majority of women were involved in all agricultural operations. Their participation was maximum in storage of foodgrains. Farm women must be considered as a visible workforce in agriculture and their work must be recognized, counted and valued to attain prosperity of the rural economy.

References

Bhalla, G.S and Signh, G.R. *'Recent Developments in Indian Agriculture: A State Level Analysis'*, Sponsored by Planning Commission, Economic and Political Weekly, March 1997.

Bhullar, B.S., Dhawan, K.C. and Mital, J.P., *'Energy Scenario of Indian Agriculture and its Future Requirement'*, Energy Oxford, 18, 657-64, 1993.

Chaubey, P.K, *'Employment-Unemployment* in Alternative Economic Survey, 2000-01.

Reserve Bank of India, *'Handbook of Statistics on Indian Economy - 1998-99*, 2001.

Shariff, Abusaleh and Gumber, Anil, *'Employment and Wages in India: Pre-and Post-Reform Scenario'*, The Indian Journal of Labour Economics, No. 2, Vol. 42, 1999.

Singh, A. *'Measurement of Energy Use in Agriculture'*, Outlook on Agriculture, 22, 119-21, 1993.

Singh, A. Singh, A.J. and Singh, A., *'Economic Analysis of Energy Use in Punjab Agriculture'*, Indian Journal of Agricultural Economics, 53, 241-55, 1998.

24

Problems of Women in Unorganised Sector

Mangaiyarkarasi

Globalization, Technological advancement, Social Development and Economic necessity have pushed the women to enter the employment outside the home. Though the women are said to have equal status to men and also constitute half of the population of the world, they are the most suffering community in the universe in every corner of the society. The range may be varying to women in different field, but it is quite high to women working in unorganized sector.

Women continue to work longer hours for less pay and also forced to work in worse jobs than men in every country in the world. Many countries in the Asian and Pacific region are like developing countries elsewhere, encountering the fact that the effects of development on women's participation differ from those experienced by men.

According to the report's author, ILO Economist Ms. Lin Lim, "The bottom line is that while more and more women are making the great majority of they are simply swelling the ranks of the working poor."

The working environment of women in unorganized sector are often poor, involving long hours sitting in one position, breathing cotton and wool fiber, chemicals, eye-strain from doing very fire work and poor lighting.

The focus of the present study is to analyze the problems and issues faced by a specific group of women in unorganized sector.

Facts and Factors on women in the Economy

- In 1994, approximately 45% of the world's women between the ages of 15 and 64 were economically active.
- In east and south-east Asia, women provide up to 80 % of the workforce in export processing zones.
- In developed counties, women work at lease two hours per week more than men and often 5-10 hours per week more. In developing countries, women spend 31-42 hours in unpaid work, while men spend between 5 and 15 hours in such work.
- Women make up nearly 70% of the world's poor and more than 65% of the illiterate.
- Everywhere, women are paid less than men, and there is no indication that this will change soon. The majority of women continue to earn an average about three-fourths of the male wage outside of the agricultural sector.
- In industrialized countries, much of the growth in women's labour force participation has been in part-time jobs. Women make up between 65% and 90% of all part-timers in OECD countries.

Since times immemorial, women have constituted an effective part of the working force in India. They worked along with the male members of the household in sowing seeds, weeding, transplanting, watering the fields, harvesting the crops, lending cattle, poultry and also helping in family enterprise, such as Beedi-making, Rope-making, Potting etc. They do all this in addition to their normal domestic work as house wife and thus always played a duel role in the society.

Women's entry in to the labour force is based on a sexual division of labour in which women are concentrated in industries and occupations requiring fewer and simpler skills and providing lower wages and poor working conditions. In the manufacturing sector, women are thus found overwhelmingly in the garment/textile and electronics/electric industries. In the trade and service sectors they tend to work as peddlers, domestic servants and in sex-related industries.

Women workers in unorganized sector account for over 40 per cent of the female labour force in the manufacturing sector. Given this predominance and concentration of women within manufacturing, it is worth to analyze the conditions, problems and issues that women encounter in unorganized sector.

Objectives

- To study the work pattern of the respondents and the wages earned.
- To study the job satisfaction of women and problems, if any, faced by women in workplace.

Now women from middle class families are working in factories in increasing numbers. Does this mean that industries are favoring women workers? How the work environments become a bed of roses for women? Are their grievances and problems redressed? Due to employment what is the position of women in society?

To get an answer to all these question, I have conducted a research study in near by village of Pondicherry. The researcher collected and interviewed women worker in packaging industry in Pondicherry city. The researcher collected the data from 30 respondents.

Most of the data collected reveal that though it is a tiring job which taken lot as Manual labour, the individuals feel that they are independent, they are kept occupied and that get to know many things around them and also socialize. The analysis of the background of the respondents show that though they are less educated and from rural background, they are aware of the happenings in the world probably due to socialization in the factory.

The analysis of the data collected on 30 samples and talked based on the range shows that regarding work pattern 8% are less satisfied. 78% are moderately satisfied and 14% are highly satisfied. The analysis of the wage pattern reveals that there is no one highly satisfied with the wages, 6% are moderately satisfied and 94% are highly satisfied.

They are not much satisfied with the work pattern, but they are highly dissatisfied with the wages and working environment. They are forced to in poor light, unsanitary toilet, no proper ventilation and no provision lunch and relax time. There is no occupational safety and health for women workers, in order to alleviate and eliminate environmental and workplace hazards, especially those affecting pregnant and lactating women, as well as measures to reduce occupational stress from, among other factors, "long hours, monotonous assembly line tasks and sexual harassment". Hence, most of them having few health problems and they are not in a position to leave their job also, due their family economic condition.

The formal inquiry apart from interview schedule also reveals that, the respondent fell that for their particular job only the specified amount could be given but it is not enough as per the living condition. The factories do not give any other allowance and benefits that are really attractive. The women workers also have a feeling that though they do more of manual labour than men, they are less paid comparatively. The work in the factory increases their self-esteem more than the work as a maid-servant. The women workers feel independent and experience sense of recognition. The salary of the workers is used for household commitments at home. It also observed in this study that few of the respondents experienced with harassment from their male boss. If the employer is unsympathetic towards worker, he expects too much of work beyond their capacity, which leads to stress and tension results in drastic changes in their health.

Suggestions

- Women are by and large employed in manual labour, they should be given technical guidance where they can also work in automatic machines with men i.e. women can also be made a skilled person.
- The women workers should be made aware of their legal rights.
- The factories should abolish male female wages differences.
- Recreation should be provided to the workers in the weekends to refresh themselves.

- The factories should provide minimum facilities to the worker, according the Factories Act, 1948.

25

Problems of Plantation Labourers in Tamil Nadu

P.G. Balasubramanian

Plantation worker means a person employed in a Plantation for hire or reward, whether directly or through any agency, to do any work skilled or unskilled.

It proves major employment to tribal living in hill areas. Plantation Labour force is slightly different from agricultural practices in plain areas. The pattern of employment is based on organized and unorganized sector. Because, Tea, Coffee industries require both skilled and unskilled labour force.

Tea is labour intensive crop whereas, coffee is less labour intensive. Coffee is a seasonal crop and different activities associated during its growth period do not require a permanent labour force. More labour force is required during the month of March and April when Coffee bears fruits. The need for labour is less when compared to tea cultivation.

Working Environment

Mostly, leaf plucking is handled by women labourers in Tea Estates. Remaining works are (carriage of leaves, burning, bearing, and processing) handled by male workers. Similarly, during harvesting time most of the work (70 per cent) is carried out by women labourers in Coffee Estates. In Lower Pulneys Hills

(Kodaikanal Regions) around 40 per cent of the work force is carried out by women workers from places, such as Batlagundu, Periyakulam, Pattiveeranpatti.

According to Plantation Labour Act 1951, any worker should not be deprived of their rights during their work. In Tea - Coffee Estate, labourers are indulged in extra work during seasonal time (In Tea Estate-Surplus leaves, Coffee Estate-harvesting season). But, the remuneration is not provided by all estates, for example; in Tea estate actual quantity of leaf plucking is 16 Kg per day. In stead of 16 Kg, they collect 25 Kg.Then, remaining 9 Kg which is considered as extra wage of Rs.2 per Kg. In short, if they want extra Rs.18, they must do extra work after 5 P.M to 9 P.M. This will lead to burden of work. Otherwise, the owner of estate will send out the workers.

Wage

According to wage premises Tea Estate workers are getting Rs.75 per day for male and female, if they belong to permanent labourers. Whereas, they belong to Daily wage and contract basis, the payment of wage is based on the quantity of work. But, this would be an exploitation in the form of workload and long working hours. Similarly, in Coffee Estates at Kodaikanal region, the workers get Rs. 65 for male and Rs. 50 for female on the basis of permanent. But, most of the labourers are engaged in the form of contract work. Some of the Tea Estates in Nilgiris, the wage has gone down from 75 to 70 Rupees. These estates have become tougher on all workers.

Social Security in the Plantation Labourers

International Labour Organisation has defined social security, as the protection which society provides for it's members, through a series of public measures, against the economic and social distress, that otherwise would be caused by stoppage or substantial reduction of earnings resulting from sickness, maternity, employment injury, unemployment, invalidity, old age and death, the provision of medical care and the provision of subsidies for families with children. Thus idea behind social security is that members of the society who contributed or are contributing to the wealth and welfare of the country should be protected against certain risks in adequate measures.

In social security there is a common thread of natural desire of communities for greater protection. Protection from life problems, from uncertainty, disease and deprivation; Social security protects members of the society by collective action against economic hardships and social risks which individual can not provide by his own ability and resources. The concept of social security is based on ideals of human dignity and social justice. Even though, social security measures are availed to plantation Labourers they can not access it properly, because most of them are engaged by the owners through daily wage and quantity of work basis.

Crisis of Plantation Workers in Tamil Nadu

Employment in plantations is not lucrative for the wards of labourers in plantations. Many of them have learnt certain technical skills. They earn upto Rs.800 – 1500/- per week in Coimbatore and Thiruppur. The parents who toiled in the plantations life-long tend to take voluntary retirement and settle down in Coimbatore and Thiruppur. Tea estates are not attractive any more as a place for employment. There is shortage of labourers in the plantations. The Plantation Companies think it is not wise to recruit new labourers on permanent basis, as it would warrant payment of all kinds of social benefits as per the Plantation Labour Act, Industrial Dispute Act, Bonus Act and so on. One of the options left for the plantation companies was to go on for 'mechanization'. But, technically, the topography of Nilgiris, is said to be unsuitable for mechanization. This is one of the reasons why plantations are still employment abundant industries. Therefore, either they employ casual labourers from the plains, or make use of the local tribals who have not till now sought employment in the plantation sector.

Generally, workers paid lower wages for increased workloads. They are suffering from hunger and malnutrition. They face increasing job insecurity. Since the late 1990s at least 60,000 workers have lost their jobs as tea price has fallen and plantations have closed down. At least thousands of workers are threatened by further closures. On the plantations that remain open, workers are suffering wage cuts, tougher picking demands, increasing short term, insecure contracts and appalling living and working conditions

References

The Plantations Labour Act, 1951 (Act of 69 of 1951), Madras Book Company, Chennai.

Reshma Arora, *"Labour Law"*, Mumbai; Himalaya Publishing House, 2000.

Babu, P. Remesh, *Labour Relations in small holding Plantations : The case of Rubber Tappers in Kerala.* N L I Research studies series No: 053/2004, V.V.Giri National Labour Institute-NOIDA, 2002.

Nagaraj.K & Vedavalli.L, *Contractual Agreements in the Tea Plantations of Tamilnadu,* N L I Research studies series No: 054/2004, V. V. Giri National Labour Institute-NOIDA, 2004.

Sivananthiran A. & Venkatarathnam C.S., *"Labour and Social issues in Plantations in South Asia: Role of Social Dialogue"*, South Asia Multi Disciplinary Advisory team (ILO – SAAT), New Delhi, 2002.

Palanithurai, *"Indian Tea Knocked out of the cup"*, Global & Local–A bi-monthly newsletter that generates discussion on globalization and decentralization, Rajiv Gandhi Chair & The Ford Foundation, Issue No. 5, July-August 2006.

Agarwal,R.N. and Goldar, B., *"Economic reforms and employment in India projections for the year 2001-02"*, Indian Journal of Labour Economics, Indian society of Labour Economics, Delhi, No. 4, Vol. 38, pp.577-95.

Aggarwal, A. *1991 Estimates Of Fixed Capital Stock In The Registered Manufacturing Sector In India*, Working Paper No. 937, Indian Institute Of Management, Ahmedabad.

Banerjee, B., *"The role of the informal sector in the migration process: A test of probabilistic migration models and labour market segmentation in India,"* in Oxford Economic Papers (Oxford, Oxford University Press), pp. 399-422. 1983.

www.citu.org.in/tapansen06.html-24k.

www.southasianmedia.net.

www.sed-trade-forum.itcilo.org.

www.aidsouthasia.undp.org.in.

26

Female Agricultural Labour in the Present Scenario

S. Baluchamy and C. Senthil Kumar

In India, women's contribution to the farm sector is largely ignored and inadequately understood very few scientific and empirical attempts has been made to examine the actual participation of female labour in crop production and other supportive works at the farm level. Farm cultivation is the main areas of economic activities for rural women. The National Sample Survey has shown that the percentage contribution of women in agriculture is higher than man.

Women play a considerably dual role in agriculture. Since time immemorial women have framed and organic compound of the working force. They along with the male members of the household are sowing seeds, weeding transplantation, watering the fields, harvesting etc. They do all this in addition to their normal domestic chores as a house wife. Thus, women always play a dual role in the society.

According to the National Commission on Labour an agricultural labour one who is basically unskilled and unorganized and has little livelihood and the personal labour" [Report of the National commission on labour, 1969].

Condition of Female Agriculture Labour

"Once the rain fails every thing fails" the entire village is now sitting ideal. The women labour of course started going out of the stand place. The women labour are the worst hit, they cannot go any where else. Drought has created new tension in living. They loose temper. There is a tension of society writ large in their face. They don't know what to do.

Women in Agriculture

Economist has observed that the societies that practice of shifting cultivation, participation as women in agriculture in fairly high. Apart from the type of agricultural practice, the kind of crop practiced and the availability or non- availability of third labour are other factors that have been observed to influence the participation of women. Female work participations high where hired labour is liberally used. Mechanization of farming does not seem to affect the participation of women adversely. In developed countries whose farming is highly mechanized the women workers have generally increased approximately to the size as the male work force.

Wage Structure for Female Agricultural Labour

The wage boards and other wage fixing bodies set up under the minimum wage act 1948 have been taking into account the equal pay principle while recommending wage scale. But difference in the wage as men and women still exist. Mode of payment to female workers is mostly contractual and on piece rate basis. A women member of an agricultural labour family works in the field but for the same back banking toil she does not receive even that pittance of a wages asks received by her male counter part.

Causes of Female Agricultural Labour's

The causative factors to push the female to engage in agricultural coolie works are identified because of the following factor:

- Large percentage of illiteracy among the female in rural areas,
- Low income of their male counterpart, due to inadequate family income,

- Non availability on non-agricultural employment opportunities within the village, and
- Lack of interest among the female to get training in the skilled profession.

Classification of Female Agricultural Lahourers

The majority of rural women else out their livelihood by working on land in a number of ways. Based on this, rural women are classified into four categories. The following are the different categories of agricultural labourers:

1. Land less women
2. The near land less women
3. The small peasant women
4. The high peasant women

The women of the first two categories are forward in large number.

This study was undertaken primarily to understand the plight of female agricultural labour of micro level in the form of an empirical study amongst these laboures in peravanpatty village, Dindigul district. The study in order to analyse the status differentials if any of the female agricultural labourers belonging to various social divisions. Certain crucial factors such as castes, pattern of employment, wage, income proportion of female income contribution, expenditure, importance in family, decision making, dependency, education, involvement of local affairs and other related relevant particulars of female agricultural labourers particularly their socio-economic problems, treatment accorded both within and outside were effectively used to identify the status of female agricultural labourers belonging to various social divisions in the village.

Objectives

(I) To study the socio- economic condition of selected female agricultural labourers,

(II) To analyze the female agricultural labourers and land owner production relations.

(III) To examine the wage structure prevailing in the study area,

(IV) To identify the problems faced by the female agricultural labourers.

Methodology

The respondents were selected randomly in the respective village. Random sampling method was adopted for the collection of data from the respondents, 50 respondents were selected out of 250 respondents. Data for the present study have been collected from both primary and secondary data. The personal interview schedule was constructed for the purpose of data collection from the respondents, that study has adopted descriptive research design.

Findings

- Majority (60%) of the respondents belong to the high productive age group 15to 35. therefore the female agricultural labourers in the study village have the potential of high labourers productively and perspective employment.
- Majority (40%) of the respondents getting the wages per day is Rs. 26-30. therefore wage per day is very low in the study area.
- Half (48%) of the respondents the annual income is Rs. 6001-7500.
- Majority (54%) of the respondents feels that the nature of wage payment is very delay.
- Majority of female labourers go to near by villages like Sedapatty and Sempatty especially during paddy cultivation seasons.
- Majority of the respondents were engaged in harvesting, sowing seeds respectively.
- Majority (70%) of the respondents has change the land owner because of high wage offer. Majority of female agricultural labourers is changing the land owner as the reason for high wage as the study area.
- Majority of (84%) the respondents have participated in the decision making.

Suggestions

In the light of the findings the following suggestions are made to improve the status of women agricultural labourers.

- Since female agricultural labourers are unaware of various social welfare legislations and provision available to various social divisions. The voluntary agencies may be in collaboration with governments must give wide publicity through community organization, particularly the minimum wage act deserves mention here should be effectively implemented.

- The government must include some agro based work also in the minimum wage act. This would enlarge the scope of work performance allied sector by women in villages.
- It is necessary to reduce the working hours of the female from present 10 hours to 8 hours. It is possible only when the land owners sympathetic towards agricultural labour. Hence, the land owners must voluntarily come forward to do this.
- Land reform act must be strictly enforced by the government and surplus lands taken must be genuinely distributed among landless agricultural labour.

Conclusion

The female agricultural labourers manifest lower status in all walks of social life, particularly to socio – cultural, educational, economic and political. In that study area female agricultural labourers agri productive age group, most of them literate their annual income is not poor, they are lived in tiled type house, they getting wage from land owner very low. Most of the female labourer involved in harvesting and sowing in their agri field, their relationship to the land owner is very good and also they were got daily wages from them. They got work per month 10-20 days as this work source they got from co-worker, mainly they are engaged in daily wages, most of them working experience are more than 10 years.

27

Women Workers in Unorganised Sector

K. Praveena and M. Mahalakshmi

India is known for its huge geographical spread and magnitude of its population. It has a huge working population of 406 million (based on NSSO survey of 1999 – 2000) almost 92 per cent of the work force is in the unorganized sector. There are numerous occupational groups pursuing economic activities from generation to generation without formal schooling and scattered all over the country with diffused employer – employee relationship.

Meaning of Unorganised Labour

Unorganised sector is not a homogenous category, but is spread over the economy in a variety of forms. Workers in the UN organized sector is an apprentice, casual, or contract worker, home – based worker, service provider, or self employed person engaged in any industry.

Women in Unorganized Sector

In recent years, the issues relating to empowerment and advancement of women have gained much attention among the policy – makers, anthropologists, social workers and the government are for preventing and eliminating all forms of women exploitation and atrocities committed on them by their employers, colleagues and even friends.

However the women working in the unorganized sector still remain at the periphery even when they constitute almost 96 per cent of the total unorganized work force in the country. In spite of all the efforts by the government as well as the institutions in the non-government sector; the situation of these women is still far below the satisfactory level. Exploitation in this sector is on the increase. There is no job security. These women are paid less and are deprived of other essential benefits. They are forced to work even late in nights without any protection or safety. Some of the young women are even subjected to sexual exploitation. There are virtually no medical facilities, rest rooms and crèche facilities. The employers callously ignore labour laws.

Women Employment in Unorganized Sector in India

During the second half of this century, as a result of the globalization of economy, there are new trends, which have created new opportunities for employment for women all over the world. In many regions, women's participation in remunerated work in the formal and non-formal labour market has increased significantly and has changed during the past decade. While women continue to work in agriculture and fisheries, they have also become increasingly involved in micro, small and medium enterprises. Women's share in the labour force continues to rise and almost everywhere women are working more outside the household.

In India, the sharing of economic activity by women is nothing new. From time immemorial women have been working both in the home and outside, though not in strict sense of earning wages. According to the 1991 census, women constitute a significant part of the work force of India. But female work participation rate has increased over the years and that too in the rural sector. Rural women are engaged more than the urban women.

Women in Agriculture

With the growth of industrialization and urbanization labourers migrate to urban areas in search of employment, in the absence of assured source of employment in rural areas. In urban areas, women are generally employed in informal sectors like weaving, handi-craft, tailoring, sale of fish and construction activities.

Unorganized women labourers are outside the reach of most laws, which seek to protect labourers, security and living conditions. They are exposed to various exploitations and discriminations.

Indian women constituting nearly half of the total population, play a crucial role in the domestic sphere and also in the rural field, particularly in the agricultural sector. Yet, our traditional attitude is to treat women as second-class citizens. This is so in spite of the fact that women have proved their mettle in every walk of life. Their contribution is not given due credit.

The largest number of working women in India is engaged in farming operation either as cultivators or as agricultural labourers, they take up a wide variety of activities like sowing of seeds, transplanting, weeding, harvesting, preparation of compost and manure pits, application of manures, storage of seeds and food grains. An active farm woman spends eight to nine hours on the farm during the peak agricultural season.

Female agricultural labourers are indeed among the poorest section of Indian society with the lowest wage levels and highest unemployment. Poverty is pushing a growing number into agricultural wage work who were not previously in the labour force or were self employed cultivators and artisans. This trend is often referred to as the feminization of the agricultural labour force. Despite their increasing prominence in the agricultural labour force rural women are not being absorbed in many of the jobs outside agriculture that are developing in the rural areas. These avenues of employment often require specific skills from women and their socialization to seek out and adapt to non-traditional work situations.

Gender Discrimination

Women experience gender discrimination in labour market due to many reasons. Women have lower accessibility than men to productivity augmentation, opportunities like schooling, required training and experience continuity in career and regional mobility. This is referred to as pre-market determination since low level education, work experience, training and constrained mobility are not consequences of labour market discrimination but the consequences of the discrimination prior to entering the job market.

Women receive less favourable jobs than men or they will not get any job because of their lower education and experience. If tastes for remain the same and qualifications differences are expected, then employment discrimination takes place. Women get lower wages than men for the same job. This is identified as wage discrimination. It can occur in different forms such as collective agreements, which can explicitly discriminate against women by creating sex-specific wage groups with a lower pay for women.

The presence of vast multitudes of rural women as workers and producers in the rural unorganized sector where earnings are low, employment seasonal and insecure, supportive services woefully inadequate or even non-existent, growth opportunities few and collective organization weak, has brought into sharp focus the failure of the main stream to alleviate their predicament. While it is true that workers, irrespective of sex, are exploited in the unorganized rural sector, women suffer more.

A further discriminating feature is differential wages. It is now common that women get paid much less than men, often for performing similar work. Their earnings are low because wages are discriminatory and work is seasonal and they are the first to be dislodged when work is scarce. Much of the work that women perform is either not recognized or is subbed as subsistence activity.

Problems of Women Workers in the Unorganized Sector

The unorganized sector is characterized by lack of stability and durability of employment, low wages, lack of job security, absence of social security, unduly long hours of work, non payment of overtime wages, no leave, unclean, unhygienic and unsafe working conditions, vulnerability to various occupational diseases, accidents causing serious injury also resulting in death or disablement. There are various categories and sub-categories of unorganized labour irrespective of typology such as bonded labour, contract worker, inter state migrant labour, building and construction workers, of stone quarries, leather, tribal collectors of forest produce, salt workers, agriculture workers, fisherman and women etc.

Minimum Wages based on Worker's Need

The unorganized sector is characterized by a combination of factors. The most important factor is that the unorganized sector workers are not adequately protected. They donor have employment security' they receive low returns or wages, there is no clear and fixed employer – employee relationship, they donor have access to social security. Of course, this does not mean that there are no laws or scheme for them. A few of the labour laws such as the minimum wages act and the labour act are meant specifically for them, such as Jawahar Rozgar Yojana, Integrated Rural Development Programme, etc.

Unfortunately in recent years, there has been a tendency to devalue the minimum wage and bring if closer to the poverty line or pauper wage. The latest attempt in this direction is the formulation of the 'floor level minimum wage', which further minimizes the minimum wage. However, every expert body has defined the minimum wage at the poverty level. Even the national commission on rural labour, it its own study, laid down the following principles.

1. The minimum wage is not the pauper level or poverty level wage.
2. The minimum wage must ensure the preservation of the level of efficiency of the workers; and
3. It must provide some basic amenities like health and education of children.

What these principles together indicate is that the minimum wage level is that below which wages should not fall. If they fall below, that efficiency of the worker will also fall.

Suggestions

There are a number of labour legislations enacted in independent India to regularize and regulate the employment procedures, wage rates, payment of wages as well as to provide various facilities like accommodation, drinking water, medical assistance, canteen, leaves, compensation etc. for the workers in unorganized sector as well as the organized sector. But unfortunately, these acts have not been effectively implemented, particularly in the unorganized sector, making the life of its workers extremely sub-human.

There is an urgent need to organize the women labourers to fight against their problems and so collective action is necessary in the form of union/association to create awareness about their rights and privileges.

The NGOs can play a useful role in making the labourers aware of their rights and responsibilities.

Conclusion

Even though, the unorganized sector has been the most vulnerable and ignored sector in India, but it holds an inevitable place in Indian economy. Thus, there is no exaggeration in saying that the backbone of Indian work force is the unorganized sector and not the organized one.

Yet there is a tendency to ignore this vast mass of work force, as these millions who belong to unorganized sector are politically power less and economically weak. More than 60 per cent of the population of the country depends upon the earnings of the unorganized sector workers for their livelihood. Hence, there is an urgent need to give top priority to the issues and problems of the workers of unorganized sector workers.

References

Balakrishnan,A, *Rural Landless Women Labourer - Problems and Prospects*; Delhi: Kalpaz Publication, 2005.

Dutt & Sundharam; *Indian Economy*, New Delhi: S.Chand & Company, 2002.

Economic Survey (2004-2005).

SECTION – C

ISSUES OF TEXTILE LABOURERS

28

Plights of the Kanchipuram Silk Weavers – A Perspective

N. Lalitha and D. Badrinarayanan

Weaving is one of the most ancient occupations in India. It is rather one of India's pride treasures that have commanded respect even from the early days of known history. The industry has been an employer of millions of people over the years and the art of weaving is predominantly a family enterprise. Though various changes in the policy and structural levels has necessarily in fluxed non-traditional members also to join weaving, the art has a lineage of generations and even today there is a oral transfer of knowledge which dominates over the academic training institutes. A child in the weaver's household, with its nimble fingers, starts to play with the waste yarn and spindles which becomes the first 'hands-on' experience of it in later years. Thereafter, it is a natural graduation over a period of time which makes the child an adept in the craft.

The weaver and the loom are mentioned in the classical Indian texts such as the Rig Veda and Atharva Veda. In these texts, the gradual spreading of darkness and light over the earth is likened to the weaver throwing a shuttle on the loom. 'tant' is the Hindi word for loom, and the weaver in many parts of the country is known as tanti. In mythological texts, Lord Vishnu is often portrayed as Tantuvardan, or the divine weaver, who wove the rays of the sun into a garment for himself. Evidence of madder-dyed fabrics was found in Mohenjadaro and Harappa. The Sangam classics (1 B.C. to 6 A.D.) record weaving of silk and cotton cloth. Weavers attained importance during the Chola and Vijayanagar dynasties, when they produced for the temples.

Indian textiles, as mentioned earlier have commanded respect across the globe with patrons crossing seas to acquire a piece for them. The silk garments, in particular have a peculiar history of musing even the royals of royal. They were adored as the masterpiece of handicraft, hence formed the major part of offering to the deities during worship. The Kings positioned next to God were undoubtedly the second in the line to be adored with garbs of silk. Because of such associations 'silk' commands the holy status, even today. Seldom is a marriage occasion planned without a silk robe for the bride and bride groom. Thus, silk, since ages, has become the part and parcel of our culture and gives us a unique identity across the globe.

Weavers – the men who create magna carta living in misery:

All the eulogy has to be confined to the art; when it comes to the artisan, the story is gloomy. The Handloom Census of India, undertaken in 1987-88, places the number of handloom textile workers at 65.3 lakh persons, making them the single largest group of artisans in India. Despite their large numbers, they produce merely 26 per cent of the country's total cloth output. Today, it is the intermediate technology of power looms that threaten the survival of handlooms much more than the mills, from which competition has been contained as an effect of the government policies.

The socioeconomic condition of the handloom workers continues to be precarious, despite the fact that of all the artisan groups in India, they have enjoyed the greatest infrastructural and financial support from the government ever since independence. The programme for development of handlooms was intensified after 1976, when, as a result of the recommendations of the High Powered Committee headed by Mr. B. Sivaraman, a number of schemes were initiated. The major thrust of these schemes was the development of handloom co-operatives and marketing

Capacity Installed	*UNITS*	*1999-2000*	*2000-01*	*2001-02*	*2002-03*	*2003-04*
Looms (Organised sector)	Lakh No.	1.4	1.4	1.41	1.37	1.05
Powerlooms	Lakh No.	16.3	16.62	16.66	16.93	18.37
Handlooms	Lakh No.	38.91	38.91	38.91	38.91	38.91

Source: JSN context analysis

facilities. However majority of the weavers still fall outside the co-operative fold, and continue to sell their products through intermediaries.

Historically, it is possible to discern two streams of development within the Indian textile industry. First, that of resident weavers in villages meeting the local need for coarse cotton fabrics; secondly, of weavers under the patronage of local nobility producing finely woven fabrics for the urban elite. Understandably, the two groups were affected by the growth of the textile industry within the country, and overseas, in different ways.

No significant changes occurred in the organization of production of the village weavers. Weaving continues as in the past, to be a household activity, with all the members of the family contributing to their labour. With the growth of the textile industry, however such household units started to rely increasingly on mill spun yarn instead of homespun yarn. Further, the advent of synthetic fibres and cheaper mill cloth, rapidly pauparised such artisans. Today, rural weavers have to augment incomes through on or off farm work in order to survive.

Kanchipuram Silk Weavers

The silk weavers of Kanchipuram have settled about 4 centuries earlier. Kanchipuram being a temple city and the capital of various South Indian dynasties like Pallava, Chola and Vijayanagara, has nurtured this industry with royal patronage. Earlier the industry was under the control of a few merchants, but later due to the growth of Co-operative movement the weavers themselves started gaining the control of the industry through their Co-operative Societies. The first Co-operative society. Kamatchi Amman Society, was formed in 1949 with 79 members. Now there are 23 such Co-operatives functioning in Kanchipuram, most of them under the control of the Government of Tamilnadu. There are nearly 61,000 weavers in the industry (34,000 under the Co-operative fold and 27,000 in the private sector) making it the major occupation of the town. Most of the weavers belong to the Saurashtrian community, while there is a significant population of weavers of Tamil as well as Telugu origin.

The industry is predominantly a cottage industry in nature with the production facility located in house of the weavers. The weavers may do a job work for their cooperative society or for private parties, which can also be a private master-weaver.

The art-work in a Kanchipuram silk sari makes each one of them a unique piece of art and has earned a reputation worldwide for its finesse.

Methodology

The study is descriptive and Kanchipuram town is the area of study. About 45 weavers from the fold of Cooperatives, independent category formed the sample. The sample respondents were chosen using simple random sampling technique. The study employed both primary and secondary data. Primary data were collected from the sample respondents using unstructured interview schedules. Secondary data were collected from published documents of the Government and other journals.

Problems faced by the Kanchipuram Weavers

Though the product has a worldwide fame, the plights of the weaver who creates such a value-laden product are manifold. An attempt has been made to classify the problems faced by weavers in terms of production, marketing, technological, personnel and financial. A detailed account under each category is given below:

Production Aspect

The introduction of computerized designing of the silk sarees also necessitates some changes in the loom. The alteration of an existing loom or installation of a new loom requires a capital investment of a few thousands which is far beyond the capability of most of the weavers.

The art of weaving involves a lot of concentration and physical strain which makes the weavers unable to work more than 8 hours in a day.

Though there could be a higher demand for silk sarees during the month of festivals and marriage season, but the capacity of production is limited and the scope for expansion is also very limited.

Fluctuating prices of the silk yarn and the gold zari which form the main raw material component of the industry, affects the production badly and the weavers do not have a possibility to plan their investment in such a scenario.

The power looms hijack the yarn meant for handlooms in bulk is also a major problem faced by the weavers.

Technological Aspect

The looms made of wood bulge during the rainy season which renders it inoperable and subsequently the weaver goes jobless.

Though there has not been much changes in the looms, it is still unclear that whether the infusion of new technology alone would provide the competitive edge. Moreover the high cost involved in upgradation of looms prevents a large number of weavers to upgrade their looms, since they are already in penury.

Marketing Aspect

The weavers attached to co-operative societies get a higher price for their products, but the products even with minor defects may get rejected there.

There is a growing preference among customers for powerloom and mill cloth, and this in turn affects the demand for handloom silk cloth. This shift can also be attributed to the reasons like the higher price of handloom cloth, inability to maintain uniform quality and design and preference for synthetics.

Wide prevalence of sarees with fake zaris at a cheaper price and lack of awareness among the buyers is a major problem faced by weavers who produce genuine varieties. Absence of trademark and distinguishing brand identity to original silk is also perceived to be a major reason for this state of affairs.

Personnel Aspect

Studies reveal that the wage component in the apparel industry is a meager of one percent**, but even in high value goods like that of Kanchipuram Silk, the wage component of the weaver is well within 10 per cent of the total value. It is a sad fact that the artisan who creates a high value for the product through his dexterity is paid the least part of the share in its value. This is another major problem faced by the weavers.

Since the art of weaving is highly traditional, external training has not been an active component in the industry. Though there has been training programmes conducted for the members of co-operatives, the weavers working in the other systems of independent weavers and master-weaver, seldom get the opportunity of attending any training programmes. This is a grave risk in the aspect of their talent becoming obsolete and there is a possibility of their talent becoming obsolete.

The politicization of the labour union and the Co-operative movement has distanced them from their primary objective of uplifting the standard of the weavers. The wage structures pronounced by these institutions are not finding their place in reality.

Weaving being a lesser lucrative profession it does not find takers among the younger generation which poses the danger of paucity of skilled labour for the profession. It is also a fact that the weavers, based on their toil in the industry, feel that their generations should be out of the profession for a prosperous life.

Financial Aspect

Many of the weavers, in absence of capital base resort to moneylenders and big merchants for loans at high rates of interest, which at times makes them, pledge their skills for a highly lesser rate of wage. Cases of weavers selling off their children as labourers for their debts are also not uncommon. Absence of strict implementation of agreed wage structures multiplies the plight of the poor weavers.

Suggestions

- Regulation of pricing mechanism for the silk yarn and supply of zari at subsidized prices shall reduce the burden of the weavers
- Loan schemes with easy installments at a lesser rate of interest should be introduced to upgrade the weaving facilities which shall be of help to the poor weavers
- Transparency in the functioning of Co-operatives and labour unions and de-politicization of these institutions are essential

to make these institutions effective and relevant to the needs of the weavers

- Periodic training programmes for the weavers will help them in upgrading their skills and help them in increasing their efficiency
- Direct procurement from the weavers by Government shall help to eliminate middlemen from the channel and make the weaver to gain the most in the business
- Promotion of a unique brand name and distinguishing trade mark to identify original silk sarees can help preventing the fake goods gaining entry
- Though the plights are many, it is possible to wipe them away, if an effective partnership is worked out among different stakeholders of the industry and the government.

References

Jaitly, J.; *The Craft Traditions of India*, Lustre Press; New Delhi; 1990; p. 55

M. Vijayabaskar, *Garment Industry in India*, in Gopal Joshi (ed.), Garment Industry in South Asia – Rags or Riches?, South Asia Multidisciplinary Advisory Team, ILO, NewDelhi, 2003, pp. 51.

SRUTI, *India's Artisans: A Status Report*, 1995.

JSN School of Management Services, *Context Analysis for EU-India ECCP SME-LEARN-NET Project*, 2005.

29

Impact of Globalisation on Rural Girls in Textiles Industries

A. Thomas Willam and G. Albin Joseph

Tamil Nadu is one of the major players in the Indian textile industry in terms of production and export of yarn, fabrics, knitwear, made-ups, and garments. Consequently, it is a major consumer of cotton and other raw materials and intermediaries. However, the markets for all these items are greatly influenced by international trends as well as the trade polices of the Government of India. At present; in Tamil Nadu despite its significant presence in the industry, is not actively associated in the policy making processes of the Govt. of India. It is felt that in all such matters, the state should actively be involved in the decision making process.

The Changing Global Order

The features of the new global order quickly crept in; in the form of the GATT treaty. Among other factors it hastened globalization. It brought down national borders with the intent of integrating economics into a single market. Its impact is unprecedented. The anticipated immediate implications of the agreement have been felt. Globalization enriches the rich and impoverishes the poor and unfortunately the victims are non-players. On the other side the huge preponderance and rapid growth of the informal as compared to the formal sector is the result neither of Globalization nor lack of flexibility in the later, but of Government policies favouring the former, combined with the employer preference for a minimum of regulation, are preferably none at all.

The globalization phenomenon was manifested in the many policies of Government. In implementing trade liberalizations, imported products compete with local produce. Multinational companies have to contend with not only the other MNCs and local enterprises but also internally among their many different producing units intending to survive. Many of them decided to relocate to other countries where doing business; is cheaper. Many small and medium enterprises (SMEs) and local manufacturing firms had to re-engineer or restructure their business. Those who failed to adopt were forced to shut down. Thousands of workers found themselves without jobs and without any ready alternatives for employment. The governments' safety net programs were nowhere to be found.

Workers will increasingly find themselves forced to eke out a living in the informal economy. The normally labor-intensive manufacturing firms will be outpaced by a very dynamic service and contractual sector that could break down the structures and dispel the powers of the large bureaucratic corporations.

Social security and social protection programmes and related concepts are radically being eroded. Increasingly women and other vulnerable sectors of the society are pushed into insecure and precarious forms of labour.

Developing Alternatives

Mere safety nets may not suffice. Many workers are seemingly on the brink of extinction, replaced by machines run by a core of highly-technical workers. Established social protection mechanisms will not save them from poverty and powerlessness unless systematic and structural reforms are introduced. This time, the workers have to be part of the shaping of these reform measures.

There is a continuous advocating of social reforms that would humanize globalization and ensure a more sustainable development. Social reform should encompass among others.

Regulations insuring the exercise and promotion of rights and welfare are on the creation and the preservation of jobs. Social reform should also establish programmes and policies that will strengthen and expand social safety nets particularly for the more vulnerable sectors of economy.

Opening Gates for Casual and Vulnerable Groups

Women and children are employed for lesser wages, and going in for more and more mechanization (Hannan, 2005). Women from the critical core input for the development of any economy, they contribute to two thirds of the world's work hours; produce 50 per cent of the world's food supplies, account for 60 per cent of work force and contribute up to 30 per cent of the official labour force (1994). One fourth of the households world wide are headed by women and in the other one third of the households 50 per cent of the total earning are contributed by females (1995).

To quote the World Bank (1995), "Women as the group are among the poorest of the world's poor". The discrimination and marginal treatment on women inflicts permanent poverty in terms of health, knowledge, skills and aspirations and are relegated to the status of the secondary members in the family and backward citizen in the society. Indian women by and large have been socially, economically and politically.

Women suffer from feminization of wages. Statistically women receive ten to 60 per cent less wages than that of men for the same quantum of or more work (1993). Rural women's earnings are only ten percent of that of their male counterparts for the same work done. (1992).

Increasing number of women are entering the labour force as compared to men, and that too primarily in the informal sector; men start loosing jobs or pushed into casual work with a loss of steady income, women start looking for work outside the house to desperately maintain retain minimum standard of living (Sparr & Pamela (Ed.) 1994).

From 1981 onwards the rate of female employment increases exponentially (UNICEF, 1989). It is also acknowledged that the increasing female labour force participation, primarily in the informal sector has been observed in all developing countries where structural adjustment has been accompanied by prolonged recessions (Latin America, The Caribbean and Africa).

Thus the structural adjustment policies lead to fall in real wages, unemployment and reduced availability of and cut in subsidies on basic goods and services. All these affects women in their role as producers, mothers, household managers, community organizers, and the implications are invariably negative in terms of reduced incomes, standard of living and greater a burden on unpaid work (Ghosh & Jayathi, 1996).

The economic changes of the 1980s triggered a sharp reversal in the trend towards improvement in health, nutrition and educational standards of children (Cornia, et. Al. 1988). The textile industry after mechanization, completely altered the required skill structure and enable the capitalist to recruits the cheap labour of women and children. The unmarried and young women are employed at relatively miserly wages. A large section of women entering the labour market in the industrialized world. It is not just that the part-time jobs exclusively taken up by women. Unfortunately, for most women the labour market offers little else. In many of the OECD counties (Germany, UK, Japan) part time employment constitutes as much as 45 per cent of women's total employment. In other countries, the percentage is anywhere between 35 per cent to 45 percent (World Employment Report, 1998). The workforce in the export units consists largely of young women who are single with no previous experience.

It is a recent trend that many textile industries closed their gates for permanent employees and opened widely to young and casual labourers and daily wages in the name of 'training'. Almost all the textile industries select unmarried young girls from certain specific locations – normally from far off distances to be employed in their textile units.

These girls and young women were appointed by middle men – who could earn good income as commission both from the industry and from the labourers, - exploiting their poverty, illiteracy, ignorance on one side; false promises in the form of advance money, jewels and utensils at the end of their tenure on the other – could successfully recruit them and dump in these textile units.

Legally speaking they are selected (not hired) for a training programme – like apprenticeship for a period of two or three years.

The unmarried young girls fall into their prey as they are motivated, instigated and forced to the unfavorable situation. Geographically districts like Viruthunagar, Ramnad, Tirunelveli, Tuticorin supply those young girls to districts like Coimbatore, Erode, Karur and Nammakkal where these textile units are abundant in number.

Objectives of the Study

1. To understand the working conditions and wage patterns
2. To observe the level of "concept of welfare" prevailing in these textile industries in the context of globalization
3. To study the problems of women and girl workers in the work and stay places and
4. To understand the general status of these women/girls in the textile industries

Methodology and Study Area

A Focused Group Discussion is conducted among the young girls who finished their contract or training for two years in these textile units revealed dangerous observations. The study area is two select villages of Viruthunagar district where this phenomenon is rampant due to failure of agriculture, poverty and other related reasons.

Major Observations

Hours of Work

- Non-regulation of working hours/extended working hours
- Women workers are compelled to see extra working hours or shift
- Workers have to work twelve hours per shift
- Each shift lasts for more than eight hours and mostly ten hours per shift.
- Poor working condition exits in terms of excessive hours.

Welfare

- Workers no adequate drinking water proper toilet facilities, health centers, rest room.

- Female workers are affected by serious stomach pain, heart pain, Ashthma, Anemia,
- Female workers have no maternity benefits
- Medical allowance is given for affected workers by accidents at working sites
- Workers are deprived of welfare measures like Provident Fund, ESI, Gratuity, etc.
- Women workers in general are not allowed to use toilet facilities if and when they need
- Poor health and safety conditions are reflected in the number of factory accident cases.
- Several injured workers failed to claim compensation from the management
- Three are no legitimate benefits (ESI, PF & Maternity benefits) under national and state labour laws.

Wages

- The workers are paid low wages
- Wages are not increased for several years
- Wages is not given at the time of leave due to accident
- Gender discrimination in wage policy
- Wage for one shift is at the range of Rs. 40/ to Rs. 60/-. For unskilled workers and many of the women and children earned less than this amount for unskilled work.
- Skilled workers earned in the range of Rs. 60. to Rs. 80/ bearing those workers in few mills were trade unions are allowed.
- wages in textile mills low particularly in the textile mills without trade unions

Trade Unions

- Most of the mills have trade unions.
- In case there are trade unions; it is inactive for workers and acting as support to the management.
- Non-cooperation of trade unions solving the problems of workers.
- Trade union leaders are corrupt.

Problems and Status of Workers

- Women laborers are subject to sexual abuse by co-male workers, mill vehicle drivers and supervisors.
- The job is not permanent
- Working sites are far away from their residence.
- Male workers are forced to evicted by compulsory voluntary retirement scheme
- Girl children, adolescent or unmarried girls are preferred by textile mills.
- Married women workers are forced to leave textile mills.
- Women reported face verbal abuses.
- Female workers are like bonded laborers
- Mill workers are weak socially and economically
- Health conditions of women workers are very poor
- Affected mill workers are suffering for their daily bread that led then to migration, broken family, denied of their children education
- The employed women workers having problems in marriage due to poor conditions of health
- Women workers are subject to sexual abuse and beating
- Workers are not provided with welfare measures
- Workers are denied to organize themselves as trade unions.

Major Issues

- Absence of employment guarantee for workers
- Gender discrimination in wage policy
- No minimum living wages
- Absence and non-cooperation of trade unions
- Non-regulation of working hours
- Denial of collective bargaining
- Workers are denied to organize
- Compulsory voluntary retirement scheme
- Labour laws are not properly implemented
- Labour rights are refused
- Non-implementation of laws and rights of women workers
- Increasing health hazards particularly for child labourer and women workers

- No proper safety measure provided
- No welfare measure like ESI. PF and Gratuity
- No accident benefits
- No Bonus regulations
- High level trade union leaders re not qualified and trained
- All trade unions are affiliated to political parties and the Political leaders interventions are increasing in trade union activities
- No proper welfare facilities

Conclusion

The globalization opened up employment opportunities in various quarters and it did so for the women labour force also. More and more young women are recruited and observed in various industries and textile industry is no exception. But unfortunately the real fruit of globalization is not to be enjoyed by these women and young girls due to its paradoxical effect. They are otherwise become victims of globalization in terms of their casual and temporary employment nature, the poor health and welfare provisions and more so as an unorganized sector in the organized sector and thus they form a new group of labour. Though it seemed to be great opening in the beginning, in later years the labour force could experience much serious repercussions in terms of employment, wages, hours of work, safety, security and other related issues.

References

Bannerjee, N., 1984, *Women's work and discrimination*, paper presented at a conference in Bogota, Columbia.

Baud, *Women's Labour in Indian textile industry*, Tilburg Institute of Development Research, Tilburg, 1983.

Business Standard, *Garments export register 4% Decline*, pp. 21 and 22, April, 2001.

Ghosh & Jayathi, *Macro Economic trends and female employment; India in Asian context*, paper presented at a seminar on Gender and Employment in India, Dec. New Delhi. 1996.

Govt. of India, *Fourth World conference on Women*, Dept. of Child and women, 1995.

Hensman, R., *The impact of industrial restructuring on Women, Men and Unions,* in Class formation and political transformation in Coast colonial India, Sathyamoorty, T.V, (Ed.), Oxford University press, Oxford, 1996.

Hersh, Jackques, and Brun, Ellen, *Globalization and the Communist Manifesto*, Economic and political weekly, No. □3, Vol. XXXV. 15 Jan, 105 – 108, 2000.

Mahendra Dev., S., *Economic Liberalization and Employment in South Asia,* Economic and political weekly, No.12, 8 Jan, Vol. XXXV. & 40 – 51, 2000.

Madhubala, *Women's Issues from the periphery to centre*, Journal of Rural Development, 1992.

Mathew, A.F., *Rethinking Globalization*, paper presented at UGC National Seminar on Globalisation and India's Environment/, SNDT Women's University, Mumbai, 15 to 16 Feb, 2001.

Sparrl & Pamela, *Mortgaging Women lives*; Zed press, 1994.

Sen, Ilina, *Industrial restructuring and women workers; A case study* in (Ed.) Nithya Rao, Louis, Rural and Sub sahara, site of change; the Structural context fro empowering women in India, Fes and UNDP, 1996, pp. 168 – 185, 1996.

UNICEF, *The Invisible adjustments – Poor women and economic crisis*, Santiago, 1989.

World of work, International Labour Organisation, No.17, 1996.

Yasodha, S., *Women Employment in India*, Allied Pub., New Delhi, 1993.

30

Labour Disaster in Textile Industry in India after Globalisation

S. Kasi and R. Sundaresan

Textile industry's predominated presence in the Indian economy is manifested in its significant contribution to the industrial production, employment generation and foreign exchange earnings. The industry is a key area; where India has an opportunity for success and a global scale given the low cost of labour. Conversely textile industry is a labour intensive industry, which has the potential to generate job for larges number of people. It provides employment to about 35 million people, together with allied sector; it will provide employment to over the 91 billion people by the end of tenth plan (2002 – 2007).

This paper presents the case of Indian textile labour issues after the globalization. Globalisation is considered as an important reform package for this sector. It has four parameters.

(1) Reduction of trade barriers so as to permit free flow of goods across the national frontiers.

(2) Creations of an environment in which free flow of capital can take place among nation states.

(3) Creation of an environment in permitting technology.

(4) In developing creations of an environment in which free movement of labour can take place in different country of the world. The advocate of globalisation more especially from developed countries accepts their detention of globalization of this sector. Work force restriction involves shifting out of labour from that different field of the sector.

However labour supply is more elastic at any given point of wage rate in India but such a technology may hold in this sector so the employment growth declined drastically after globalization. It is now an established fact that the growth rate of the economy in the nineties continuation of the eighties. However the story of dismal employment growth in the 1990s is now well - accepted phenomenon. The textile and clothing industry is one of worst affected industries under globalization.

The textile industry has a complex structure existing at several stages like spinning, weaving and stitching. Yarns are converted through weaving process to fabric process, fabric made ups or garments. There is one additional dyeing process. This study aims at how globalization encourages or obstructs the different stages of the laborers in this sector.

Methodology

This study uses different stages of the textile industry, data of different years in order to examine the textile labourers. This study covers post reform period from 1990 – 1991 to 2004 -05 and only on organized sector; more appropriate variables are used to identify the real task of labour being employed in the textile industry.

Industry wise Level of Employment and Wage Growth

This part analyses the textiles labourers in the different stages of the textiles sector after the globalization. Here this analysis covers only the employment aspect in the textile sector.

The industry has several vast sectors within it, such as mill sector, the clothing or garment sector, the handloom sector and the power loom sector. Each of these sectors employs lakhs of workers and also contributions significantly to the national income.

The tradable commodities under textiles include readymade garments, cotton yarns and fabric silk and woolen products.

Sector – wise Employment Growth Ratio

Trends in employment growth rate displayed in this table show the clear pattern of all the sectors in textiles industry, clear pattern of de growth of employment generation in mill sector, the clothing or garment sector, the handloom sector and the power loom sector. Textiles include readymade garments, cotton yarns, fabrics silk and woolen products.

The table shows that sector wise employment growth of the textile industry. The textile industry within the textile shows a declining employment growth after the reform period in 1991. The employment growth was 9.1 percent in 1991. it has declined gradually year by year, this sector has witnessed high degree of technological improvement, imports of new machines etc, at present the employment is at very low level of 5.2 percent in 2004-2005 Almost 4 percent of employment declined in this sector so there is no possibility to for more labour absorption in the sector.

Cotton Textile Sector

Cotton textile sector of the textile industry indicates the instability declined after the reform period. In 1990-91 there was 9.2 percent growth level of the employment after that it has declined year by year; in recently the growth rate is 5.3 percent in 2004-05.

Cotton Blended Yarn

Cotton blended yarn is the sub sector of the textile industry. It utilizes more work forces among the textile sector but after 1991 it utilized the labour force only at low level. In 1990-91 the growth on employment was 10.3 percent, after 1990-91 it declined drastically and in 1991-92 it was only 8 percent. There is a crisis in this sector where thousands of workers are getting regular employment. In 2004-2005 the growth rate was only 5.6 percent. It pathetic situation as far on the textile labourers are concerned.

Cloth Sector

Cloth sector is the apparent of the textile industry. The employment growth was at high level in 1990-91 which was 14.2

Table: Employment Growth Rate in different sectors in Textile Industry (In percent)

Sectors / *Year*	*Textile*	*Cotton*	*Cotton &Cotton Blended yarn*	*Cloth*	*Synthetic Textiles*	*Synthetic Yarn*	*Synthetic Fabric*	*Textile processing*	*Readymade Garment*	*Silk*
1990-91	9.1	9.2	10.3	14.2	4.9	5.0	3.1	3.6	7.0	2.5
1991-92	8.2	8.7	8.9	13.6	4.4	4.5	3.1	3.4	7.2	2.2
1992-93	7.3	8.6	8.1	12.4	4.2	4.2	3.3	3.3	6.0	2.1
1993-94	7.6	8.9	7.9	10.7	5.0	5.1	3.3	1.9	4.7	1.6
1994-95	6.5	8.3	8.0	9.4	4.6	4.7	3.1	1.4	4.1	1.6
1995-96	5.6	7.5	7.8	7.7	4.4	4.5	3.0	1.5	3.9	2.6
1996-97	5.7	7.9	7.6	7.8	4.6	4.8	3.4	1.7	4.1	3.8
1997-98	6.7	7.3	6.3	9.1	4.6	4.6	3.5	2.0	5.1	3.2
1998-99	6.9	6.8	6.3	8.0	4.7	4.8	3.3	2.1	4.9	3.2
1999-00	6.5	6.5	6.2	7.3	4.4	4.5	3.3	2.3	5.1	5.1
2000-01	6.2	6.4	6.1	7.0	4.1	4.2	3.9	2.2	4.7	8.1
2001-02	6.5	6.1	6.1	6.5	4.2	3.6	3.7	2.0	5.2	5.3
2002-03	6.2	5.8	5.9	6.1	3.6	3.3	3.5	2.2	5.6	6.9
2003-04	5.8	5.3	5.6	5.0	3.3	3.1	3.9	2.3	5.6	8.2
2004-05	5.2	4.8	4.5	4.8	3.1	2.8	2.2	2.2	5.5	7.0

percent. After reforms it has declined gradually and in 2004-2005 it has grown by 5 percent

Synthetic Textile and Yarn

Synthetic textile sector is a major segment of the textile industry. Its contribution to the employment creation was 4.9 percent in 1990-91. It has declined 3.1 percent in 2004-05. Synthetic yarn sector has contributed the labour at 5.0 percent in 1990-91 and in 2004-05 has declined to 3.1 percent level. Making condition a distract impact of the globalization process in employment generation in Textile industry.

Readymade Garments and Silk Sector

The ready made garment and Silk sector has emerged as the most globalize sector in the world today. Readymade garment sector alone workforce only at 7.0 percent in 1990-91 and increased it shows fluctuation trend with slight increases and falls on the different periods which is not a health trend. At present it has only 2.9 percent and Silk sector work force of the employment increasing trend. It was only 2.5 percent in 1990-91 it increased up to 7.0 percent level. The silk sector after the reform period might have been using labour deepening technology.

Summary and Conclusion

There is a decline trend in employment generation in the textile sector since reform period. It appears clear that the employment growth rate was at higher level during pre- reform. The employment in the textile sector is terribly low during after the reform period. This will have its impact on the incidents of poverty, especially in the rural area. This may also affect the labour productivity. The capital intensive technology adopted in textile sector since globalization has been the major obstacles in the employment generation even at low wage rate.

The new technology adopted in the industry is not only labour-saving but also cost effective in this respect. It is suggested that may take some policy measures to create more employment opportunities to compensate for the lapse in employment in the textile industry. For example government may promote the development of man-made fiber sector. It can be generate more employment opportunities.

31

A Study on the Socio-Economic Conditions of the Sales Women in the Textile Shops in Dindigul Town

S. Sathes Kumar and G. Bhuvaneswari

The organizational behaviour approach deals with peaceful and appropriate climate are essential for working class people. But with the variation of sectoral approach of employment and functional performance, organizational change has been emerged. Such as primary sector employment scenario is different from service sector (especially working environment).

In spite of increasing trend in productivity of service sector job satisfaction is reduced to women labourers in the context of drastic changes of employment opportunity due to globalised economy. In this respect, the service sector and unorganised women labourers particularly, working in private industries may have restricted their rights and social responsibilities. Due to this the working class younger generation of women are facing a lot of problems regarding their working environment, wage, security measures etc.

Working conditions and the like, is based on the presumption of an employer-employee relationship. In this context, it is very important to study the condition of women in the textile sale sector of Tamilnadu. This study is about the women working in the textile sale sector in Dindigul urban area. Dindigul being a major town in Tamilnadu, it will depict the typical situation.

Conceptual Framework

Working class women are doing all type of job/work. Women play a vital role in the economy. They are involving in many types of works/jobs. But at the same time, they are facing a lot of problems in their field of work physically and mentally. They mostly prefer to do the work in the unorganised sectors. In any organisation, women are predominant. The first and foremost problem faced by women are economic backwardness and underemployment.

In this context, it was felt necessary to study the problems faced and prospects of women who are working in the unorganised sectors, and how they are tackling their problems, which will give more confidence to their lives, what are the actual problems faced by working girls in their families due to their absence in home, how can they overcome those problems. Hence, the study is undertaken.

Objectives of the Study

1. To study the socio-economic characteristics of women sales force in the textile shops in Dindigul town.
2. To find out the income earning of sales women from the textile shops,
3. To analyse the working environment of sales women in the study area,

Methodology

This study is making an attempt to find out the working pattern and practices of working environment in the garment shops in urban areas. This study is basically empirical in nature based on descriptive method. 80 respondents (women) were selected those who are working in small and medium garment shops in Dindigul town. The primary data were collected from the respondents through personal interview regarding their problem, prospects and working environment. The secondary sources of information are gathered from various published documents.

Sampling Techniques

For selection of respondents, convenient sampling method was followed in the study area. Medium size shops only were selected in Dindigul town. In total 80 respondents were selected from 14 garment unit in Dindigul.

Profile of the Women Workers in the Unorganised Sector

Dindigul town in situated between lower Palani hills and Sirumalai hills. The road connections are highly accessible in NH 7.

The availability of job opportunity is more or less equivalent to both organised and unorganised sectors. But, a large number of manufacturing concerns and industrial area is very low when compared to that of Coimbatore. But at the same time, the nature of working environment in informal sector women labour is common for all. In this connection, this study has reflects that behavioural pattern of sales women, working environment, nature of job etc. in small and medium scale garment selling units.

There are about 10 large-scale textile shops and about 25 small and medium scale textile shops functioning in Dindigul. In the large-scale textile ships there are at least 30 sale girls, in the medium-scale shops a minimum of 7 and in the small-scale shops a maximum of 5 are working as salesgirls.

Area of Population : Total geographical area of the city is about 1401 square kilometer. Population of Dindigul city is about two lakhs according to 2001 census.

Literacy : The literacy rate of Dindigul is 78.69 percent.

Occupational Profile : The city houses various types of factories and industries ranging from tiny to medium, business estabilishments, public and private undertakings etc. In the industrial sector, tanneries and lock and iron-safe manufacturers occupy a major part. Different types of workers such as main workers (66,475) marginal workers (2,732), cultivators (676), agricultural labourers (268) and other workers (62,192) are the working force of the city and non-workers were 64,376.

Data Analysis and Interpretation

This chapter deals with anaysing and interpreting the collected information from the respondents. Those data compiled in the form of structural basis i.e. tabulation and coding.

Table – 1 : Distribution of Age and Marital Status

Particulars	*No.*	*Percentage*
Age Group		
15-20	39	48.8
21-25	19	23.8
26-30	11	13.8
31-35	8	10.0
36-40	3	3.8
Total	**80**	**100**
Marital Status		
Unmarried	54	67.5
Married	14	17.5
Widow	6	7.5
Divorcee	6	7.5
Total	**80**	**100**

Source: Field data

Table depicts that more number of teenage girls i.e. girls in the age of 15-20 are working (48.8 percent) and all of them were unmarried. The other age groups, which are 21-25, 26-30, 31-35 and 36-40 are less in numbers and respective percentage are 23.8, 13.8, 10.0 and 3.8. This shows that the owners of the garment sales centers prefer the young girls.

Summary of Findings and Conclusion

Based on the findings, conclusions were drawn. Suitable suggestions are also for equipping the women who are working in textiles sales units.

Findings

- Majority of the owners of the garment sales centers prefer the young aged girls i.e. who are in the age group of 15-20 years,

- Majority of the women workers belong to backward class,
- More percentage (62.5 percent) of women workers are having high school education and there are no illiterate women workers in the sales units,
- Majority (95 per cent) of the women workers are working above 8 hours in a day,
- Half of the respondents families depending upon income from the present job,
- Nearly half of the respondents families (46.3 per cent) are having debts,
- Half of the respondents (50 per cent) are getting salary of less than Rs.1000 per month,
- 33.8 percent of the respondents are getting overtime allowances during the festival seasons,
- majority of the respondents (76.3 per cent) are getting bonus every year,
- More than half (68.7 per cent) of the respondents are not getting medical expenses from the shops they are working, 47.5 per cent of the respondents told the reasons that the shop owners' won't give the medical expenses,
- Majority of the respondents (82.5 per cent) have not availed the medical facility in the year 2005,
- Majority of the respondents (62.5 percent) are in the tendency of saving a portion of their salary, they expressed that the reasons for not saving is their family debt (18.7 percent), insufficient wages (12.5 percent) and not having tendency of saving (6.3 percent) of the respondents,
- 66.3 percnet of the respondents are not getting salary for the leave days,
- 62.5 percent of the respondents are not getting any medical leave and special allowances.
- 70 percent of the respondents are not working in the shift system, due to non acceptance by their parents, getting enough salary, not necessary to work in the shift system,
- majority (60 percent) of the respondents are getting concessions from the shop owners,
- Majority (72.5 percent) of the respondents are provided with minimum facilities like toilet, water etc.,

- Majority of the respondents (90 percent) are harassed by the male co-workers like comments, teasing etc.
- Out of 80 respondents, 15 (18.8 percent) of them are facing problems from the public, who come to the shops, like unnecessary comments, behaving indecently.

Conclusion

To conclude that the above analysis made in the study, which has a large number of sales girls who belonged educational background and nuclear family. Their working environment/ atmosphere is not much with the level of social security norms. But at the same time, their behavioural approach and job satisfaction also not highly concentrated. The garment shop owners also more or less concentrated about the welfare of sales girls of their shops, because their vision is only earning profit and its maximization. According to the unorganised sector workers, social security 2004, the social security measures and norms would not be enforced by the government because most of them belonged to contract and casual and daily wage earners. In this regard, garment shop sales girls are belonging to monthly wage earners.

The job satisfaction and working environment depends upon the willingness of sales girls. There is no rigidity among owners and sales girls in the form of durable in continuation of garment sales work.

Suggestions

The following are the major suggestions for strengthening the betterment of garment unit sales girls.

- The garment shop owners must adopt the time factor of working hours of sales women (not exceeding the specified working hours).
- The owners may be ready to give medical expenses, medical allowance along with medical leave facility for their sales girls to meet their medical expenses. This can be for the betterment and beneficial of sales workers.
- The owners should try to provide the salary for the leave days to their sales girls. Because they (sales girls) are getting a meager amount of salary,

- Unnecessary punishment, scolding, wage cut may be avoided by the garment shop owners.

32

Present Scenario of Women Workers in Textile Mills

A. Venkatachalam and S. Siyamala Devi

Today's working women are economically independent and this makes them conscious of their rights. Working outside the family has broadened their outlook also. In India, the employment of women has a sustained increase, despite the several hindrances to their harmful employment in a continuing basis in industry, commerce and services. The argument usually advanced against employment of women is that they are too much involved in home making, food preparation, childcare and all the other domestic chores. In three decades back, in scientific planning for development there was a failure to recognize that women are half the labour force. At present this is fully recognized for accelerated economic development and scientific of man power.

The textile industry is one, which is offering more opportunity for the employment of unskilled women labour. Though women are not new to the industry, their employment in the past was confined only to one or two departments viz. reeling and winding. The present scenario is quite different, in these industries, where women are widely employed in many departments and in more than one shift. It is proposed to examine the various problems faced by the women workers in Textile mills.

Women Employment in Textile Mills

It is found that the Growth Rate of women employment has a positive trend of 55.31. It is inferred that in 6 years women employment has increased by nearly more than one third. The important reason contributed towards this increasing trend is better discipline, easy supervision and passive union activity of the women workers. The trend towards positive increase is generally attributed to the following reasons.

- Impact of labour laws that aim to protect health and welfare of women workers.
- Impact of policies aiming at equalization of wages between men and women and,
- Structural changes in industry through rationalization and modernization.

The analysis of data and information regarding the contributing factors which helped and induced the women to become industrial workers reveals that there are pushing and pulling factors for their entries. The growth and development of textile mills in the study areas has opened the avenues of employment opportunities both for men and women. There are certain specific activities namely; cone winding and spinning could be carried out more efficiently only by women. Accessibility of the work spot, group of women employed, operation of shift system of work, employment through out the year, possibility of getting permanent job with regular salary and fringe benefits such as maternity leave, bonus etc., are the identified pulling factor the following are the reported pushing reasons by the respondents to become industrial workers.

- Irregular and uncertainly of income to the family thro·ıgh out the year.
- Inability to meet the basic necessities of family members.
- Necessity to earn money for marriage, and
- To support economically their parents.

Absenteeism

Absenteeism is a major problem of the textile mills. Absenteeism in its widely used sense means failure of workers to report for work, when work is available to them. It may be classified as follows:

- Leave sanctioned by management called a "Authorized Absenteeism",
- Absence without prior permission known as "Unauthorized Absenteeism" and
- Absenteeism due to sickness and accident called as "Certified Leave"
- It is reported that no one availed the unauthorized leave. It is because of the fact that their pay will be cut and they will be punished with fines. The various reasons for taking leave are:
- Socio-economic factors like living conditions health of the workers. Social norms and values.
- In plant factors like the attitude and practice of management and working conditions.
- Liberal scheme of granting certified sickness leave.
- Other unavoidable factors like accidents and personal matters.

Maternity Benefit

The Maternity Benefit Act of 1961 applies to factories covered by the E.S.I. Act. It is administered by the State Government. In Tamilnadu, a women worker who has put in 160 days of service immediately preceding confinement is eligible for maternity leave of 12 weeks with full pay. It prevents the dismissal of women workers during the period of maternity leave. The study reveals that the percentage of women availing of maternity benefits was 6. It is inferred that the number of women claiming maternity benefit and cost of it is a negligible factor in the employment of women.

Creche Facility

The Factories Act of 1948 and its amendment in 1976 provide for crèche in a factory employing 30 or more women workers. According to the provision of this Act an ayah/nurse has to be appointed and biscuits, toys and milk are to be given to the children. The crèche has to be located near the work spot of women.

This reveals that only 4% of the women workers have availed of this facility. It is reported that in textile mills under conservative management women workers are discouraged from bringing the children to the crèche, which are being used as store rooms. It is also reported that the sick children and healthy babies are put together in crèches leading to "Cross infection". It is suggested that the management should come forward to overcome these difficulties.

Membership in Union

A trade union is a voluntary organisation of workers to promote and protect their interest by collective action. It may be defined as an organisation of working class in its struggle against the all preventing power of the capitalist class. The principle business of a union is collective bargaining. Unions symbolize workers rights to organize, the press for their rights is a collective way and to go on strike.

It is revealed that the trade union leaders are satisfied with the membership of women in their union, as far as subscription and participation in strike are concerned. They are most regular in paying subscription and participate in strikes willingly. But they refrain from participating in gherroes, picketing and demonstrations. The trade union leaders feel women workers are most reluctant to serve as representatives in committees and show least enthusiasm in attending union meetings.

The management of Textile mills feel that women workers prefer to stay away from work during strikes and do not indulge in any violent or silent demonstrations. It is also felt that collective bargaining will be easier, if more women become active members and office bearers.

Continuity in the Present Job

It is observed that a majority of women workers opined that they would like to continue their service till their retirement. The main reasons reported by them are:

- They want to be "independent" and not a "dependent" member in their family.

- They would like to continue their economic support to their families with a view to support their children in education, employment and marriage.
- They pointed out that the future benefits from their service such as additional increments, provident funds etc., and
- They have also pointed out that they would like to spend their time "productively" than remaining idle.

Physical Problems

All the respondents have unanimously reported that they are facing physical and psychological problems. As mill workers they have their duty for 8 hours in the mill. As women, they have their household works both before going to their duty and after returning home. On account of this, they have hardly few hours of rest. They are not able to spare time for even reading news papers and magazines and there by improving their knowledge with the audio and visual media.

In the mill they have to stand in front of huge machines throughout their 8 hours of work per day. All of them have reported that they get leg, hip and knee pain. 10% of the respondents have reported that continuous work under such condition has resulted in uterus problem and this has very much affected their health. The researcher could observe the respondents above 40 years of age look very old, restless and tiresome both physically and mentally. These could be attributed to their physical and mental stains both at home and in the mills.

Conclusion

Increasing in productivity is the ultimate object of every industrial organisation especially after the introduction of Liberalization, Privatization and Globalization. The provision of labour welfare is the most important one to attain the above objective. The labour welfare implies providing better working condition. Job performance of workers based on appropriate working condition. So, it is necessary to solve the multi dimensional issues ranging from economic, social and environmental to psychological.

33

Labour Issues in Textile Industry

M. Karuppanalagu

Potential risks of injury in the textile industry, as in other manufacturing industries, due to physical hazards are associated with accidents with machinery and equipment, vibrations of the equipment, dust, heat and noise. This includes the risk of injury and chronic exposure. Hazards resulting from worker exposure to noise and particulates such as dyes, cotton dust and small fibres require careful design of textile mills to protect human health. Machines equipped with individual dust collectors minimize ambient dust levels. Raw material fibres are generally outside of the respirable particle range and usually do not pose a health risk. Mechanical injury is possible with improperly designed equipment and inadequate guarding of equipment. Wet processing operations use both chemicals and high temperature. Steam systems if low pressured however minimize the risk of pipe ruptures.

Both the International Labour Organization and individual countries recognize the need for worker safety vis-à-vis physical hazards.

Workplace Noise

The maximum noise levels in the textile industry are in the spinning and weaving sections. Incorporation of noise reducing parameters in the basic design of textile machines is a complicated process. Which involves a compromise between productivity and cost on hand and noise pollution on the other hand.

In woven cotton fabric finishing, noise is primarily due to poor maintenance of machinery rather than the processes per se.

Typical noise levels reported in the textile industry in India usually range from about 70 to 114 dBA. The Indian Standards Institution has yet to stipulate tolerance limits for noise pollution in textile industry.

The detrimental effects of noise on human beings are shown below:

Table -1 : Effect of High Intensity Noise on Human beings

Frequency Hz	*Noise level dB(A)*	*Effects observed*
100	110	Stimulation of receptors in skin
2000-2500	150	Mild warming of body surface
100-10,000	105	Significant changes in pulse rate
	140	Pain in ear
	130-140	Changes in muscle tone, increase in tendon reflexes and incoordination.
	160	Minor permanent damage, if prolonged
	190	Major permanent damage even in short time
50	120	Vibration of muscle in arms and legs
700-1500	130	Resonance in mouth, nasal cavities and sinuses

Source: S.R. Bhatt, K.Subramanyam, K.R. Swami, Noise Pollution in the Textile industry: A Review. ENG/131: 1982, Ahmedabad Textile industry's Research Association.

Equipment Related hazards

Hazards associated with equipment include accidents due to:

- Moving machinery
- Pressure vessels
- Running nips

- Electrical installations
- Heat and steam

Hazards due to moving machinery are primarily due to lack of sufficient machine guarding. Accidents could also be caused by running nips. These nips occur when material runs on to or over a rotating cylinder e.g., where a belt runs over a pulley wheel, a conveyor over a roller etc. Typically accidents arise due to running nips because an operator gets his clothing caught in a nip or slips and falls into one while trying to make some adjustments to the material running on to the cylinder or cleaning rollers or because the machinery is started up by mistake.

Apart from moving machinery, hazards are also associated with unsafe electrical installations, improper handling, lifting and carrying practices, handling of corrosive chemicals, pressure vessels, steam etc.

Electrical hazards are primarily due to failure to isolate or earth equipment or due to temporary or defective equipment.

Steam systems if low pressured however minimize the risk of pipe ruptures and consequently minimize injury.

Safety Recommendations

General guidelines

- Least possible fibre damage should be ensured during production to minimize textile dust.
- Fibre dust should be removed thoroughly by mechanical surfaces treatment such as sanding or napping.
- Sufficient lighting and protection from glare should be ensured.
- Cushioning of equipment to make them vibration free.
- The temperature and the quality of air in the working space should be appropriate.

Machine Guarding

- Machine guarding should be ensured to control hazardous points on machinery particularly the moving parts.
- Efficient mechanical appliances should be provided to move driving belts to and from fast and loose pulleys and driving belts should not rest or ride on revolving shafts when the belts are not in use.

- Secured fixed fencing is the preferred method of guarding machinery. The fixed guards should be securely bolted position and in good condition. It should be removable only by the use of tools and should not deteriorate as a result of frequent removal and replacement for maintenance. The fencing should enclose the parts guarded completely. Complete fencing is normal for machinery such as revolving shafts, belt drives and gear wheels while partial fencing is often used on calendars.
- Partial fencing may be complemented by distance fencing which prevents the operator approaching too close to the machine.
- Some other methods of providing protection on these lines are feeders, interlocks and trips. Feeder devices such as slides, or rollers are used to allow material to be fed into a machine without the necessity for a worker to put his hand in.
- In cases where access to the machinery is needed for maintenance etc., interlocks may be used which prevents access until the machine is stopped and prevents start-up while it is unguarded. The mechanical and electrical condition of the interlock guards and adjustments of automatic guards should be proper.
- Trips which are used in the cases of machinery where fencing is not possible, should be maintained well. Operators should be trained in the use of these protective systems while being trained to use the machinery.
- Oiling and greasing points should be extended to a safe place clear of moving parts and should be easily accessible.

Running Nips

Protection for running nips should be ensured and the preferred form of protection is complete fixed fencing. Partial fencing, distance fencing, feeders, interlocks and trips are also sometimes used. Often several measures are used in combination. However, it is essential to ensure that the operation and maintenance of these protection devices is done well.

General Guarding

- General area guarding is to be ensured to control hazards due to unprotected floor openings, slippery or defective floors, stairway surfaces, inadequate illumination etc.
- Installation, inspection, testing and maintenance of electrical equipment should be done only by competent electricians.
- Electrical equipment should be regularly inspected and serviced. Equipment on which repair is to be done should be disconnected from the supply until the work is completed. Defective equipment should be taken out of use and completely disconnected from the supply until it is repaired.
- Temporary wiring should be avoided as far as possible but if used should be to a safe standard and properly earthed. It should be replaced by a permanent installation as soon as possible. Circuits should not be overloaded as this increases the risk of fires.
- Regular maintenance of equipment, guards, and other safety features of equipment is essential.
- Proper material handling practices such as limiting of loads as to size and shape for handling by hand and mechanization for heavy or bulky loads. Lifting appliances should be marked with safe working load to minimize accidents due to overloading. The ergonomics of the handling task should be right. Training in matters of handling should be provided to prevent injury.

Personal Protective Equipment

The various tasks for which some form of protective clothing or equipment is necessary includes working with:

- Corrosive chemicals
- Toxic chemicals
- Dusts
- Hot environments
- Noisy environments
- Fire fighting

It is essential to ensure adequate personal protective equipment such as eye protection (e.g., eyeglasses/goggles during use of solvents), ear plugs, nose masks and breathing apparatus (wherever applicable).

In dusty operations dust/mist half-face disposable respirators should be used. Where the chemical composition of the dust poses a hazard, for example lead or cadmium containing pigments, a high efficiency respirator is appropriate.

Protective clothing should be regarded as a last line of defence. It is much preferable to remove or control the hazard if this is practicable.

Worker Safety and Chemicals

Hazardous materials in processing of woven cotton fabrics include chemicals used as raw materials such as the caustics, oxidizers, acids, solvents and dyes as well as wastes such as waste oils, degreasing compounds and residues, vat clean-out materials, boil-out wastes, spent caustics and acids, spilled or otherwise off specification chemicals and waste treatment sludges.

Potential risk of injury due to hazards associated with chemicals includes both immediate and chronic exposure. Hazards resulting from worker exposure to solvents and dyes require careful design of textile mills to protect human health.

Most textile chemicals are relatively non-volatile so that vapour emissions are not excessive. However, wherever there are vapour emissions from volatile solvents they should be controlled through suitable management practices. Rigorous house keeping measures will reduce the risk from indoor exposure as well as from accidents. Enforcement of a plant hygiene programme is necessary. Caustic and acidic compounds should be handled by trained personnel who are familiar with proper safety procedures and the risks from exposure.

The problems associated with most of the chemicals are primarily related to skin contact with or inhalation of harmful chemicals. Exposure and toxic effects should be avoided, preferably through prevention.

Flammable liquids should be segregated for storage and handled according to fire code zoning restrictions. Corrosive materials such as acids and caustics and corrosive wastes require proper handling with the latter requiring neutralization before discharge into biological waste treatment systems.

Table – 2 : Toxic and Harmful Substances Used During Cotton Woven Finishing

Textile Process	*Toxic Substance Used*
Scouring	Chlorinated products, caustics
Bleaching	Hypochlorite (chlorine bleaching)
Dyeing & Printing	i) Azo-dyes containing aromatic amines ii) Dyes containing traces of heavy metals such as Arsenic, Lead, Cadmium, Mercury, Nickel, Copper, Chromium, Cobalt and Zinc iii) Formaldehyde as a mordant
Finishing	Formaldehyde as a cross linking finish, urea formaldehyde as F.R. finish
Garment Manufacture	Stain removers containing chlorinated products
Packaging	Wooden boxes treated with insecticides.

Source: Adapted from Cleaner Production in Textile Wet Processing, A Workbook for Trainers, March 1996, UNEP, Paris.

Handling of residues and sludges which are high in water content, contain toxic organics require skin protection.

A clearly identified first aid box in charge of a responsible and trained person should be maintained. Suitable eye washing and emergency shower facilities should be provided and maintained in good condition.

Clearly marked emergency exits and fire prevention facilities should be installed.

Special requirements for storerooms such as separate storage areas for chemicals and facilities for easy cleaning should be introduced.

Source: Industrial Pollution Prevention and Abatement-Chapter on Textiles Industry, March 1994, The World Bank, UNIDO,

Table – 3 : Impacts of Hazardous Substances on Human Health and Environment

Process Description	*Effect/Purpose*	*Chemicals employed*	*Possible health and safety related problems*
Bleaching	Whitening	Hydrogen peroxide Sodium hpochlorite	Respiratory and skin allergies
Optical brightening	Brilliant white	Organic substances	Skin allergies
Dyeing	Diverse range of colours	Diverse dyestuffs Heavy metals Carriers (Benzidine dyestuffs, carriers)	Skin allergies Carcinogenic
High-grade finishing	Prevention of shrinking and creasing	Urea formaldehyde Melamine formaldehyde	Skin allergies Strong suspicion of carcinogenic properties
Sanforizing Sanor plus	Prevention of creasing and shrinking	Urea formaldehyde Melamine formaldehyde	Skin allergies Strong suspicion of carcinogenic properties
Sanfor setting process	Prevention of creasing and shrinking	Ammonia (mechanical compression)	Respiratory discomfort due to ammonia vapors
Mercerization	Permanent luster	Sodium hydroxide Ammonia	Corrosive
Flame-proof finish	Prevention of flame formation	Halogenated hydrocarbons Phosphorous compounds	Possibility carcinogenic, Allergenic substances
Softening	Improvement of the handle	Quaternary ammonium Siloxanes Fatty acid-modified melamine resins	Possibly skin allergies

UNEP; Environmental Quick Scan Textiles, Compiled by CBI and SIDA by CREM, 1996.

General Recommendations for safety with chemicals

Improvement of working conditions should include:

- Avoidance of dust, soil and noise in the factory in addition to minimizing the use of harmful chemicals and industrial hygiene standards.
- It is essential to implement good working practices and personal hygiene.
- Eating, drinking and smoking should not be undertaken in the work area.
- Employees should wash their hands before engaging in any of these activities.
- Food, beverage or cigarette machines should not be present at te work station.
- Work clothes should be kept separate from street clothes.
- Storage and handling of hazardous materials should be done only by trained employees in designated areas.
- Work areas should be kept clean and tidy. In regular instructions the employees have to be informed about possible risks and they have to be urged to adopt good working hygiene.

The storage of different chemicals in the warehouses and stores should be in accord with the safety rules. Chemicals should not be over stocked. The warehouse inventory should be systematically maintained and computerized and also preferably linked to the management information system of the company. This will allow for updating and the proper follow up for the expiry dates or proper stocking of suitable chemicals. Proper training and upgrading of the warehouse staff and management in this domain is a must.

In order to ensure chemical safety, the following checklist may be used:

Materials Handling

- Maintenance of inventories of hazardous substances – storage according to the specifications in the MSDS as well as according to the local legislation - e.g., in India as specified in the Manufacture, Storage, and Import of Hazardous Chemicals Rules – 1989.

- Segregation of incompatible chemicals.
- Use of appropriate containers as specified in the MSDS
- Regular monitoring of containers for leaks
- Use of covers on containers
- Proper labeling
- Transport as per the local legislation using a TREMCARD system
- Control of emissions during usage
- Chemical substitution to minimize toxicity
- During disposal ensure segregation of different wastes
- Label the wastes
- Maintain a schedule of disposal
- Develop emergency response plans, impart training for implementation of the plan, maintain spill kits, first aid kits etc. handy and inspect them regularly for their efficacy.

References

Samir Amin, *Capitalism in the Age of Globalization*, Zed Books, London.

Veronica Beechey and Tessa Perkings, *Matter of Hours: Labour Part-time Work and Labour Market*, Polity Press, Cambridge, 1987.

Isa Baud and Ines Smyth (eds), *Searching for Security: Labour's Responses to Economic Transformation*, Routledge Studies in Development and Society, 1997.

Michael Chousodovsky, *Globalisation of Poverty*, Other India Press, Goa, India, 1997.

Peter Custers, *Capital Accumulation and Labour in Asian Economies*, Vistar Publications, New Delhi.

Human Development Report 1995, 1997.

Valentine M. Moghadan (ed), *Patriarchy and Economic Development*, Clarendon Press, Oxford.

U.Kalapagam, *Labour and Gender Survival in Urban India*, Sage Publications, 1994.

SECTION – D

MIGRANT LABOURERS IN VARIOUS INDUSTRIES

34

Status of Migrant Laborers and Peace Trust Intervention for Safe Migration

Anitha and J. Paul Baskar

Emigration of workers to other countries and regions has been an ongoing process since time immemorial .The opening up of world markets and increasing globalization has resulted in a large number of Indian workers emigrating to foreign countries especially to the gulf region for approximately around 3.5-4 million workers Majority of migration includes unskilled and semiskilled workers who are considered to be the major economic players of the nation. These workers are more vulnerable being marginalized on the agenda of human rights and health care. Hence an appropriate strategy need to employed to strengthen and safeguard the rights of Migrant workers. The paper will discuss in detail about the status of migrant workers and the underlying part of Peace Trust in promoting safe migration.

Migration-A Developmental Issue

Definition : According to ILO, "Migrant can be defined as a person who is to be engaged, is engaged or has been engaged in remunerated activity in a state of which he or she is not a national"

Globalization and large scale Economic development is developing countries create a strong desire for industrial for families to upgrade their living standard. The gaps between rich and poor widen and these marked differences contribute to large scale of labour and service flow. Current data reveal that 30% of Indian population has found to be migrated. When the developed countries open their market in the developing countries import their technology and modern goods, the indigenous industries are destroyed. This increases movement of people across borders legally or illegally from rural to urban (or) from poorer to wealthier countries. Most of the migrant workers are unable to find a decent job due to insufficient job vacancies are forced to stay without income and shelter. Hence International Migration may not be viewed simply a problem of modern slavery. It also means more than a reflection of less access to necessary information, emotional, social or financial support especially those who are illegal migrants are highly vulnerable to detentions exploitations.

Migration and Human Rights-Intersecting Issues

Migrants are a particularly more vulnerable population, but they have often invisible on the international human rights agenda. Migration and human rights intersect at a number of points. While international Human rights law recognizes the right to leave one's country, there is no corresponding right to enter another country without the state permission. This complex relationship is multifaceted occurs at all migratory levels like country of origin, during transit, and in the country of destination. Skilled labourers may face fewer problems but the vulnerable group is unskilled and semiskilled workers who form the majority are more prone to human rights violations. This may include violations on economic and social rights, health care, education and adequate housing. The main reason behind is that the migrants are strangers to society, unfamiliar with the national language,laws,practices and hence less able to assert their rights.

Need For Safe Migration

International Migrants are the major economic players of the Nation; the savings remitted by migrants abroad constitute the largest source of foreign exchange for India. Which is clearly evident from the Global development finance report stating that Indian worker remitted more than US$ 10 billion in 2001.Migration can narrow the trade gap, increase foreign currency services, facilitate department servicing, reduce poverty and above all support sustainable development. Migration offers benefits to both ending and receiving countries. Receiving countries are able to fill in labour shortages and offset demographic pressures, hence by allowing managed migration which would ensure that returning migrants bring back new skills, contacts and financial resources that enhance the growth rate of local economy. Hence it is the duty of both the ending and receiving countries to ensure a safe working environment for migrants. Statistics show that there is a dramatic increase of women willing to work as domestic laborers abroad. Attempts need to be made to advance the life of our migrant workers working outside their country of origin. Employing a new approach with relevant Strategies is the only way to produce more effective and practical programmes and practices. A labor frame needs to be employed for supporting and strengthening the rights of migrant workers. Hence any intervention must therefore consider direct and indirect impact on a person's right to mobility.

A Systemic Approach

Peace trust has been adopting a rights based approach to promote safe migration .It has been working for the welfare of Migrants since 1999.The approach includes participation, empowerment and linkage. The objective of the approach is to empower migrant workers with adequate knowledge by involving community participation. Due to globalization and oil markets, gulf region are opened up to many Indian workers. Our study makes it true that most of the workers from our area are being employed in Middle East countries. They are the unskilled and semi-skilled laborers being employed in construction sites, hotels, fitters, and carpenters. Some of them are also working as undocumented labourers. Many of them were cheated by the agents and not paid properly. These workers are more vulnerable being marginalized on the agenda of human rights and health care.

Migration in Relation To HIV/AIDS

According to National sample survey, In India 24.7% of the population had found to be migrated which was estimated to be around 264 million migrants. Most of these migrant workers are highly mobile and often live in unhygienic conditions, with longer working hours. Relative isolation from the family and geographical mobility may foster casual sexual relation ships and make them highly vulnerable to STD's and HIV/AIDS. Migrant workers have little access to information on AIDS and STD due to language and cultural barriers in their existing country. These workers when returning or visiting their home community may infect their wives or other partners. Hence adequate knowledge on migrant's vulnerability towards AIDS with proper counseling is needed. This is possible only by an organization, which can take up such a promotional role.

Peace trust underlying objectives aim to promote safe Migration through providing adequate knowledge on Migration and Health. Some of them include:

- To equip migrant workers with adequate knowledge on Migration and health care before departing to their working countries and by educating their peers in the working countries with the obtained knowledge.
- To assess and analyze the knowledge and attitude of people on Migration and health.
- To strengthen the spouse and Migrant associations and empower them with knowledge on migration and health
- To disseminate the information on Migration and its vulnerability on HIV/AIDS through advocacy the issues and to propagate with the available medias

Selected Area for Intervention

Sivagangai dist is among the few districts of TamilNadu where a quite large number of people migrate to foreign countries as unskilled and semiskilled labourers .The selected area of Intervention covers 10 panchayats in Sivagangai.The area is declared as low risk area by AIDS control sectors since there is high number of migration. This is the main reason behind the neglection of governmental schemes for HIV/AIDS prevention in the region. Current statistics from Government hospitals show that 204 were tested positive out of 327 persons who approached for testing. Out of this, 80% of them belonged to Migrant community.

Interventions at Grassroot Level

Migrants and their spouses are being equipped with adequate knowledge on Migration and health by providing them training programmes and by organizing associations for them. Interventions are being given by grouping them as

- Pre departure trainees
- Peer educators
- Returnees-Migrants association
- Spouses of Migrant workers-spouse associations

This grouping helps to reach out to the problem multidimensionally. Apart from that our information booth are providing guidance and counseling to the migrant labourers.

Participatory Action Research

An action research was conducted in the intervene area with the aim

1. To understand the knowledge of people with regard to migration in the study area
2. To assess and analyze existing problems and identify the measures to be implemented
3. To involve community participation in action research programs
4. To meet the training needs of migrants

Implementation of the Findings

- The findings of the research program are implemented in every training program to fulfill the objective of meeting the training needs of the migrants.
- PAR findings are published in the Quarterly and email newsletters that has been circulated to the Migrants
- The assessed knowledge of the people help to simplify the training programs or modify the programs to focus on the area of intervention .For ex: more focus had been on condom usage as the study revealed lack of knowledge on condom usage.

Ø The periodical research program being targeted on the same samples helps to formulate the intensity of the training program and the needed measures to adopt to increase its reachability.

Ø The research gaps are fulfilled in the adjacent action researches, which helps to provide a holistic view of the study area.

Developed Strategies

Strategies have been facilitated to ensure safe migration of Migrants. Some of the major concerns include:

Regulating Immigration status of Migrants in their working countries by providing them access to Information. This includes training Programmes, training Manuals, Migrant diaries which include legal laws of the working countries, rules to be followed

Overcoming the Language barriers by educating some simple words of the working countries.

Educating safe money transfers to send their earnings. Advocacying governmental level to adopt policies to encourage safe investment of remittance to their home countries.

Ensuring proper health care and adopt safe life style. Migrants are being provided awareness on HIV/AIDS with high concerns on condom usage.

Empowering spouses of Migrants to be economically productive by implementing micro finance credits and vocational skills. Psychological counseling and guidance are additional interests rendered. Three spouses from the area had attended the conference on reproductive and sexual health was the part to be highlighted.

Peace trust believes that exploitations or violations of human rights in the working countries are also included in the agenda of trafficking. Hence Case handlings are being carried out and any migrant labor being exploited in the working country is given support and adequate measures implemented for their rescue.

IEC-Information, Education and Communications

A continuous News monitoring has been done with the international newspapers highlighting the theme of safe Migration.

Website radio Pasumai Ulagam has been propagating the voice of Migrants internationally especially to the receiving countries.

Networking with the NGOs and Indian Embassies worldwide helps to render timely help for the migrant workers who are in need.

Newsletters via in Email is being sent monthly to more then 200 beneficiaries.A quarterly Newsletter Kadal Kadantha Thozhilali reaches 1500 beneficiaries worldwide.Governmental schemes on migration issues, HIV/AIDS details are the highlighted topics included.

Conclusion

International Migration is a complex task to understand. Peace trust intervention aims to provide a safe working environment for the migrants especially unskilled and semiskilled workers who are considered to be highly vulnerable. Peace trust believes that enlightening the Migrants with labour opportunities and working rights help each migrant to have equal treatment in their working countries. Our attempts ensure that every migrant should not be subjected to any kind of exploitation, discrimination or abuses and hence lead a life of dignity.

References

Alam, S.M. and Alikhan, F. (1987), Perspectives on Urbanization and Migration : India and USSR, Allied Publishers.

Bardhan, K. (1977), "Rural Employment, Wages and Markets in India, A Survey of Research," Economic and Political Weekly, Review of Agriculture, June 25.

Bhattacharya, Prabir (1998), "The informal sector and Rural-to-Urban Migration : Some Indian Evidence, Economic and Political Weekly, Vol. XXXIII, No. 21, May 23, pp. 1255-1262.

Das, Biswaroop (1993), "Migrant Labour in Querries and Brick-kiln : A Overview," Centre for Social Studies (Mimeo), Surat.

35

A Case Study on the Problems of Women – Migrant Labourers in Madurai City

S. David Amirtha Rajan and P. Gnana Soundari

The concept of migration is not a new term in Indian context. At the time of British period, for establishing railway track and industrial development, rural labours were migrated. In the course of migration, the labourers were exploited to the core. The woman labourers were cheated and their moral life becomes a question. Even they involved in immoral activities for the sake of their earnings. The same trend also exists even now in many places. Now, the need of migration is quiet different, because of urbanization. This also creates a lot of change in the life of migrant. In many cases, they are conditioned to involve in immoral activities such as prostitution, selling country liquor, and so on. This kind of news becomes common in daily news. Therefore, there is a need to analyse the problems of woman-migrant labourers in Madurai City. This is developed on the basis of the following objectives.

1. To study the migration in general.
2. To identify the reasons for migration among women.
3. To study the problems of the respondents.

The causes of migration have changed over time. Throughout most of history, migration followed the movement of people as they acquired new territory or merged with other people. Movement was therefore a matter of conquest, settlement, intermarriage, or the religious conversion of prior inhabitants. Migration was often voluntary, not dictated by a simple struggle to survive.

From then until late in the nineteenth century, the slave trade changed the nature and volume of migration. On historical maps of migration, slaves account for several thick lines connecting Africa to the Americas, especially South America. A set of thinner lines connects Africa to Europe, the Middle East, and the Persian Gulf, where many slaves were also taken. A small number of indentured servants went from Brittain to Australia. In all, roughly 14 million people are thought to have moved under force during these four centruries.

By contrast, from 1500 until the early 1800s, probably only 2 or 3 million people crossed national borders voluntarily. A few arrows point across the migration map from Europe to North America. Others go from Europe to South America. One arrow goes to South Africa, and one to the South Pacific. A few point between African countries, and one goes from China to Taiwan. Those are all of the flows large enough to warrant arrows.

Individual voluntary migration became a major trend for the first time in the early 1800s. European feudal systems were disappearing and steamships were available to move people around quickly and easily. Around 60 million Europeans left for new lands in search of economic, religious, or political freedoms during the following hundred years. About 12 million Chinese and 6 million Japanese left their homelands for other parts of southern and eastern Asia, and a million and a half left India for Southeast Asia and Africa.

But nothing on those historical maps prepares the viewer for the sheer mass of people etched into current maps of migration, where as may people can move in one year as moved in entire previous centuries. The total number of international refugees during just the last four decades of the twentieth century probably exceeds the total for involuntary international migrants in all previous history. Today, every region either sends or receives migrants. Nor would anything on those historical maps even hint at the remarkable diversity of reasons people now have for leaving their homes and countries. Today's migrants tell an extraordinarily varied catalog of stories – far more diverse than the tales their predecessors offered.

Apart from the long-established migratory pressures of war, persecution, and the pull of economic opportunity, migrants are now responding to scarcities of land, water, and food that are more wide-spread than ever before. They are leaving because of overcrowding in decrepit squatter settlements that now house huge numbers of people, because of post-Cold War changes in political climate, and because of widening disparities of income.

This is why most of the world's migration has yet to happen. As these pressures grow and converge, in countries not yet in the news, new waves of migrants are likely to appear. They will tell stories about water scarcity or about falling life expectancy, or other issues not yet a part of our thinking on national security and not yet understood as forces capable of driving migration. Yet these forces are liable to accelerate, contributing in many developing countries to an unstable mixture of rapid economic change, social disintegration, and unrelenting demographic pressure.

And then there are migrants who are trying to improve their standards of living. Some may be getting out of crashing economies while it's still possible to leave with their lives mostly intact. Others are simply pursuing better opportunities and could easily have remained at home. In total, these economic migrants number around 100 million.

Migration

Humen have always been wanders. The most ancient myths and stories include tales of individuals setting out to explore new lands and unfamiliar peoples. Massive population movements to escape natural disasters or political persecution are recorded in the histories of many ethnic groups.

International migration – which refers to the movement of people from one country to another to take up residence – is a relatively recent development, however. It is only in the 20th century that the system of nation-states, passports, and visas developed to regulate the flow of people across national borders.

In 1995, 185 countries were members of the United Nations. Nearly all have passports to distinguish citizens from foreigners, controls to regulate movement across borders, and policies, and procedures for allowing foreigners to reside within their borders.

Why People Migrate?

Most of the world's nearly 6 billion people never cross a national border. The fact that only a small share of people actually move suggests that the decision to move is not taken lightly, and that most countries discourage immigration.

What causes the relative few to leave their homelands and move to another country? There are countless reasons an individual may decide to move, but most reasons for crossing international borders for temporary or permanent settlement may be classified as fundamentally economic or non-economic. In addition potential migrants are influenced by pull, push, and network factors. The major underlying factors that encourage migration are depicted in Table 1.

Individuals may be influenced by one factor (for example, a job offer), but also motivated by non-economic factors, such as the chance to join family members or the desire to experience life in another country. Poor job prospects at home might provide a push forward the decision to migrate. Networks interact with the push and pull factors by providing the information and means necessary to move.

Pull, push, and network factors rarely have equal weights in any particular migration stream. And, the importance of each factor changes over time. Pull factors – such as foreign worker recruitment to meet labour demands – may initiate migration streams. Push and network factors then gain importance as a migration stream matures.

Economic Restructuring

The job situation in many developed countries is complicated by a shift away from agriculture to industry and service jobs. Between 1950 and 1990. The share of the world labour force in agriculture fell from two-thirds to one-half. In developing countries, the proportion dropped from four-fifths to two-fifths over the period.

Table – 1 : Factors Encouraging Migration

Type of Migration	*Pull/Demand*	*Network*	*Push/Supply*
Economic	Guest workers programs	Job information from employers, the media, compatriots	Unemployment/ under employment
	Recruitment	Labour recruits and smugglers	Low wages
	Company transfers		
Non-economic	Family reunification, marriage	Transportation and communications networks	War
	Personal desire to live abroad	Communities of family and friends	Political and religious persecution
		Refugee assistance organizations.	

Agriculture's labour force share is expected to drop further during the 21st century, as the agricultural revolution – which has re undermine the ability to control or monitor the foreign workers.

Second, programmes cause less labour market distortion if there are strong labour market institutions (such as labour unions and regulatory agencies to enforce labour laws) that allow host governments to determine whether foreign workers are needed and to monitor the effects of the foreign workers on the native labour market.

Third, governments can (and increasingly do) use employer taxes or levies to minimize the wage or labour market distortions caused by foreign workers. These fees also help to pay some of the inevitable settlement costs of workers and families. Governments can use economic incentives to promote the return of guest workers by, for example, retaining a share of the workers' wages until they return to their home countries.

The present study is carried out among the women working in various fields like teaching, hospital services, software institutes and retail shops. 40 respondents have been selected at convenience, ten respondents from each of the four categories. A questionnaire was prepared to collect data from the respondents. The information on personal data and reasons for migration and problems of migration are collected. The data collection was carried on during the first week of February 2006. The collected data have been analysed and summarized as follows.

The percentage of women migrants in the age group 15 – 20 is 60 per cent and 21 – 30 is about 30 per cent and above 30 years is 10 per cent. It is revealed here that the young women below the age of 20 years are able to migrate themselves early due to their lass commitment at home.

Only 25 per cent of these respondents are married, and 75 per cent of them are unmarried. This shows that for unmarried women it is possible to move from one place to another.

Nearly 90 per cent of them are educated Higher Secondary and above i.e. up to post graduation, 40 per cent of them got technical education in computer systems. Only 10 per cent are with High School education.

Table – 2 : Distribution of the Respondents by the Reasons of their Migration

Reason	*Categories*				
	Teaching	*Hospital Services*	*Software institutes*	*Retail Shop*	*%*
Low income	3	2	2	3	25
Unavailability of work	1	2	4	5	30
Indebtedness	1	-	-	2	7.5
Family problems	2	1	-	-	7.5
Illness	2	2	-	-	10
Low pay	1	3	4	-	20
Total	10	10	10	10	100

Source : Primary Data

Main reasons for migration are low income, indebtedness, irregular availability of work, irregular wages and less wages. It has been presented in Table – 2.

It is inferred from the Table – 1 that 25 per cent of the migrant women labourers have migrated because of their family income is low and they are forced to go for jobs to increase their family income. 30 per cent of them migrate due to the non-availability of work at their native place. The reasons of indebtedness and family problems constitute a total of 15 per cent of the respondents which are not major problems. 10 per cent of the respondents felt that due to their health problem they migrate in order to get good medical treatment. The rest of the 20 per cent informed that they are not getting this much pay they get in their earlier jobs.

Regarding the problems faced by the respondents, it is observed that though they migrate from one place to another still they are nor able to fulfill the purpose for which they migrate. The problems faced by them are long hours of work, feel loneliness without relatives nearby, long distance of work place, cost of living high and no job security.

It is inferred from Table –3 that in their present job they have to work for long hours especially the respondents of hospital services expressed that during emergency and overcrowding days they are not allowed to go home on time. They have to work till the situation becomes normal.

22.5 per cent of the respondents felt that though they earn high pay they incur high expenses also, which does not make much change in their standard of living. 20 per cent of the respondents have expressed that in their migrated job they have to travel long distance in order to reach their work place. 17.5 per cent of the respondents viewed that they have no job security unless they perform well. The rest of the 10 per cent of the respondents felt that their family as a whole missing their relatives and for each social functions they have to go often to their native place which requires more expenses.

To conclude that the women migrant labourers are much satisfied with their present job and migration is unavoidable for them

Table – 3 : Distribution of Respondents based on Problems

Problems	*Categories*				
	Teaching	*Hospital Services*	*Software institutes*	*Retail shop*	*Percentage*
Long hours of work	3	5	2	2	30
Loneliness	1	-	-	3	10
Long distance	4	1	2	1	20
Cost of living high	1	3	5	-	22.5
No job security	1	1	1	4	17.5
Total	**10**	**10**	**10**	**10**	**100**

Source : Primary Data.

References

Singh D.P., *"Women workers in unorganized sector"*, Deep and Deep Publication Pvt. Ltd, New Delhi, 2005.

Balakrishan A, *"Rural Landless Women labourers-problems and prospects",* Kalpaz Publication, Delhi, 2005.

Economic Survey 2003-2004.

Dutt & Sundaram, *Indian Economy*, Sultan Chand & Sons, New Delhi, 2004.

36

Challenges Faced By Entrepreneurs in Informal Sector Enterprises in Dindigul District, Tamil Nadu - A Micro Level Study

K. Ravichandran and K. Dhevan

Informal Sector is that segment of laboUr market in the developing countries that has absorbed significant numbers of jobseekers, mostly in a pattern of self-employment. The informal sector, with its enterprising individuals and groups can be looked as both the casualty and cure to many ill effects of globalization (Isagani Antonio F. Yuzon, D.P.A: 2004). Globalization led to shift from secured self-employment to more precarious self-employment, as producers and traders lose their market niche. With these shifts, while more and more men enter the informal economy, women tend to be pushed to the lowest income end of the informal economy. On the other hand expansion of the informal economy in many countries was the significant effect of globalization on informal employment which generate new opportunities for those who work in the informal economy in the form of new jobs for wageworkers or new markets for the self-employed (Marillyn Carr AND Martha Alter chen: 2001).

Focus of the Study

The subjects of informal sector (IFS), rural non-farm sector (NFS), and micro enterprises (MES) have been an area of interest to the academicians, researchers and policy makers during recent past. The term IFS was first coined by Hart (1971) in a study of Ghana. However, the official use of IFS was first appeared in the reports prepared under the ILO Programme in the beginning of the 1970s on Ghana and Kenya. The term, which is commonly used to refer to that segment of labour market in the developing countries that, has absorbed significant numbers of jobseekers, mostly in a pattern of self-employment, and workers in very small production units.

Low levels of capital, skills, access to organized markets and technology; low and unstable incomes and poor and unpredictable working conditions have often characterized informal activities. Such activities are often outside the scope and purview of official statistical enumeration and government regulations, and beyond formal systems of labour and social protection. Some studies opined that the smallest enterprises are the most likely to be informal. The resolution concerning statistics of employment in the informal sector adopted by 15th International Conference of Labour Statistics held at

Geneva during 1993 was as follows: The informal sector is regarded as a group of household enterprises or unincorporated enterprises owned by households that includes: (a) informal own account enterprises which may employ contributing family workers and employees on an occasional basis; and (b) enterprises of informal employers, which employ one or more employees on a continuous basis (ILO: 2002). ILO characterizes the informal sector as: Informal units comprise small enterprises with hired workers, household enterprises using mostly family labour and the self-employed. The informal sector can be categorized into the small or micro-enterprise sub-sector, the household-based sub sector and the independent service sector comprising of domestic helpers, street vendors, cleaners, street barbers, shoe shiners and casual labourers. (Amit Mitra: 2002) Mrs.Renana Jhabwala (SEWA) insisted to follow household approach rather than the enterprise approach to capture the informal sector for the purpose of measuring its size. The household approach includes big chunk of workers like home based workers, women agriculture workers, and street vendors whereas the household approach captures the informal workers in the informal sectors (www.def_measure.htm).

With the structural changes, the rural non-farm economy is conceptualized again as a part of this informal sector. And thus the rural non-farm sector plays a crucial role. It accounts for a large proportion of total rural employment (the range is from 20 to 40 percent) and total rural income ranges from 20 to 50 percent in Asia. As far as India is concerned, about 370 million workers constituting 92 percent of the total workforce were employed in the unorganized sector as per NSS survey 1999-2000 (www.labour.nic.in.pdf,p.4). In rural India, as compared to the entire population, Informal sector workers include all workers in informal enterprises, some workers in formal enterprises, self-employed workers, and those doing contract work for informal or formal sector enterprises and contractors. (Paola Kantor: 1997) It also becomes an important source of income for women, small farmers and landless workers. As Hernando de So to and others have shown, the informal sector is made up of entrepreneurs who produce legitimate goods and services without proper permits and legal status because they are locked out of the formal legal economy by a maze of regulations, excessive procedures, high tax rates and other barriers to market entry (John Sullivan & Jean Rogers: 2004). All unincorporated proprietary and partnership enterprises were defined as informal sector enterprises in the NSS during 1999-2000. (GOI: 2001). According to SEWA in India, this sector includes home-based workers, vendors, manual laborers and service providers; It accounts for up to 70 percent of gross domestic product and over 40 percent of exports; of the total workforce, 93 percent operate within the informal sector, and 60 percent of these are women. (Mary Treacy: 2003). Informal sector played in some of the major structural changes in the Indian economy during 1970s when there occurred an occupational shift out of agriculture, with the share of agriculture in employment declining and that of non-agriculture increasing (Prabir Bhattacharya: 1998). All these studies have not paid much attention on the level of income earned by an individual in the informal sector, and if they are entrepreneurs their level of investment, future plans, challenges, etc.

On the other hand most of these activities are termed as Micro enterprises' and are of small, part-time, mostly businesses that are highly labour-intensive in nature. Their activities depend to a large extent on the local and regional demand. Micro enterprises can be effective tool for poverty reduction, employment generation, empowerment of women and enterprise development. However, in the liberalization era these micro enterprises face lot of challenges and many of them have become bankrupt. Meantime the emergence of Self Help Groups (SHGs) boosted the micro enterprises, which further contributed for the widening of the pool of entrepreneurship available to society and it broadens the base of the private sector. With the background, two different studies were conducted to analyze the nature of enterprises of individual entrepreneurs and of the entrepreneurs promoted by these SHGs to understand their socio-economic background and the challenges faced by them.

Objectives

The present study has the following objectives.

1. To study the socio-economic status of sample respondents
2. To study the nature of business of the sample respondents, and
3. To find out the challenges faced by micro entrepreneurs in informal sector in Dindigul district.

Methodology

Survey method was used for the study. Both primary and secondary sources of data were used. Respondents for the study were selected purposively i.e., 100 individual entrepreneurs and 100 entrepreneurs promoted by SHGs in Dindigul district were interviewed with structured pre-tested interview schedule.

Dindigul District Profile

Dindigul District of Tamil Nadu is one of the very few districts, which have two distinct agro climatic zones viz., semi and tropical climate and subtropical climate. The district is located between 10.050^0 and 10.09^0 north latitudes and 77.30^0 and 78.20^0 east latitudes. The net irrigated area is 99380 hectares, which is about

42 per cent of the net sown area of 236,457 ha. The district is drought – hit and has a poor groundwater status. It has received less than average rainfall (836 mm) during the last two years. Very small land holdings of less than one hectare accounting for 67 per cent of the total holdings. A wide range of fruit, flower and vegetable, food crops like paddy, maize, pulses and oil seeds like groundnut and commercial crops such as sugarcane and tobacco are grown in the district. It is also specially known for the cotton spinning mills, handloom art silk saris in addition to the other industries, particularly lock, safe manufacturing and tanning. At present development of infrastructure started picking up which helps all-round development of the district.

The district has 7 taluks, 14 development blocks and 357 villages covering a geographical area of 6267 sq. km. There are 22 commercial banks operating with the network of 138 branches in the district, 60 per cent of which are located in rural areas. The Dindigul DCCB with its 28 branches as well as 197 affiliated PACB and 6 PARDBs play an important role in financing for agriculture and rural development. The institutional credit flow in the district has achieved above the targeted level during the past. It was planned to distribute Rs. 43100 lakhs during the year 2004 – 05 for agriculture and other priority sector.

At present, there are 3485 SHGs functioning of which 2945 SHGs functioning in rural areas. Their internal lending amounts to Rs.1473 lakhs.

Major Findings

Men and Women in Informal Sector: In the case of individual entrepreneurs, majority (83 percent) of the sample respondents were male. It shows that there is wide gap in the male female entrepreneurship ratio. This lower participation is also observed while calculating the number of female workers per thousand male workers, in the rural non-farm sector and farm sectors (Mitra: 1993). However, the proportion of women and men non-agricultural workers in informal employment is roughly equivalent in Asia (ILO: 2002). In the case of entrepreneurs promoted by SHG, all the sample respondents were female.

Prime Working Age : It was found that today's youth show keen interest in self-employment as majority of the sample respondents in both the category was in the age group of less than 35 years. Though it is not just the young or old who make up the informal sector, in the total informal sector labour force, the prime working age group (25-44) constitutes majority (Nurul Amin A.T.M.: 2002).

Educational Status : Majority of the respondents in both the category was having only primary education. The skill and technology base of these people is not conducive to move up to the economic and social ladder. These constraints are accentuated by lack of access to micro-finance, new technologies and information (Amit Mitra: 2002).

Marital status : Majority of the respondents of the individual entrepreneurs (68 percent) was married whereas only married women or those women who are the bread winners of the family were encouraged to become members of SHG (TNCDW: 2001).

Family Type : 70 percent of the respondents of the individual entrepreneurs were from nuclear family, where as it was found 80 percent in the case of SHG entrepreneurs.

Community: Generally entrepreneurship culture rests with the upper strata of the community. In this study also, it was found that 92 percent of the respondents belonged to Backward Class Community. But it was reverse in the case of the respondents of SHG where majority of them belonged to most backward and scheduled caste category. The caste and ethnicity are the major issues among majority of the illiterate or those below the poverty line belonging to scheduled castes and scheduled tribes (Amit Mitra: 2002). If opportunities are given, their entrepreneurial talents would fade away these issues.

Monthly income : A large proportion of the respondents (58 percent) have a monthly net income in the category of less than Rs. 3,000. But all the SHG entrepreneurs were come under this category.

Type of Entrepreneurship and entrepreneurial activity : It was found that all the individual and group respondents were adoptive / imitating and first generation entrepreneurs. Majority were in vegetable business and tailoring in the former case whereas coconut thatches and petty and teashop business were common in the latter case. It was also found that self-employment is more important as a source of employment among women workers than among men workers (ILO: 2002).

Ownership on Shops : Majority of individual entrepreneurs were (89 percent) having their shop in rented houses but it was only 11 percent in the case of SHG entrepreneurs.

Experience in Business : Majority (34 percent) of the individual entrepreneurs was having less than 5 years of experience in their business. Likewise, 80 percent of the group entrepreneurs had less than 5 years of experience (Kalyani & Chandralekha: 2002).

Level of Investment : Majority (31 percent) of the individual respondents made an initial investment below Rs.20000. But 90 percent of the SHG entrepreneurs made an initial investment below Rs.5000.

Borrowings : It was found that 65 percent of the respondents have contributed their own money to their business, while only 35 percent of them borrowed from various sources. All these 35 per cent of the respondents borrowed loan from non-institutional source like, moneylenders and friends. In the case of SHG entrepreneurs' majority of them borrowed from their SHGs only. On credit supply, group approach serves as collateral and can reach millions. A success story of that magnitude has still to emerge (Nurul Amin A.T.M.: 2002), (Ravichandran.K & Revathi Bala M: 2004). The dawn of SHG uprooted informal sources in rural credit markets.

Employment Generation : Majority of the sample respondents has generated employment opportunities to others.

Business Objective : Earn more money, become the role model to others, self identity, and providing employment were the objectives of the business found among the respondents (Ravichandran K. & Revathi Bala M: 2004). While earn more money was the major objective of the respondents in the first category, self -identity was the objective in the case of SHG respondents. Similar findings were also reported among women entrepreneurs by Ganesan R. et.al: 2002 and Kalyani & Chandralekha: 2002.

Causes for Success : Majority (43 percent) of the respondents reported that 'family support' was an important factor, which contributed to success in their entrepreneurial activity. Nanda

Gopal R. & Chinnaiyan P also reported similar findings: 2004. However, for the majority of the SHG entrepreneurs their SHGs' support was the major factor for their success, which was followed by family support.

Future Plan : Majority (39 percent) of the respondents has reported that expansion of their business was their major future plan. The SHG respondents opined that generating employment opportunities was their future plan.

Challenges before them : For majority of the respondents in the first category competition from new entrepreneurs and large-scale units were the major challenge. Apart from that increasing cost of production and technology, globalization, poor information flow about updated technology and market trends and train the unskilled labourers are the other challenges met by the sample individual entrepreneurs. For the SHG respondents, the fear about the discontinuance of their SHG's /NGO's support in the future was the major challenge. Advertisement of products, marketability, social stigma, creation of demand for the product, learning technical know-how and practice of machine handlings were also challenges before the SHG women entrepreneurs.

Conclusion

The study found that entrepreneurial activity has improved socio-economic status of the sample respondents. It was also found that one common factor for the success of entrepreneurs in both the categories is their family support. All of them were new generation entrepreneurs so that they need institutional assistances and training for their development. The challenges before these entrepreneurs were the emergence of new rural entrepreneurs, competitions from large-scale units, change in technology in their respective trade, non-availability of support from the Government specifically for rural entrepreneurs and the future role of SHGs in promoting entrepreneurs. However, these have not affected their interest, infact increased their interest in their respective business.

The Policy Implications of the Study are

IFS being a labour intensive sector could generate more employment opportunities to the unemployed youth in the country. Hence, Government could think of establishing a separate cell to promote IFS, especially in the rural area by providing all infrastructure facilities.

It was found that majority of the respondents were not having any idea about the Government schemes and programmes for the micro enterprises. It is the potential area for the NGOs to work for the welfare of the entrepreneurs in IFS.

The success of SHGs lies on their capacity to develop more number of micro enterprises. During the study it was found that the members lack the skill to identify entrepreneurial activities in their environment. Always they have been concentrating on the micro credit. Agencies involved in Entrepreneurship Development Programmes may intensify their strategies to tune the interest of members of SHGs. In fact, many SHGs in other parts of the country have become successful micro enterprises. Their successful experiences can be emulated.

Appendix

Table-1 : Entrepreneurs in Informal Sector

Sl.No	*Indicators*	*Individual Entrepreneurs N=100*	*Entrepreneurs Promoted by SHG N=100*
1.	Sex – Male	83	-
	Female		100
2.	Age – Less than 35	61	46
	35-50	32	42
	Above 50	7	12
3.	Educational Status – No formal education	-	33
	Primary education	52	63
	Secondary education	27	4
	College education	12	-
	Technical education	9	-
4.	Marital Status – Married	68	100
	Un Married	32	-

(Contd.)

(Contd.)

Sl.No	*Indicators*	*Individual Entrepreneurs N=100*	*Entrepreneurs Promoted by SHG N=100*
5.	Community – Back ward	70	38
	Most backward	25	16
	Schedules caste	5	46
6.	Monthly income – Less than 3000	58	100
	3000 – 6000	23	-
	Above – 6000	19	-
7.	Type of Entrepreneurship	Adoptive	Adoptive
8.	Ownership of Shops – Own	11	89
	Rented	89	11
9.	Experience in business-		
	Less than 5 years	34	100
	5- 10 years	33	
	More than 10 years	33	
10.	Level of Investment		
	Less than 5000	27	90
	5000 – 10000	19	10
	10000 – 20000	23	-
	Above – 20000	31	-
11.	Borrowings – Less than 5000	17	85
	5000 – 10000	15	15
	Above 10000	3	-
12.	Employment (No of persons)		
	No employment	40	48
	Up to 2	58	52
	Above 2	2	-
13.	Business objective		
	Earn More Money	28	-
	Role Model for Others	25	-
	Self Identity	21	100
	Providing Employment	26	-

(Contd.)

(Contd.)

Sl.No	*Indicators*	*Individual Entrepreneurs N=100*	*Entrepreneurs Promoted by SHG N=100*
14.	Causes for success -		
	Family support	43	32
	Personality	30	-
	Financial stability	18	-
	Effective Management	6	-
	Educational status	3	-
	Support by SHG	-	68
15.	Future Plan		
	Business Expansion	39	45
	Gain good will and customer satisfaction	27	-
	Generating more employment to others	19	55
	Adopting new technology	15	-
16.	Future challenges		
	Emergence of new entrepreneurs	34	-
	Competitions from large scale units	52	-
	Change in technology	9	-
	Non-availability of support from Government	5	-
	Future role of SHGs	---	75
	Others	---	25

References

Amit Mitra, *Training and skill formation for decent work in the informal sector: Case studies form South India*, p.3&6, 2002, www.ilo.org/public/english/employment/infecon/download/mitra.pdf

Ganesan R. Dilbagh Kaur & Maheshwari R.C. *Women entrepreneurs: Problems and Prospects*, The journal of Entrepreneurship, Vol. 11(1), p. 82, 2002.

GOI, *Informal sector in India-1999-2000*, NSSO, May, p. 3, 2001.

ILO *The World Employment Report*, p.167&168. www.wiego.org/papers/unnirani.pdf 1998

ILO), *op.cit*, p.23, 2002.

ILO, *Women and men in the informal economy: A statistical picture*, Geneva, p.11, 2002.

Isagani Antonio F.Yuzon D.P.A, *The informal sector as cure for globalisation* www.economics.bham.ac.uk/seminars/external/2004/manjitpdf, 2004

John Sullivan & Jean Rogers *The informal sector development and Global economy*, http://www.Sais-jhu.edu/programs/i-dev/syllabi/informalsector.html, 2004

Kalyani W. & Chandralekha, *Association between socio-economic demographic profile and involvement of women entrepreneurs in their enterprise management*, The journal of entrepreneurship, Vol. 11(2), p.225&233, 2002.

Koteswara Rao, M(ed)., *Growth of Urban Informal Sector and Economic Development,* Vol.II, Kanishka Publishers & Distributors, New Delhi, 1994.

Martin Partrick *Self - Employment and Successful Entrepreneurship*, Kanishka Publications, New Delhi. 1999.

Mary Treacy, *International Trade forum–Issue 4*, p.6, www.tradeforum.org.htm, 2003

Marilyn Carr & Martha Alter Chen, www.ilo.org/public/english/employment/infeco/download/wp1pdf, 2001

Mitra, Arup, *Rural Non-Farm Employment, Poverty and Women*, The Indian Journal of Labour Economics, 36(3), p. 459. 1993.

NABARD, *State Level Credit Seminar, State Focus Paper,* Chennai, 2002-03.

NABARD, *Potential Linked Credit Plan*, Dindigul District, 2003-04.

Nandagopal R. & Chinnaiyan P., *Success factors: Entrepreneur's perception*, Southern Economist, Vol.43 (10), September, p.16, 2004.

Nurul Amin A.T.M., *The informal sector in Asia from the decent work perspective – Working paper on the informal economy,* ILO, Geneva, p.3&54, 2002

Paola Kantor, *Informal sector: Lifting the shroud*, Economic & Political Weekly, Vol.32 (40), October, p. 2512, 1997.

Prabir Bhattacharya, *The informal sector and rural to urban migration-some Indian evidence*, Economic & Political Weekly, Vol.33 (21), April-June, p.1255, 1998.

Ravichandran K. & Revathi Bala M., *'Challenges faced by entrepreneurs in informal sector enterprises in Dindigul District – A Study'*, the paper presented in UGC sponsored national seminar on Challenges before Indian Entrepreneurs in the 21st century held on 10th April 2004 organized by Adirampattinam Khadir Mohideen College, Adirampattinam, April 2004, p.7, 2004.

Ravichandran K. & Revathi Bala M., Role of Cooperatives and SHGs in rural credit market, CAB Calling, RBI, p.10, 2004.

Singh, Surjith, *Urban Informal Sector,* Rawat Publications, Jaipur, 1994

TNCDW, *Group Hand Book*, Mahalir Thittam, p.3, 2001.

www.def_measure.htm

www.labour.nic.in.pdf,

www.peoplesmarch.com/archieves /2004/Oct 2k4/Impact.htm

37

Socio-Economic Conditions of Unorganised Labourers with Special Reference to Auto-Drivers in Madurai City

David Amirtha Rajan and P. Gnana Soundari

The present era of WTO and globalization makes a change in lifestyle of all people in this world. This also provides new outlook to their living conditions to some extend. On the other side due to globalization the gap between rich and poor has been widened. In continuation of this, it could be visualized that the socio-economic condition of the unorganized labour may become worsen than over. This condition may lead the labour into a pathetic situation. Then their survival may be questionable. This may reflect in the life of all type of unorganized labours. Therefore, in this context an attempt is made to study socio-economic conditions of unorganized labours in Madurai City. This study is conducted on the basis of the following objectives.

1. To assess the working condition of the unorganized labourers
2. To study the social condition of the auto drivers
3. To analyse the economic condition of auto-drivers

In recent years, the issues relating to empowerment and advancement of human beings have gained much attention. The policy-makers, anthropologists, social workers and the government are leaving no stone unterved for preventing and eliminating all forms of exploitation and atrocities committed on the unorganized workers by their employees.

Labour force working in the unorganized sector still remain at the periphery even when they constitute almost 91 percent of the total work force in the country. In spite of all efforts by the government and the non-government institutions, the situation is still for below the satisfactory level. These workers are paid less and deprived of other essential benefits and they have no job security.

The most common characteristics of this sector are the small size of establishments, often consisting only one individual with a couple of hired workers, casual nature of employment, ignorant and illiterate workers, superior and dominating employer and scattered nature of establishments. The workers in this sector work as pieceworkers, the self-employed workers, the paid workers in informal enterprises, the unpaid workers in family businesses, auto drivers, vendors, the casual workers without fixed employer, the sub-contract workers linked to informal enterprises and also the sub-contract workers linked to formal enterprises.

The National Commission on Labour (1966-69) in chapter 20 of its report, covered the following categories of workers under the heading 'Unorganised Labour : (i) contract labour including construction workers, (ii) casual labour, (iii) labour employed in small scale industries, (iv) handloom / powerloom sectors, (v) bidi and cigar workers, (vi) employees in shops and commercial establishments, (vii) sweepers and scavengers, (viii) workers in tanneries, (ix) tribal labourers, and (x) other unprotected labour.

The commission described the characteristics of unorganized sector as : (i) casual nature of employment, (ii) workers are illiterates and ignorants (iii) small size of establishments with low capital investments, and (iv) superior strength of the employers operating single and in combination. According to the National Perspective Plan for Women 1988-2000, employment in the unorganized sector is characterized as : (i) low pay, (ii) long hours of work, (iii) low productivity, (iv) low skills, and (v) low job security.

Even though, the unorganized sector has been the most vulnerable and ignored sector in India, but it holds an inevitably very important place in Indian economy. The structural adjustment programs and technological innovations in last decade of the 20th century in India have pushed a majority of workers in this sector, consequently making it the largest sector of Indian economy. According to one statistics, 93 percent of the India's total working force is in this sector. They along with their family members and the marginal farmers and self-employed workers, constitute 95 percent of the country's population, thus leaving just 5 percent of the population of the country covered by organized sector. (Panda : 1999). The accepted figure of employment of this sector is 93 per cent of the workforce, including agriculture and the contribution to total net value added by industry stood 63.5 per cent in 1992-93 (Vasaria & Jacob, 1997).

Table – 1: Trends of Employment in Organised and Unorganised Sectors 1961 to 1991

Year	*Organised Sector*	*Unorganised Sector*	*Total*	*Share of Unorganised Sector Employment*
1961	14.60	174.10	188.70	92.26
1971	20.20	206.70	226.90	91.10
1981	22.90	214.00	236.90	90.33
1991	26.70	259.38	286.08	90.66

Note : (Quoted in EPW, July 13, 1996 by G. Parthasarathy, 'Unorganised Sector and Structural Adjustment)

Sources:1. Five Year Plan Draft, 1978-83, Planning Commission.

2. Economic Survey, 1994-95

3. Sarvekshana, Vol. III, No 1, July 1979.

Tables 1 and 2 provide further insight into the importance of the unorganized sector for India. In 1991, the share of the unorganized sector in our economy was as high as 90.66 percent while Table 2 shows that, in 1996-97, the share of unorganized sector to the national income was about 35 per cent.

Table – 2 : Share In National Income of Various Sectors

S.No	*Sector*	*1980-81*	*1990-91*	*1994-95*	*1996-97*
1.	Agriculture	38.08	31.46	30.69	27.37
2.	Government	17.50	23.90	24.50	27.37
3.	Private Organised	12.50	12.30	13.30	13.20
4.	Unorganised	31.92	32.34	31.51	34.83
	Total	**100.00**	**100.00**	**100.00**	**100.00**

Source : NAS 1997. Central Statistical Organisation, New Delhi.

Thus, there is no exaggeration in saying that the backbone of Indian workforce is the unorganized sector and not the organized one. Yet there is tendency to ignore this vast mass of work-force as these millions who belong to unorganized sector are politically powerless and economically weak. More than 60 percent of the population of the country depends upon the earnings of the unorganized sector workers for their livelihood. Hence, there is an urgent need to give top priority to the issues and problems of the workers of unorganized sector. (Social Action: April – June 1997, Vol. 47, No. 2).

The present paper studies the socio-economic profile of the auto-drivers in Madurai city. Auto-drivers in the auto-stands of Keelavasal, West gate, South gate, Goripalayam, Tallakulam, K.K. Nagar, Anna Nagar, P&T Nagar, Simmakkal and Ellis Nagar are taken into consideration. 50 auto drivers are selected. Scheduled questionnaire was framed to collect information. The data collection was conducted in the last week of January 2006. The collected data are analysed and summarized as follows.

Table - 3 : No. of Respondents Area Wise

Areas	*No. of Respondents*
Keelavasal	3
South Gate	4
West Gate	5
Tallakulam	9
Goripalayam	8
K.K. Nagar	4
Anna Nagar	4
P & T Nagar	3
Simmakkal	5
Ellis Nagar	5
Total	**50**

Source : Primary Data.

The sample selection is spread over the Madurai City Limit. To study the social conditions factors like age, education religion, marital status family size, and number of children are collected.

Age : The age composition of the respondents suggest that the majority of the auto drivers are young as almost more than 80 percent are found to be less than 30 years of age further break up of the under 30 group showed that 40 percent are between the age of 18 to 25 and 60 percent are between 26-30. The another 20 percent are between the age of 31-40 years of age.

Religion : As far as the religion wise distribution of the auto-drivers is concerned, the information showed that majority (88 percent) are Hindus 8 percent Muslims and 4 percent are Christians.

Marital Status : The data on marital status of the respondents revealed that 46 percent are married and 54 percent are unmarried.

Educational Background : An analysis of the level of education of the respondents indicated that 52 percent of them are illiterate they said that though they studied upto 5th standard they do not remember anything. Another 30 percent studied upto 10th standard and 12 percent studied higher secondary and 6 percent obtain undergraduate degree through open universities.

Family size : The data showed that 68 percent of the respondents families have the 2 to 5 members in their family whereas 32 percent families have 6 to 8 members. The members in the bigger families comprised of parents, brothers and sisters of the husbands of the respondents and their children.

Number of Children : It was found that 36 percent of the respondents have 3 to 4 children while 10 percent have only 2 children and the rest 54 percent are not married.

To study the economic conditions of the auto-drivers apart from family income, amount of savings, debit and sources of borrowings are considered.

Family Income : With regard to the income of the family for the whole year it was found that 72 percent are able to earn Rs.20000 to Rs.25000/- and 12 percent Rs.25000-30000 and 16 percent Rs.30000-35000.

Savings : Most of the auto-drivers and their families are not able to save any money out of their limited income. There are just 26 percent who replied that they are likely to save some money. It was found that 14 percent are to able to save upto Rs.3000/- annum whereas 12percent could save between Rs.3000 and 5000 per annum. The savings of the families of auto-drivers are very less and are not sufficient for improving their quality of life.

Amount of debt : The data revealed that more than 3/4th of the respondents i.e. 78 percent are under some debt 50 percent have an amount of debt less than Rs.5000/-. There are families whose debt also between Rs.10000-15000. The data showed that 46 percent among the debtors have borrowed money from their relatives and 34 have borrowed money from their friends and 20 percent have borrowed money from private money lenders. However, 22 percent of the families have no debt on them.

Summary

The present study observes that there is an urgent need to make some suitable amendments in the existing labours legislations so far as the auto-drivers is concerned. It is practically not possible to cover all the aspects of the respondents. Under the supervision of the state level, a common welfare fund can be constituted with the help of well-wishers and NGOs to help the auto-drivers in the aspects of loans, health and their children's education. The government authorities at the local level should give a considerable attention to the auto-drivers as they play a pivotal role in transport.

References

Singh D.P., *"Women workers in unorganized sector"*, Deep and Deep Publication Pvt. Ltd, New Delhi, 2005.

Balakrishan A, "*Rural Landless Women labourers-problems and prospects*," Kalpaz Publication, Delhi, 2005.

Economic Survey 2003-2004.

Dutt & Sundaram, *Indian Economy*, Sultan Chand & Sons, New Delhi, 2004.

38

The Plight of Migrant Workers in the Context of Globalisation in Hosiery Industries in Tiruppur

G.Albin Joseph and A. Thomas William

The globalization phenomenon was manifested in many forms such as policies of Government. In implementing trade liberalizations and competition of local products with imported products compete with local produce. Multinational companies have to contend with not only the other MNCs and local enterprises but also internally among their many different producing units intending to survive, many of them decided to relocate to other countries where they are doing business is cheaper. Those who failed to adopt were forced to shut down. Thousands of workers found themselves without jobs and without any ready alternatives for employment.

It was observed by Russel Brown (2003) that there were no trade union and lot of irregularities of violations of laws, international agreements, and trade regulations found while the studying situation of women workers in Jamaica.

Goolsby (2001) described that in China, the interplay between labour conditions, national sovereignty, free market labour, and global human rights offers description of five possible approaches for addressing labour violations. They have their own country's Municipal laws, advancing labour rights through permanent normal trade relations, applying business codes of conducts, implementing international Organisation's mechanisms for promoting compliance with treaties, and promoting greater awareness among Chinese workers of their own legal rights through Communications media such as the Internet.

Women workers faced poor nutritional status who are working in the garment industries (Joseph, 2004). It was also observed that anomalies in the dietary pattern of women workers in the garment industry and it called for more detailed investigation.

Due to massive rural unemployment that has been accentuated by serious drought conditions in about sixteen states today, there is wide spread migration of agricultural workers to other states and cities. The situation especially in Karnataka is very serious especially in the border districts in northern and western Karnataka. A large number of workers have migrated to Maharastra and Goa in search of work A larger number of workers are pouring into capital Jaipur from surrounding districts. Of them, 50 per cent belong to Sc and ST communities and another 37 per cent to the OBC's. Their number is increasing everyday (Hannan, 2005).

Study Area

The governments' safety net programmes were nowhere to be found. Many small and medium enterprises (SMEs) and local manufacturing firms had to re-engineer or restructure their business. In this context Tiruppur Hosiery industries are no exception and they designed their business activities accordingly. Tiruppur is the basin of the garment oriented industries and considered as the prominent one in the state of Tamilnadu. Migrant populations from various parts of Tamilnadu and other neighbouring states such as Andhra, Karnataka and Kerala throng Tiruppur region, since then the region woos those indigent and unskilled workers for its knitwear and its ancillary industries that amount to more than 4500 industrial units in and around Tiruppur town. As the hosiery industrial sectors open channel for employment opportunities many migrants from various parts come to Tiruppur for survival.

Population growth rate in Tiruppur is more than 100 per cent, which is the largest recorded growth rate in the country. The direct garment workers in Tiruppur are more than 4.00 lakhs and indirect workers constitute more than 2.00 lakhs. The concentration of the migrants from southern parts of Tamilnadu is high among other parts and they constitute 62 percent. Typical profile of the migrants shows that men and women in the ages of 16 – 55 years are working as Helpers, Ironers, Cutters, Singars, Flat locks, over locks,; - living in a constraint room. Unvaried minimum wages for their survival, assigned in contract works.

In this context , a study is conducted to understand the plight of migrant workers in Tiruppur with the following objectives

Objectives of the Study

1. To analyze the problems of the workers with regard to the wage pattern
2. To find out the working conditions at the time of work.
3. To measure the labour exploitation in terms of wages, hours of work etc.
4. To examine the labour welfare facilities available, if any.
5. To understand the psychosocial aspects and abuses for the focused group.

Methodology

A structured Interview schedule was used to data collection from a randomly selected four units. The are120 samples selected from among the migrant workers from these four units. Focused group discussion was also conducted in four different places convenient for the respondents to understand the psychological and emotional aspects and abuses of the workers. The study is descriptive in nature.

Major Findings

- The collected data after analysis using computer showed the following observation.
- It is apparent that majority of the workers are in the adult age group of 28 to 37 years.

- Least percentage of workers fall in the old ages of 48 years and above.
- Nearly four-fifth of the workers are in the productive young ages of 18 to 37 years.
- Women workers are observed high in garment industries in equal proportion with the men workers.
- Many workers (45.83%) are engaged as helpers in pressing and packing sections.
- A sizable proportion (16.67%) of the workers are employed in the garment industries as singars.
- There are 12.50 percent of them are engaged in over lock, 10 percent of the workers in checking section, 8.33 percent of the workers in flat lock division and 6.67 percent of the workers engaged as rectifiers.
- More than three-fifth (67%) of the workers have school education in the continuum of first to twelfth standards, paradoxically, one-fourth (25%) of the workers have not stepped into school and smelled the tasted of the education.
- More than two-fifth (43.33%) of the workers are falling in the income group of Rs.1001 to Rs.2500 and followed by 31.67 percent of the workers who in the income range of Rs.2501 to Rs.4000, 11.67 percent in the range of Rs.4001 to Rs.5500, 9.16 percent in the continuum Rs.5501 to Rs.6500 and just 4.17 percent in the monthly income group of above Rs.6500.
- More than half of the sampled workers are working for more than two years and less than three years.
- Most of the workers worked more than 15 hours. Hours spent by the workers at work spot are 90 hours per week (51.67%), 84 hours per week (23.33%), 72 hours per week (15.83%) and 60 hours per week (9.17%).
- Rest hours for the workers are 1 hour for taking food and tea and snacks (73.33%), half an hour for taking food (22.5%) and more than one hour (4.17%).
- Compensation off available is for the workers. (29.16%) is regular weekly off,(36.67%) once in a month and (17.5%) one day off in a fortnight.

- Majority of the workers did not receive bonus.
- Seventy Nine percent of the workers are being engaged in continuous work for 3 to 4 shifts once in a fortnight in a span of last 6 months.
- Three-fifth of the workers does not receive any overtime payment.
- Most of the workers (87.5%) are not enlisted in any trade unions.
- Most (37.5%) of the workers get wages in the ranges of Rs.71 to Rs.90, followed by 23.33 percent of the workers in the earnings of below Rs. 70, 22.5 percent of the workers are paid in the wage ranges of Rs. 91 to Rs.110, 11.67 percent of the workers in the continuum of Rs.111 to Rs.130 and 5 percent of the workers earned wages above Rs.130.
- Majority of the workers are having grievances to make demand for wage regulation, in need of incentives, to resolve problems with superior or manager, to make structural adjustment in the working conditions and provide adequate safety and health measures.
- A majority (76.67%) of the workers are not enjoyed the payment for health and security benefits such as life and medical insurances, saving plans, and supplement worker benefits.
- A preponderance (98.33%) of the workers are not paid for the labour contract negotiations, which is based on special duties.
- None of the workers had enjoyed the financial legal services, recreational programmes and educational services.
- Most of the workers (76.67%) had stated that they didn't have cafeteria facilities instituted by the garment industry.
- A less proportion (17.5%) of workers had expressed that the supervisors are fair in doing coordinated work. The managers and supervisors of the garment industries need to be given proper orientation on workers' perspectives.
- From the focused group discussion, the data reveal that psychological and sexual abuses are high in Tiruppur industries.

Conclusion

Though Globalization has brought in more packages of employment and opportunities it promotes more casual and temporary employment and workers face very deplorable conditions and exploitation takes its own advantage. The morality, ethics and personality of the workers are at the stake. The workers should be treated as human beings with all their entitlements.

References

Hensman, R., *The impact of industrial restructuring on Women, Men and Unions*, in Sathyamoorty, T.V, (Ed.), Class formation and political transformation in Coast colonial India, Oxford University Press, Oxford, 1996.

Hale, Angela, *What hope for "Ethical" Trade in Globalized Garment Industry?*, Antipode 32:4, 349-356, 2000.

Teerink, Rensje, *Migrations and its impact on Khandeshi Women in the Sugar Cane Harvest*, in Loes Schenk-Sandbergen(ed), Women and Seasonal Labour Migration, Sage (IDPAD), New Delhi, pp. 210-300, 1995.

Clay, Lisa (Student author), *"The effectiveness of the worker rights provisions of the generalized system of preferences: the Bangaladesh case study"*, Transnational Law & Contemporary Problems, no.1, Vol.11, p.175-201, Spring 2001.

Russell-Brown, Sherrie, *"Labor Rights as Human rights: The Situation of Women Workers in Jamaica Export Free Zones"*, Berkely Journal of Employment and Labour Law, no.1, Vol. 24, 2003.

Goolsby, John.H (Student author), *"Is the Garment Industry Trying to pull the wool over your Eyes?*, Law & Inequlity: Journal of Theory and Practice, no.2, Vol.19, p. 193-227, Summer 2001.

Bannerjee, N., *Women's work and discrimination*, paper presented at a conference in Bogota, Columbia, 1984.

Baud, *Women's Labour in Indian textile industry*, Tilburg Institute of Development Research, Tilburg, 1983.

Business Standard, *Garments export register 4% Decline*, 21 to 22 April, 2001.

Hersh, Jackques, and Brun, Ellen, *Globalization and the Communist Manifesto*, Economic and political weekly, Vol. XXXV. No.3, 15 Jan, 105 – 108. 2000,

Mahendra Dev., S., *Economic Liberalization and Employment in South Asia,* Economic and political weekly, Vol. XXXV. No,1 &2, 8Jan, 40 – 51, 2000.

Mathew, A.F. 2001, *Rethinking Globalization*, paper presented at UGC National Seminar on Globalisation and India's Environment/, SNDT Women's University, Mumbai, 15 to 16 Feb.

Sen, Ilina, *Industrial restructuring and women workers; A case study* in (Ed.) Nithya Rao, Louis, Rural and Sub sahara, site of change; the Structural context fro empowering women in India, Fes and UNDP, 1996, pp. 168 – 185, 1996.

39

An Analysis of Migrant Labour

S. Alagu Marimuthu

Migrant Labour

The migrant labour system has always existed, not only in South Africa, but also around the world. The experience is similar across cultures. It comprises of members of a peasant rural community or traditional society, which due to various pressures be they ecological, social, political or cultural, who are forced off the land to go and obtain cash and sell their labour on the market in an urban environment. When they do this, all sorts of new dynamics are set up in their own culture. They're exposed top new systems of thinking, new value systems, new cultures and new World views. The traditional culture does not prepare them for this so it's a very rude birth. In South Africa the first real waves of migration onto the labour market occurred with the discovery of gold and diamonds. People from all over South Africa and beyond travelled to Johannesburg to sell their labour on the labour market. Originally the labour pool was male gender based, and only later women joined the labour pool in order to work in the domestic arena. Although enforced by government the need to procure a job became part of the male rite of passage and rural tradition. You were considered a successful peasant farmer to the extent that you went off when you were a young man, found a job, came back when you had enough cash, started to have your own children, set up a family and ran the farm plot at home. Then in a cyclical fashion, your sons went off and sent you cash, and in this way you had a sustainable way of life. You produced a little bit of surplus.

Migrant Labour, term applied in the United States to labourers who travel from place to place harvesting crops that must be picked as soon as they ripen. Although migrant labour patterns exist in other parts of the world (e.g., Africa, Australia, Canada, Europe, and South America), none compares with the extent and magnitude of the system in the United States. Migrant labourers may travel on their own or they may be transported by a contractor who has agreed to supply the farmer with the needed workers. They may be urban dwellers who go on the land only for the season or migrants whose only means of living is to follow the crops from one place to another. Efforts to enforce sanitary conditions, prevent child labour, and protect the workers from exploitation met with only slight success until the 1960s.

In the 1930s, a combination of droughts, the depression, and the increased mechanization of farming prompted a migration of small farmers and labourers from Arkansas, Kansas, Oklahoma, and Texas to the W United States. It was estimated that this type of permanent migrant worker, without home, voting privileges, or union representation, numbered more than 3 million. John Steinbeck's The Grapes of Wrath is a dramatic representation of the life of those migrants. In World War II another type of migrant worker sprang into being with the need for labour in the defense industries. These uprooted workers experienced housing problems, but they were protected by wage and hour laws that did not apply to agricultural labour.

Since the 1940s, thousands of workers each year have been brought into the United States from foreign countries, principally from Mexico. Migrant labour, which remains almost exclusively agricultural, continues to receive little legal protection. However, in the mid-1960s, under the leadership of Cesar Chavez, organization of migrant workers began in the West, mainly in California. In 1970, after years of strikes, marches, and a nationwide boycott, more than 65% of California's grape growers signed contracts with the AFL-CIO's United Farm Workers Organizing Committee headed by Chavez. That organization, which became a full-fledged union as the United Farm Workers (UFW) in 1972, had some success in negotiating contracts in other states as well. However, it found itself locked in a fierce struggle with the Teamsters Union, which also claimed to represent migrant labourers and succeeded in renegotiating many of the UFW's contracts in California. The Teamsters' attempt to break up the UFW led to many strikes and some violence. The rivalry also significantly reduced UFW's membership (down to 24,000 members in 1996, compared to 100,000 in the late 1970s).

Growth of Migrant Labour

Migrant labour is an issue of growing importance as a number of factors - including growth in international trade, rapid population expansion, higher rates of urbanization, the widening gap between rich and poor, and economic and political oppression - have led many people to seek better economic opportunities elsewhere, either in other parts of their country or other parts of the world. The International Labour Organization estimates there are roughly 96 million migrant workers and their dependents in the world today; some experts predict that the number will double in the next twenty years.

Often employed in low-skilled, low-paying jobs, migrants tend to be the most vulnerable class of employees. These workers are often handicapped by inadequate training and language skills, face discrimination in pay and other employment conditions, lack legal protection, and are sometimes victims of xenophobic harassment. Some are held in virtual forced labour by having to pay large "deposits" to their employers and/or to surrender their passports until they have worked for a stipulated amount of time. Some are forced to pay excessive recruitment fees, and to sign contracts stripping them of their essential labor rights. Female migrant workers can be more susceptible than their male counterparts to mistreatment, including physical and sexual harassment. In addition, many migrant workers (particularly those supporting families in their home countries or regions) seek substantial overtime work to maximize profits, raising concerns about health and safety and product quality.

Companies operating in our increasingly globalized economy - whether large transnational companies or smaller suppliers - may find themselves employing migrant labour and will need to deal with the special challenges and issues surrounding this segment of the workforce. Companies that work to understand their relationship with migrants, develop human rights policies and practices for the protection of migrant workers, conduct outreach and build partnerships with non-governmental organizations and stakeholder groups, and monitor and publicize compliance are better positioned to benefit from the growing mobility of the world's population and the rising expectations for responsible corporate operations.

Some facts about Migrant Labour

An estimated 175 million migrant workers, permanent immigrants, refugees and their dependents were living outside their country of origin or citizenship in the year 2000.Of this total, some 86 million are economically active migrant and immigrant workers, including refugees: Africa: 7.1 million Asia, including Middle East: 25 million Europe, including Russia: 28.5 million Latin America and the Caribbean: 2.5 million North America: 20.5 million Oceania: 2.9 million women now constitute 49% of migrants worldwide and more than 50% in Asia, Europe, and Latin America, North America and Oceania. The US $100 billion sent home every year by migrant workers is a larger sum than all overseas Development assistance, and is second only to the value of global petroleum exports in international commodity trade. Developing countries lose 10% to 30% of skilled workers and professionals through "Brain drain."

ILO studies found that more than one in every three qualified migrant applicants was unfairly excluded in employment selection procedures in several Western industrialized countries: and the discrimination rate was 35%.

An Analysis

Millions of people world-wide have left their home countries in search of employment. But many are not looking simply for better work. Propelled by poverty and insecurity, they are looking for any work. Migrant labour is a key feature of globalization, and makes a significant impact on the world economy. Every year, migrant workers send home the equivalent of US$100 billion in remittances to support families and communities, while making social security contributions in host countries. Today's migrants face many challenges – including mistreatment and discrimination.

Migrant workers are increasingly in demand, not only for high-skilled information technology and professional jobs, but also for many of the low-paid, less skilled jobs in agriculture, cleaning and maintenance, construction, domestic service, health care and the "sex sector". Migrants are often relegated to the "three D" – dirty, dangerous, and degrading – jobs that national workers reject or are not available for. Many migrants are in precarious and unprotected work in the growing informal economy.

Labour migration can lead to a "brain drain" in home countries. But appropriate labour migration can also contribute to development in these countries through worker remittances and the transfer of skills through returning migrants. The freedom to move geographically, transfer jobs and change employers facilitates economic development and is essential to ensuring the most productive use of labour. Governments are, however, increasingly erecting barriers between willing migrants and strong demand for foreign labour in host countries – making it highly profitable in many cases to illegally circumvent those barriers. One result has been a dramatic rise in human trafficking.

Migration policies that are not founded on a respect for human rights can exact high costs on individual migrants and their home societies. There is evidence that 10-15% of migration today involves undocumented women and men who enter or work in a host country without authorization. Irregular migration leads to high levels of exploitation, forced labour, and abuse of human rights and dignity. The global challenge today is to forge the policies and the means to regulate and manage migration and ensure that it contributes positively to development of both home and host societies and to the well being of migrants themselves.

The Role of the ILO

Since its establishment in 1919, the ILO has worked to develop international consensus on regulating labour migration and on protecting workers employed outside their home countries. Such consensus is essential because these workers are at the mercy of the host country's laws and may not be protected by the laws of their home country. The ILO sets standards, assists member States in formulating their policies, and enhances understanding of the impact of migration policies through research and training. The ILO works for safe and constructive migration in three main arenas.

Building the knowledge base to address migration in the age of globalization. Key research themes concern the costs and consequences of "brain drain", the impact and productive uses of remittances, conditions of work for migrant workers, measuring discrimination and finding remedies to it, and exploring effective ways of ending human trafficking. The ILO is expanding its online International Labour Migration (ILM) database to provide current data on migrant worker flows and characteristics; currently some 80 countries provide data.

Enhancing good governance of international labour migration, by developing policy with governments, employers and trade unions at conferences and regional seminars and through direct cooperation. Trade unions – as representatives of the work force and employers are key partners in making viable policy and administration on labour migration. Other ILO activities include providing technical advice to governments and training officials of government agencies and employer and worker organizations.

Advancing human rights and decent work for migrants, by promoting the adoption and implementation of international norms. The ILO also encourages anti-discrimination activities by governments and workers' and employers' groups. It promotes actions that benefit high-risk groups, such as victims of trafficking and migrant domestic workers, and encourages labour inspection to enforce minimum decent work conditions in sectors where migrants are vulnerable to abuse.

International Experiences

ILO principles and training prompted the Mauritius Ministry of Labour and Industry to set up a "Special Expatriate Squad" to oversee all aspects of employment of foreign workers. Specialized labour inspectors with ILO training, interpreters and legal officers maintain direct contact with migrant workers and employers. The team vets all contracts to ensure that workers have decent working and living conditions and it coordinates between various relevant ministries.

Interventions by this unit have resolved several conflicts through dialogue involving migrant workers, employers and representatives of home countries. For example, misunderstandings regarding conditions of housing and work in Mauritius precipitated a spontaneous walkout from several textile plants by Chinese workers in March 2002. Mediation by Squad members backed by the Mauritius Minister of Labour resolved the dispute, precluding a strike and diplomatic tensions. As Squad officer M. Caremben says, "the office generates solutions between workers and employers, and its success derives from full support by the Minister and ILO inspiration."

The Ministry of Labour of Jordan's Special Working Contract to non-Jordanian Domestic Workers is expected to become a model for other countries in the region. The contract guarantees migrant workers – mainly women – the right to life insurance, medical care, rest days, expatriation upon expiration of contract, and treatment in compliance with human rights norms. The contract resulted from efforts led by UNIFEM in consultation with the ILO and partners such as the host government, the police, embassies of the workers' countries, and local women's groups.

UNIFEM reports that there are 56 million migrant women workers in Asia and Pacific. According to Irena Vojackova-Sollorano of the International Organisation for Migration, this could be taken as a positive indicator that women are becoming empowered, taking a decision for themselves to seek work outside their own country. However, women migrant labourers still come into adverse conditions once they enter into employment abroad. A combination of racial discrimination, employer abuse, lack of health services, and vulnerable legal status face women seeking low-paid jobs abroad, but still they accept these conditions over the lack of employment at home.

Conclusion

Globalization is leading to profit-driven economies that thrive on cheap and docile labour, especially of women, and societies that stress consumerism and competition. In turn, these have resulted in the erosion of human values, commodification of people (especially migrant workers), disintegration of societies, families and communities, racism, xenophobia, unsustainable lifestyles, and the degradation of the environment.

Migrant workers, whether documented or undocumented, have rights as workers and as human beings as embodied in the Universal Declaration of Human Rights, the UN Convention on the Protection of the Rights of All Migrant Workers and Members of their Families, ILO Convention No. 97 and No. 143 of Migrant Workers, and other international conventions. There is need to advocate for permanency of job and income to all workers and wants to remove system of contract labour.

The challenge to migrant workers, contract workers, support groups and the people is great. Globalisation gives rise to increasingly complex processes and situations. The relentless drive of the capitalists to pursue globalisation, and the governments' abdication of their responsibility to the people, make our tasks even greater.

References

C. McWilliams, *Factories in the Field,* 1971.

D. Nelkin, *On the Season,* W. A. Cornelius, ed., 1970.

The Columbia Electronic Encyclopedia, *The Changing Role of Mexican Labor in the U.S. Economy,* Columbia University Press, 2005.

K.C. Zachariah, K. P. Kannan and S. Irudaya Rajan, *Kerala's Gulf Connection,* Centre For Development Studies, Thiruvananthapuram.

K. Gopal Iyer, *Migrant Labour and Human Rights in India*, New Delhi, Kanishka, 2003.

40

Rural Non-Farm Employment: A Case Study of Brick Industry in Usilampatti

Fr. Soosaiappan and A. Thomas William

The work force in rural area is gradually moving out of agriculture. It is not only in India, but also 15th developing countries the rural labour force primary engaged in non farm work falls between 20 to 30 percent, which is given by world bank early 1980. In India the non-farm rural employment has witnessed a steady expansion during the last two decades. In rural area only 16.8 percent of male workers were engaged in non-agricultural activities in 1972-73, this increased steadily to 19.4 percent, in 1-77-78, 22.5 percent in 1983 and then to 25.5 percent, 1987-88. The similar type of trend in applicable to female workers also. In Tamilnadu 24.6 percent in 1972-73, 26.0 in 1977-78, 33.7 percent in 1983 and 34.8 in 1987-88.

In rural India, the population is increasing rapidly, in the long run agriculture and other land based activity could not provide employment to all the rural workers at adequate level of income. Taking into consideration of above fact the Government of India has initiated several employment generation schemes to generate the employment. To provide employment, in the name of globalization multinational companies were started some industries.

Very easily labours are available in India, with minimum wages get more profit.

The rural labour does not need technological skill to work in unorganised sector. Vaidyanathan observed that non-agriculture rural wage rate is in generally higher than the agricultural wages. Another reason is that to alleviate the poverty non-farm employment were created. The brick industries also were established. At present in and around of Usilampatti there are 120 brick industries are existing. In these industries most of the workers are working as contract labours. They belongs to near by villages and few are from the native. Almost all are illiterate and economically poor. They were agricultural labourers due to the failure to the crops and lack of rain, compel to leave the jobs for the survival they are employed in the brick industries.

The problem associated with the labourers of rural unorganized sector have many aspects, such as socio-economic, political, psychological, sociological and legal etc. The major share of workers in rural non-farm employment in Indian context is observed in the economic activities like manufacturing of wood products, paper cover product, printing, leather, and brick construction, trade, commerce, transport and service industries.

An attempt is made to study the socio-economic profile of workers in the case of brick industry. Precisely the objective of study in to examine the socio-economic profile, level of living and indebtedness in the workers families of brick industry.

Socio-Economic Profile

The socio-economic conditions of the brick industry workers are analysed in their age, marital status, family size and income. It is noted that, 64 percent of women labourers are working in the brick industries. More than half of the workers are belonging to the age group between 30-40. The age above 50 none of them working are found, because the work force was distributed on the basis of contract. At the same time, the age group 10-20 comparatively less than the age group 30-40. It shows that child labour are not much engaged here.

The distribution of workers by marital status are more than three-fourth of respondent were married. But less than one-fourth respondent were unmarried. They are belonging to the age group between 10-20.

Table – 1 : The Distribution of Workers by Age, Sex, and Marital Status

S. No	*Age*	*Sex*		*Total No.*	*Percentage*	*Marital status*	
		Male	*Female*			*Married*	*unmarried*
1.	0–0	0	0	0	0	0	0
2.	10–0	3	7	9	18	2	7
3.	20–0	3	10	13	26	10	3
4.	30–0	7	14	21	42	21	0
5.	40–0	5	2	7	14	7	0
	Total	**18**	**32**	**50**	**100**	**40**	**10**

The each and every brick industry two or more families are fully depend upon the brick industry for their livelihood. Some families all the members of the family are involved in the work. The distribution of workers by family size shows that more than half of the respondents are having small size families, in their families one or two children. The 34 percent of the families are having less than four children. Above four children are having families are only 10 percent.

Table -2 : The Distribution of Workers by Family Size

S.No	*Children*	*Number*	*Percentage*
1.	1 – 2	28	56
2.	3 – 4	17	34
3.	5 – 6	5	10

Levels of Living

In India there are many labours laws, but it remains in the book level. Most of the laws are not known to the vast majority of the workers in the unorganised sector. Government regulations provide minimum wage rates in various spheres of labour work, but these conditions are hardly observed and enforced in brick industry.

Wage Pattern

Most of the brick industries here, the work force is given on the basis labour contract. The contract wage are fixed on their following ways.

- To make 1000 brick the wage is Rs.120.
- To transform 1000 brick from making place to the brick chamber, the wage is Rs.35.
- To arrange 50,000 brick in the burning chamber with fire wood, rate is Rs.4000 (35 women labours and 15 male labours)
- To load and unload the bricks on the transport the rate is Rs.200.

There is discrimination of wages between man and women. The women gets the wage half wage of man, but type of work and times is same.

Table-3 : Distribution of Workers by Monthly Income

S.No	*Income*	*Male*	*Female*	*Total Nos.*	*Percentage*
1.	0-500	3	6	9	18
2.	500-1000	1	18	19	38
3.	1000-1500	1	8	9	18
4.	1500-2000	4	0	4	8
5.	2000-2500	9	0	9	18
	Total	**18**	**32**	**50**	**100**

Most of the families are having two or more earning members in the same brick industry. More than three fourth of the workers are women, because their wages are half of the man's wages. The 38 percent of workers income is below Rs.1000. In the brick industries they employ more women and increase and work force and finally achieve the maximum profit.

Indebtedness – A Cause for Workers

In the rural village, most of the families are facing the problem of indebtedness, especially those who are working in the unorganised sector, they are sinking in debt. The study in brick industry shows that all the workers are suffering with the problem of indebtedness. All of them were drawn loan from the brick industry owners. That was the major reason none of them move one industry to another. In other word by loan they bought the employer. Half of the respondent were drawn loan for the social economics like social customs of offering something to god and relatives on feast day, expenditure for children's marriage, Kathukuthu, the girl comes to the age, and death etc.

Table -3 : Distribution of Respondents by the Cause for their Indebtedness

S.No	*Cause*	*Number*	*Percentage*
1.	Poverty	10	20
2.	Unemployment	5	10
3.	Social ceremonies	25	50
4.	Medical	4	8
5.	Bad habits	6	12
	Total	**50**	**100**

The 20 percent of workers were taken loan because of their poverty. Another area of indebtedness is unemployment and bad habits. In unorganised sector these workers may not get work whole through the year. Rainy season the work when stopped and when the prepared bricks are not soled. The workers in the brick industry do not have time limit for their work. Morning to evening they have to work, even they have to work more. Physical force is more utilized in this type of work. It makes the person more weak and sick. Some time the person adopt the bad habit of drinking alcohol. The workers what they earn, some amount of money go for the interest, which they borrowed money from the owners. With this minimum salary they have to maintain the family. This way the major reason they could not live in standard of life and remain in the indebtedness.

Conclusion

From the last three decades the rural non-farm employment were increased and brick industries is no exception. The main reason is that the agriculture and allied activities could not provide employment and adequate income to the rural families, due to the failure of crops and rain. On the other side the brick industry does not need any technical skill and experience. At any age the workers can joint in this work, most of the family members are involved in this activities because of indebtedness due to the poverty and unemployment. The study shows that half of the respondents were borrowed money for the social ceremonies because if they spend more money on the social function, and religious activity it gives prestige to the family. And the poverty and unemployment also reason for indebtedness.

Steps should be taken for these workers to give social awareness and education so that they came out from the indebtedness. The labour Department should introduce a special wing to fix the minimum wages for women give medical facility and welfare for the workers. The labour act should be enforced in unorganised sector. Any of the non-farm sector units should be brought among the workers.

References

Koteswara Rao, M., *Rural Employment - The Non-farm sector*, Deep & Deep Publications Pvt. Ltd., New Delhi, 2004.

Narasaiah. M.L., *NGOs and Child Labour*, Discovery Publishing House, New Delhi.

Banarji. J, *"Worker's Rights in a New Economic Order'*, Biblio, Vol.IV Nos.1 & 2, January – Februrary, 2001.

Datla Kanika, *"Employers of India may lose their chain"*, Business Standard 2 March, 2001.

Economic Times, *"90m working children in India: ILO"* 29th April, 2001.

Economic Times, *"Government firm on Labour Act amendments"*, 17th April 2001.

Edwin Tina, *"Employers contribution opposed. Social security plan to exclude of land"*, The Economic Times, 18th May, 2001.

Hensman.R., *"World Trade and Workers Rights" To link or not to link?,* Economicand Political Weekly, No.15, Vol. XXXV, 8th April, 2000.

Mahendra Dev.S, *"Economic Reforms, Poverty, Income distinguish and Employment"*. Economic and Political Weekly, Vol. XXXV, No.10, 4th March, 2000.

41

Labour Migration and Sustainable Development

G. Sathis Kumar

Migration is a multifaceted and complex global issue, which today touches every country in the world. All 190 or so sovereign states of the world are now either points of origin, transit or destination for migrants; often all three at once. The UN's current official estimate remaines at 175 million migrants globally. By extrapolating the growth of the known migrant stocks for the period 1990-2000, the UN Population Division predicted a total of between 185 million and 192 million migrants by early 2005 (UN, 2004).

International migration is a global phenomenon. Many countries are sources of international flows, while others are net receivers, and still others are transit countries through which migrants reach destination countries. Such countries as Mexico and India experience migration in all three capacities: as origin, as destination and as transit countries.

The labour migration-sustainable development nexus incorporates two elements: the ways in which development processes, including development assistance, can reduce pressures for unwanted migration, particularly irregular movements of people, and the ways in which migrants can be a resource for poverty reduction and sutainable development in their home communities. With its focus on "migration and development", this paper is intended to make a useful contribution to this end.

Trends in Labour Migration

International labour migration generates a complex set of economic and social costs and benefits for the receiving country, migrant workers and their countries of origin. Families often pool their economic resources to send one member into the world to improve their lot back home; and an intricate network of recruiters, employers, immigration authorities, relatives and friends abroad makes the rest of the process possible.

Most economists welcome migration of all types of workers from lower to higher-wage countries, since it tends to allocate scarce labour resources to their highest value use, allowing maximal global production. The economic gains from immigration are small but positive, with the benefits however invariably distributed unequally. Most gains accrue to the migrants and owners of capital, and can have positive flow-on effects for global GDP levels. The "losers" are often the local workers with similar skills to the migrants, but again the overall losses seem minimal (ibid). It is also difficult to measure the longer-term integration or diversity costs of labour migration.

A number of factors have contributed to the increase in international migration, including the following:

- Economic globalization – which linked the economies of origin and destination countries together – led to trade agreements that contain provisions for mobility of international personnel, goods and services, prompting the growth of multinational corporations that move their personnel between countries and across the globe;
- Demographic trends, with many developed countries facing population stagnation and ageing while developing countries continue to grow faster than their job markets can absorb new workers;
- The transportation revolution that has made migration affordable to millions of would-be migrants;
- The revolution in communications (internet, cellular phones) that informs would-be migrants of opportunities outside their home countries and allows them to keep in touch with families and communities left behind;

The growth in transitional communities with growing numbers of persons with dual or multiple nationalities and citizenship who remain involved in the countries of their origin as well as their countries of destination.

Skilled migration patterns in the Asia-Pacific region demonstrate how sending and receiving countries with vastly different economies and approaches to migration, ranging from the giant growth economies of China, Japan, Korea and Taiwan Province of China to the poorer economies of Bangladesh, plan and manage labour migration. The benefits for receiving countries, or for sending countries with large economies, are well documented. But the costs for smaller, economically weaker sending countries, or for migrants in vulnerable situations, are not sufficiently known and factored into migration policies. There is a call for more ethical approaches by migrant receivers.

Labour Migration and Sustainable Development

The relationship between migration and development is complex and difficult to assess, yet many national and international development agencies are seriously exploring ways of reaping the development gains from migration. Public perceptions are often negative: migration grows out of and causes further poverty both in the sending and receiving country. Experts have examined the cause-effect relationship between migration and poverty and concluded that sometimes, where poverty does seem to result from migration and displacements, it is rather the result of poor policy planning.

Conclusion

Causes and impacts of migration and the policies to manage it are not easy to categorize, and even less easy to measure. We should close some of the gaps of unpredictability about migration management, not for purposes of controlling migration, but to ensure maximum benefits derived from it for migrants, governments and society. It points to areas requiring more research, such as the real impact of labour migration on development, the effect of the new liberalized forms of recruiting skilled immigrants from within a foreign community on future migration and emigration patterns; and what could today be useful indicators and determinants of costs and benefits of international migration. Exploding the myths and establishing more clearly the facts about migration and its consequences is a sure way of enabling the debates and design of migration policies to be more informed and reasoned.

References

UN, *World Survey on the Role of Women in Development: Women and International Migration*, Department of Economic and Social Affairs, UN, New York, 2004.

UN HABITAT, *Responding to the challenges of an urbanizing world,* UN-Habitat annual report 2005, UN, New York, 2005.

42

Labour Issues in Hotel Industries of Dindigul Town

M. Soundarapandian and T. Saravanan

Hotels are amongst the most visible and important aspects of a country's infrastructure. Hotel industry is closely linked to tourism industry. A number of factors like promotion of tourism and rapid industrial progress have given a boost to hoteliering. The recent liberalization of trade and opening up of economy will further lead to revolutionary growth in this sector. The diversity of experience in hotel management is greater than in any other profession. Hotel industry involves combination of various skills like management, food and beverage service, housekeeping, front office operation, sales and marketing, accounting. Today, the rise in corporate activity (leading to greater number of business trips) as well as the wish to travel on holiday has made the hotel industry a very competitive one.

The job opportunities in this sector varies within the industry and is largely dependent on the size of the hotel. The hotel chain, the clientele it caters to and the purpose it is made for. Personnel working in these departments require specific training and skills. With the greatest demand for services during customer's leisure hours one needs to be on duty during the evenings as well as holidays. The Hotel Industry requires a large amount of manpower to run its several departments – the food and beverage, housekeeping, front-desk, accounting, marketing, engineering, maintenance, service, firefighting, public relations and many more. Although sophisticated technology is increasingly being put to use, hotels cannot be successful without the personalized attention and care given by the hotel staff.

In this study an attempt is made to analyse the labour management practices in hotel industry with special reference to the Dindigul (district headquarter) of Tamilnadu.

The specific objectives of the study are:

1. To review the various human resource management functions in hotel industries in Dindigul Town, such as:
   (a) Recruitment and selection
   (b) Training
   (c) Promotion
   (d) Salary administration
   (e) Welfare measure
2. To study the background of the personnel and their attitudes towards personnel functions.
3. To identify the practical problems faced n implementing human resource functions in the hotel industries.

The data used in this study are the result of field surveys undertaken to find out the number of hotels in the Dindigul town. The total number of hotels in Dindigul town is collected from the office of the Commerical Tax Office-I in Dindigul Town. Number of tourists' arrivals in Dindigul district and Tamil Nadu and India are also collected from the office of Statistical Department in District Collector Office. Apart from this secondary data, primary data were also collected from the employees of the hotels in Dindigul town.

Structure of the Hotel Industry

Before analyzing, the Human resource management functions and practices with regard to hotel industries in Dindigul town, it is essential to know about the structure of hotel industries and its HRD functions.

To provide various services by the hotel to its customers it must have many departments and divisions, which are divided in various sub sections for a smooth flow of work in the hotel. Front office is one of the major departments as the hotel's main business is the sale of rooms and front office is the controlling and revenue collection department for the rooms division.

Functions of HRD Department in Hotel Industry

The HRD department uses following functions for the development of the employees status, living conditions and working condition:

(a) Providing continuing education to the employees for increasing their educational qualifications.
(b) In house or outdoor trainings & workshops to refresh and update their working knowledge.
(c) Maintaining good working conditions and improve on it.
(d) Providing more family benefits for the employee, like medical, eduation for wards, etc.
(e) Networking amongst employees and families through community development programmes, club activities, sports festivals, staff days, etc.
(f) Improving upon technology use in the organisation to improve productivity and working conditions.
(g) Creation of better relations between management & employees.
(h) Creation of proper channel of communications between all levels of work force.

Labour Issues in Hotel Industries of Dindigul Town

It is difficult to generalize about the range of personnel functions performed in an Indian organisation owing to a variety of factors such as attitudes, philosophy, organisation needs, and so on.

According to a study undertaken by M.N. Rudrabasavaraj, "Management of Human Resources in India: General Patterns and Principles", in June 1970, the following functions are listed on the basis of a fifty-company survey, covering a mix of firms.

1. Selection
2. Manpower training and development

3. Promotion transfers and performance appraisals.
4. Communication – top down
5. Wage and salary administration
6. Employee welfare statutory minimum
7. Union-management relations; etc.

In the present study the following budget class hotels at Dindigul town were taken as sample respondent for the purpose analyzing the human resource functions.

Table - 1 : Showing List of Hotels in Dindigul Town

Sl. No	*Name of the Hotel*	*Number of Rooms*	*Number of Employees*
1.	Hotel Paarvathy's (P) Ltd.	39	12
2.	Hotel Mahajothi	9	6
3.	Hotel Swagath	26	7
4.	Hotel Suganya	40	8
5.	Hotel Kurinji	29	5
6.	Hotel Anand	66	6
7.	Prakash Lodge	43	6
8.	Dolphin Hotels	43	8
9.	Hotel Om Saravanabhavan	22	7
10.	Hotel Vales park	31	6
11.	Hotel Gomath	48	9

Source: Primary Data.

Selection

Selection is the second phase in the process of procurement of people. It is the process of choosing the individuals who possess the necessary skill, ability and personality to do successfully specific jobs in the organisation. In Dindigul the hotel industries selects the candidates by filling the application blank and conducting interview. In the interview process the hoteliers used to ask about the person's past experience, schooling and personal references for placing them a suitable job. The selection and interview process have been complete within 1-2 weeks from the date of selection process. Candidates selected for the various categories of posts are asked to join immediately after the selection is over.

Probation

A person appointed to any post in these hotel industries shall ordinarily be on probation for a total period of 3 months. On the completion of which, he/she shall be confirmed temporarily because there is no permanency of jobs in hotel industry in the Dindigul town.

Induction

Induction is the systematic organizational effort to minimize problems facing newly recruited personnel so that they can concentrate on the work of the organisation. The induction is concerned with the introducing a new employee to the organisation, in the selected hotel the concerned superior or senior workers in the concerned hotel do industries induction.

Deputation

Deputation is the process of lending of services of employees by one organisation to other organisation of same concern. Usually the hotel industries in Dindigul town don't have any branches of hotels, hence deputation in these hotel industries usually not taken place.

Termination of Service

The appointing authority is competent to terminate the services of an employee at any time during the service, if his/her work has not been in satisfactory. No appeal shall be allowed against any order terminating an employee during the period. Usually the Managing Diretors shall take decision regarding the termination of employees in the hotel industries.

Manpower Training

Training is a well-articulated effort to promote competency in the public service by imparting professional knowledge by broadening of vision and adoption of correct pattern of behaviour among the employees in regard to their existing personnel responsibilities. Training prepares the individual to meet the requirements of his job. In hotel industries in Dindigul town, the persons selected will be treated as trainee for the period of 3 months and he have been provided effective training during these periods.

Promotion

A good promotion system is useful to the employees individually as well as to the organisation as a whole. Promotion is the transfer of an employee to a job, which pays more money or one that carries some preferred status. Thus promotion is one of the best forms of incentives, which generates the loyalty of all the employees of the organisation. There are three criteria, which can be followed for giving promotion; they are seniority merit and merit-cum-seniority.

The promotion process in hotel industries is very less in Dindigul town due to the small size of the organisation. If some employees terminated, then the existing staffs were given preference for that posts on the basis of seniority and merit cum seniority.

Wage and Salary Administration

A good wage and salary structure plays an important role in personnel management. A sound wage and salary policies and programmes are essential to procure, maintain, develop and promote employees and to get effective contribution from them.

At present the employees of selected hotels are getting the normal basic pay plus allowances stipulated on the basis of cost of living index. In selected hotel industries all the 56 employees are working on monthly salary basis. While fixing the wage and salary, the following factors are considered.

(i) Government Legislation and Public policy

(ii) Capacity to pay by the hotels

Employee Welfare

Welfare scheme is one of the techniques for motivating the employees towards the work. Hotels as a service industry should pay due regards to the welfare of their employees in order to get satisfy them as well as to behave in satisfactory manner with the guests. Such welfare schemes are not only made from ideological consideration but also for providing material incentives to the employees for stimulating them toward higher productivity. The following welfare measures have been introduced in the selected hotel industries.

(i) Provision of better working environment and lighting facilities.
(ii) Provision of some fringe benefits to the employees, viz., casual leave, medical leave, provident fund, gratuity, T.A, D.A, and bonus.
(iii) Provision of loan facilities
(iv) Provisions of uniforms to room boys and securities with washing allowances.

Retirement Administration

The personnel department maintains a record of all the employees on their appointment and accordingly also for their date of retirement. The department has to ensure filling up of such vacancies by way of promotion or new recruitment. The department also has to ensure clearing dues to the retired employee including pensions, gratuity, etc., maintaining their pension records etc. Since the hotel industries in Dindigul town are small enterprises, there are no separate HRD departments to maintain all its personnel administration. Pensions and gratuity are also not provided to the employees of the hotels on their retirement.

Conclusion

From this study it is found that there is no separate department for handling labour issues in Hotel Industries in Dindigul town. Mostly the proprietor of the hotel industry will handle all the decisions regarding the labour issues. Labour welfare is maintained in a few hotels. In most of the hotels the employees are in temporary work, job security cannot be assured in any hotel of the Dindigul town.

References

Akilesh & D.R.Nagaraj (Eds) *Human Resource Management- Indians Perspectives,* New Delhi – NIPM, Wiley Eastern Ltd; 1990, pp. 17-31, 2000.

S.L.Goel, *Personnel Management in Indian Industries*, New Delhi, Inter India Publication, 1992.

Rosemary Lucas, *"Fragments of HRM in hospitality? Evidence from the 1998 workplace employee relations survey"*, International Journal of Contemporary Hospitality Management, volume: 14, Number:5, Page: 207-212, 2002.

43

BPO: A New Revenue Strategy

S. Dhanasekaran, Well Howrae and R. Anandarasu

Business Process Outsourcing (BPO) occurs, when an organisation turns over the management and optimization of a business function such as accounts payable or purchasing to a third party that conducts the activity based on a set of predetermined performance matrics. Business Process Outsourcing is the long term contracting out of non-core business process to an outside provider to help, achieve increased shareholder value. Many IT professionals are familiar with the term "Business Process Outsourcing (BPO)", but knowing how to distinguish it from types of outsourcing requires scrutiny.

Business Process Outsourcing refers to delegation of ownership, administration and operation of a business process or processes to a third party or external service provider. Major corporations in the US and Europe are outsourcing their back office operations to India to save costs, e.g. employee payroll is maintained in India for their employees worldwide. Although these jobs usually are not IT related, their data based orientation often means that they require IT department support to be successfully outsourced.

Philosophy of BPO

The philosophy behind BPO is specific, do what you do best and leave everything else to business process outsources. Companies are moving their non-core business processes to outsource providers. BPO saves precious management time and resources and allows focus while building upon core competencies. The list of functions being outsourced is getting long by the day. Call centers apart, functions outsourced, span purchasing and disbursement, order entry, billing and collection, human resources administration, cash and investment management, tax compliance, internal audit, and pay roll. The list gets longer every day. In view of the recent accounting scandals (Enron, World Com, Xerox etc) more and more companies are seen on keeping their investors happy. Hence, it is important for them to increase their profits. BPO is one way of increasing their profits. If done well, BPO results in increasing shareholder values.

Business Process Outsourcing since its inception has been the turf of large business clients. Small and many medium sized business do not have the staff required to develop, negotiate, and manage and contracts, service level agreements and other overhead associated with doing business with the large Business Service Providers (BSP). As a result, Business Process Outsourcing has been practically unavailable to small and some medium sized business.

Why BPO

Free your resources and work on your strategy : An important aspect of Business Process Outsourcing is its ability to free corporate executives from some of their day-to-day process management responsibilities. Traditionally, executives spend 80 per cent of their time on managing details, and only 20 per cent on strategy. Once a process is successfully outsourced, the ratio can be reversed. Executives get more control over their most valuable resource: time. Time to explore new revenue streams, time to accelerate other projects, and time to focus on their customers.

Improve Process – Save Money : Companies that outsource business processes are often able to reengineer those process and capture new efficiencies. Then they can reallocate resources to other important projects and leverage their investment in technology. For example, processes that are handled in a shared production environment for multiple companies save everyone's money. In most cases, high caliber subject matter experts are brought into design and manage these processes, bringing with them best practices, innovation, and years of experience that most companies don't have access to or can't afford on their own.

Increase Your Capabilities : With this expertise often comes increased capability. In addition to doing things more efficiently, you can expand your ability to deliver new products and services to your customers. Then there are the factors of scalability and scope. Companies that want to grow internationally must continuously invest infrastructure and find talent around the world. Many outsourcing providers are already established globally and can help make the growth process run smoothly.

Dynamic Outsourcing : Business Process Outsourcing is generally categorized as being transactional, niche, or comprehensive. Transactions are generally sub-processes such as account payables, account receivables, journal, general ledger, order processing, medical transcription, etc. Niche support moves up to support a complete business process by specialized business services providers such as accounting, human resources, etc. Comprehensive usually thoroughly covers multiple business processes by one of the large Business Services Providers (BSPs).

Rather than having a contract for the support of an entire business process (or multiple processes) over a contractual period of time, each BPO transaction can be a stand-alone entity. When a process is broken down into its component parts, each transaction (sub-process) becomes much simpler and can be focused on by the appropriate people without the overhead of normal business outsourcing to a single provider. So where does support come from at the transactional level? It comes from the many small and medium sized businesses and the myriad of unemployed individual business professionals and skilled workers, which have been released due to corporate downsizing. Certainly more people are involved, but the level they can be the right people for the right job. As a stand-alone entity, a transaction is an inviting proposition for small companies and individual business professionals, which have

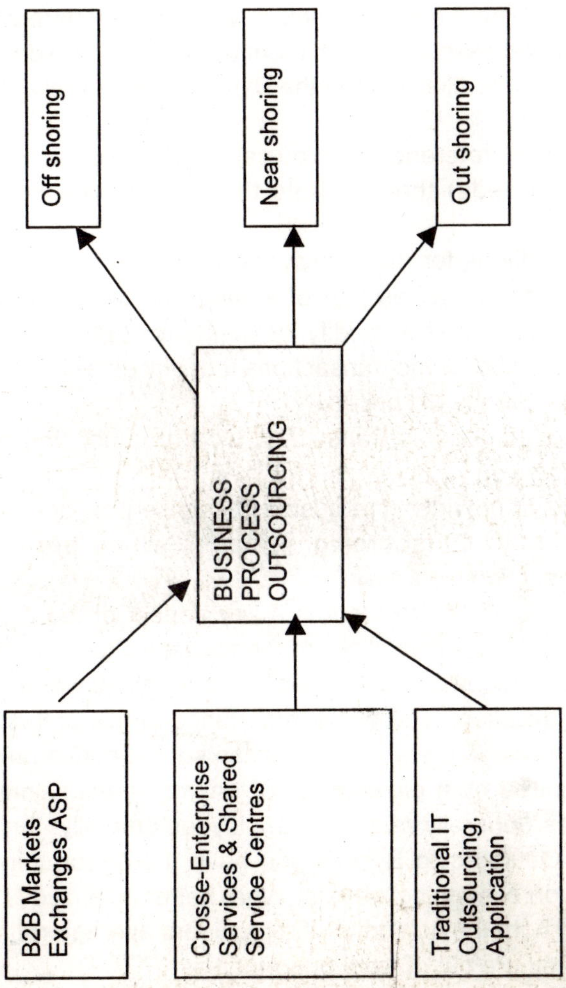
Off shoring
Near shoring
Out shoring
BUSINESS PROCESS OUTSOURCING
B2B Markets Exchanges ASP
Crosse-Enterprise Services & Shared Service Centres
Traditional IT Outsourcing, Application

special skills to bring to bear. Most large business services providers are not invested in participating in transactional business process outsourcing.

The Dynamic Outsourcing System makes transactional business process outsourcing easy, convenient, and very competitive. There are no contracts, service level agreements, or other over had associated with them (unless they are desired). As a Requester (the client role in the Dynamic Outsourcing System), you have.

- Queue preference that you can set (if the defaults do not fit your needs) that controls the transaction and bidding process.
- Instructions for the transaction that you can keep on your PC and upload as part of setting up the transaction (you may also enter or modify the instructions),
- Offer price for the transactions that places a cap (maximum price) on the bid prices.
- Rejection of any transaction work product that does not satisfy you,
- Rate of provider (the business service provider role in the Dynamic Outsourcing system), which performs the transaction work task.

The rating of providers is a key aspect of the transaction process. It is quick (two clicks of the mouse). Providers are rated by you, as a Requester, on a scale of 1 through 10 where 1 is poor and 10 is excellent. The prime importance of this of this rating is that in your queue preferences you can set the minimum average rating required by a provider to bid on your transactions. Large businesses generally rate their employees annually: through the Dynamic Outsourcing System you have the opportunity to rate providers on everything they do. What better incentive is there to do the job right the first time? If a providers average rating drops too low, they are out of work opportunities.

Business User Software Inc., and the Dynamic Outsourcing System believe strongly in small businesses and the role they plan in employment and productivity in America and around the world. Hopefully, together, many of the worthy unemployed workers can find work-at-home opportunities through the Dynamic Outsourcing System. This would be a win-win situation for all involved parties.

Rapidly changing and increasingly complex business forces are bringing fundamental shifts in management and organisation. The steady advance of technology, the complexity of business operations and the need for constant growth are conditions that require core compentence in too many functional areas. This business climate demands that companies adapt to keep up with the changes. Outsourcing has helped companies improve business focus, free management from day-to-day operations oversight and implement significant cost-saving measures. As business practices continue to change and evolve within organisations looking to remain competitive, the nature of outsourcing is undergoing a transformation in both its use and its impact. The following are the important considerations of outsourcing:

Improved business focus : Outsourcing lets a company focus on broader business issues while having details assumed by an outside expert.

Access to world class capabilities: By the very nature of their specialization, outsourcing providers bring extensive worldwide resources to meet the needs of their customers.

Redirection of resources: Every organization has limits on the resources available to it. outsourcing permits an organisation to redirect its resources from non-core activities toward activities that have greater return in serving the customer.

Benefit expenses alone add 20% to 30% to the cost for a permanent employee. Add to that unemployment insurance, workers compensation insurance, office space, equipment, software, continuous training, human resources overhead, payroll taxes, etc. and the cost can be as much as 40% to 50% more for a permanent employee versus outsourcing.

BPO in India

In order to meet the growing international demand for lucrative, customer-interaction centers, many organizations worldwide are outsourcing these services from locations like India. India has inherent strengths, which have made it a major success as an outsourcing destination.

Scope

A booming IT industry, with IT strengths recognized all over the world.

Language

The larger English-speaking population after the USA.

Manpower

- A vast workforce of educated, English speaking, techno-savvy personnel: A boon in a high-growth industry faced with a shortage of skilled workers.
- Cost-effective manpower: In a call interaction center operation, manpower typically accounts for 55 to 60 per cent of the total cost. In India, the manpower cost is approximately one-tenth of what it is overseas. Per agent cost in USA is approximately $40,000 while in India it is only $5,000.
- Technical support: India graduates about 1,00,000 engineers each year. These can be used in call centres for troubleshooting / tech. support, as the salaries are dramatically lower than in Europe or the US.

Government Policy

- The Government of India has recognized the potential of IT – enabled services and has taken positive steps by providing numerous incentives.
- IT is one of the Government of India's top five priorities.
- The National IT Task Force submitted its 108-point Action Plan to promote IT in the country. The Government of India has approved the plan and is in the process of implementing it.
- A separate Ministry of Information Technology was setup to expedite swift approval and implementation of IT projects and to streamline in the regulatory process.
- Information Technology Act 2000: The Information Technology Bill that was passed in the Indian Parliament in May, 2000, has now been notified as the IT Act 2000. The IT Bill brings E-commerce within the purview of law and accords

stringent punishments to "cyber criminals". With this, India joins a select band of 12 nations that have cyber laws.

Regulatory Enablers

- 100% foreign ownership permitted in IT Enabled Services Industry unlike other sectors where foreign ownership is restricted,
- Software Technology Parks (STPs) established,
- To provide ready to plug IT infrastructure and telecom facilities,
- Single window clearance for all regulatory compliance issues.

References

Buzzing BPO, Civil Services Chronicle, December, 2004.

Forrester Research, *BPO's Fragmented Future*, Quote Chart, INTERNET, 2005.

Sujay Chohan, *Offshore BPO*, VP for GARTNER INTERNET, 2005.

Thor Olavsrud, *Business Process Outsourcing Overhyped ?* INTERNET, 2003.

44

Economic Conditions of Girl Child Labour in Sivakasi Villages, Tamil Nadu

L. Rathakrishnan

From time immemorial, children have been contributing to the household work. The phenomenon of child labour as a problem has, however emerged relatively recently. In order to draw the attention of the human community on a global basis, the United Nations declared the year 1979 as the International Year of the Child. This declaration draw the attention of the scholars all over the world and combined efforts were made to look into the problems of child labour.

In general, the following factors attributes for the growth of child labour.

Demographic expansion, high fertility rate and the poor socio-economic conditions of family (Espenshade 1972);

Unemployment, hunger, poverty and illiteracy;

Bondage, a product of such object poverty. 73 per cent of the total child labour force in rural areas and urban unorganised sectors are put under diverse forms of bondage by their own parents or guardians (Horowitz 1969);

Limited number of schools, their absence in several interior villages, the cost of schooling as well as its restricted implication on job opportunities and dropout facilitate the growth of child labour.

The studies conducted in the area of child labour have brought out the following result. The bulk of female working child population is found in the rural areas. Significantly, while the work of girls in rural India is very visible, this is not so in the urban unorganised sector. For example, of the 45,000 working children in the Sivakasi Match industry in Tamilnadu, approximately 90 per cent of girls below the age of fourteen years (Nair 1983). Girls are found in large numbers in the coir industry of Kerala and home-based industries like incense-making and papad preparation (Jhabvala, 1982). Girls are involved in substantial numbers in the beedi industry and gem polishing industry in Jaipur, and the making of paper bags and garments, cotton-pad shelling, groundnut pad shelling, hand-embroidery, grain cleaning, block-making, sub-assembling, electrical and electronic items (Bhat 1987). Hundreds of girls are working in the lock industry of Aligarh, the brassware industry of Muradabad in Uttar Pradesh, the carpet industry of Jammu and Kashmir and Rajasthan and the Zarri embroidery industry in Varanasi (Sudesh 1988). But these are essentially invisible children who do not go to work in factories and in work shops and therefore do not come under the purview of law. A large number of girls are to be found in domestic service, bag-picking, newspaper vending and so on (Karlekan 1982).

Despite efforts from diverse corners, child labour is a common sight in Sivakasi. Against this back drop, the present study has been undertaken to throw light on the real living conditions of the working girl children in the different villages in and around Sivakasi.

Objectives of the study

(i) To examine the socio-economic profile of the child labour and factors responsible for the existence of child labour;

(ii) To analyse the impact of child labour on their families in terms of their contribution to create additional income and assets;

(iii) To identify the major causes for the existence of child labour; and

(iv) To find out the impact of child labour in terms of the changes in their consumption and expenditure pattern of the family.

Hypotheses

1. The child labour's income is an additional source of income to the family;
2. The socio-economic background have much bearing for the employment of the children;
3. Poverty is the major cause of the child labour; and
4. The changes in the consumption and expenditure pattern of households leads to compulsory employment of child labour.

Research Methods

The data pertaining to the present study have been collected from both primary as well as secondary sources. Personal interview method was adopted to collect the primary data through well structured pre-tested interview schedule. The question was administered to the respondents personally. The information was collected not only from the respondents but also from their parents since some of the information were unable to be answered by the children. The secondary data have been collected from published sources like books, journals, government reports, newspaper, and theses. The basic information about the exact number of the employment of child labour in the sample industries were collected from the industries. The children interviewed are drawn from three villages of Sivakasi panchayat union namely Maruthanatham, Moolipatti and Shankaralingapuram. 300 girl children are employed in match industries. It is decided to select a sample of 60 randomly from these three villages. A sample of 20 girl children were selected from each village randomly.

The collected data from the primary sources have been analysed through the percentage method in bivariate tables. The following model has been used in order to estimate the causes for the employment of child labour in match industry.

$$S_{GCL} = b_0 + b_1 \, DIST + b_2 \, AGE + b_3 \, EDN_{GC} + b_4 \, EDN_p + b_5 \, CAST + b_6 \, FT$$
$$b_7 \, FS + b_8 \, WR + b_9 \, Y + b_{10} \, BI + b_{11} \, A + U_i$$

where,

S_{GCL}	=	Supply of child labour in days
DIST	=	Distance of the factory from the house in Kms.
AGE	=	Age of the Girl child in years
EDN_{GC}	=	Class studied by the girl child in number of years, say 3rd standard as 3 years study
EDN_p	=	Class studied by the parent in number of years
CAST	=	Caste and community of the child – Dummy variable: 'O' for Backward Class and '1' for Scheduled Caste
FT	=	Family Type – Dummy variable: 'O' for Joint family and '1' for Nuclear family
FS	=	Family size in number
WR	=	Wage rage in Rs. per day
Y	=	Income of the family per month
BI	=	Bonus Index
A	=	Assets worth in Rs.
Ui	=	Random variable
bi	=	Coefficients to be estimated
i	=	1, 2, ... 11

Analysis and Interpretation

1. Distance and Mode of Transport

Mostly, the factories are located in semi urban areas. The workers of these factories are coming from the adjoining villages. The distance from villages to the factory ranges from 1-2 K.m. The factory is providing bus facility to the workers to fetch them to the factories and also to leave them to their residence in the evening.

2. Age distribution of the respondent

In our sample, only two workers are found in the age of 10. Mostly the employers never prefer the child workers below the age of 10. About 45 per cent of the girl child workers of our sample are in the age group of 14. Employers prefer the child labourers between the age group of 12-14 because these group children are very suited for the match factories. In the age group between

10-12, child workers normally produce less because of inadequate skills and other physical constraints.

Table : 1 Age Distribution of the Respondents

Sl.No	Villages	Age Distribution					Total
		Below 10	11	12	13	14	
1	Maruthanatham	1	2	1	4	12	20
2	Moolipatti	-	3	5	6	6	20
3	Shankarlingapuram	1	3	5	2	9	20
	Total	**2**	**8**	**11**	**12**	**27**	**60**

3. Educational Status of the Child Labour

About 55 per cent of the children have studied upto middle level. Nearly 32 per cent of the children have studied upto primary level while 13.3 per cent of the children were illiterates. This amount of illiteracty is due to poverty which causes them to put their efforts towards the earnings income. Eventhough educational facilities are available within the reach of the poor, they hesitate to avail this facility.

Table : 2 Educational Status of the Child Labour

Sl.No	Villages	1 Illiterates	2 Primary	3 Middle	Total
1	Maruthanatham	1	4	15	20
2	Moolipatti	2	7	11	20
3	Shankarlingapuram	3	8	7	20
	Total	8 (13)	19 (32)	33 (55)	60 (100)

4. Parental Education and Occupation

There is a strong relation exist between the occupational pattern of the parents and the need for children to work. Interestingly, 98 per cent of the girl children's parents are engaged in farming while the remaining parents belong to painter. Most of the parents of the children (75%) are generally had low level of education, i.e., studied up to the fifth standard. Low levels of education of the parents enable them to obtain only poorly-paid jobs which keep them, along with their children, in perpetual poverty.

Discussions with the parents revealed that two-thirds of the parents were either illiterate or had dropped out from school, and had been forced to work in their childhood. Thus, experience of the parents in their childhood has influenced their attitude towards child labour. Even to send children to lower classes, parents make a conscious choice of sending male children to school and keeping girl children at home to look after the younger siblings, or be sent to match factories as wage labour.

5. Caste and Community Background of the Respondents

Most of the girl children are from Hindu religion and the negligible number is from Christianity. About 78 per cent of the girl children are from backward community, namely Reddiar community while 22 per cent of the girl children are from scheduled caste.

6. Housing Particulars of the Respondents

40 per cent of the child labourers are living in tiled houses, 33 per cent of them are living in thatched houses and the 27 per cent of them are living in concrete houses. When we observe the electrification about 82 per cent of their houses are electrified and the remaining 18 per cent of their houses are not electrified. 90 per cent of the houses are owned by the respondents parents.

7. Type of Family

Child labour is also determined by type of family, namely whether it is nuclear or joint family. If the number of dependants of a family increases, then naturally it leads to increase in child labour as there is no other near alternative for the head of the family. In reality, an increase in joint family leads to an increase in child labour both in urban and rural sides. However, it is found from our study

Table 3 : Type of Family

Sl.No	*Village*	*Type*		*Total*
		Joint	*Nuclear*	
1	Maruthanatham	2	18	20
2	Moolipatti	1	19	20
3	Shankaralingapuram	2	18	20
	Total	5 (8)	55 (92)	60 (100)

that 92 per cent of the child labourers are from nuclear family and the remaining 8 per cent of them are from joint families. Hence the type of the parents family does not affect the children's participations in the labour force.

8. Size of the Family

The size of the family is an indicator for standard of living of the family and poverty. Any additional number of child in a family is always considered as a sin. The increasing amount of poverty is in fact associated with the number of births.

Table 4 : Size of the Family

Sl.No	*Village*	*Size*			*Total*
		Below 3	*4-6*	*7-10*	
1	Maruthanatham	3	16	1	**20**
2	Moolipatti	1	17	2	**20**
3	Shankaralingapuram	3	16	1	**20**
	Total	**7 (12)**	**49 (81)**	**4 (7)**	**60 (100)**

Table 4 gives an account the size of the family of the sample respondents. About 81 per cent of the families possess on an average size of 4-6 members. It is only 12 per cent of the families who maintain the population of 1-3 members. The size of the family with 7-10 members is very less (7 per cent). It is found from the study that the size of the family is very large. Consequently, the members in the family are either directly or indirectly employed in order to support the family. It is safely concluded from the above table that the size of the family acts as a real determinant factor for the employment of children.

9. Employment Pattern of Children

Data reveals that 76 per cent of girl children interviewed are employed in frame filling, 16 per cent in box filling, 4 per cent in box making, and 4 per cent in band rolling. All of them are causal workers. There is a sexual segregation of laboUr in the match industry. There is no upward occupational mobility for female workers and they are employed only in unskilled work. Male children and adults are employed in chemical dipping and chemical mixing, side-frame painting and other processes. In due course, they become foremen, accountants and mangers which fetch higher salaries.

10. Income of the Child Labour

The wage structure in the match industry is mostly piece-rated. For work involved in chemical mixing, chemical dipping., distributing splinters and veneers the workers are paid fortnightly or monthly. They are called company workers. Mostly, boys and male adults are engaged in such jobs. Girl children are generally paid on a piece-rate basis that has its own oppressive logic, namely long hours of work at high speed for low returns.

Table 5 : Income of the Child Labourers

Sl.No	*Villages*	*Income Size (in Rs.)*				*Total*
		Below 400	*401-800*	*801-1200*	*1201-2000*	
1	Maruthanatham	-	2	11	7	20
2	Moolipatti	-	3	13	4	20
3	Shankaralingapuram	1	9	7	3	20
	Total	1 (2)	14 (23)	31 (52)	14 (23)	60 (100)

Table 5 shows the income of the child labourers. About 52 per cent of the workers are earning income between Rs. 801-1200 per month. About 23 per cent of the workers are earning income between Rs. 401-800 per month. Another 23 per cent of the workers are earning income between Rs.1201-2000 per month. Only 2 per cent of the workers are earning below Rs. 400 per month. It is generally seen from Table 5 that more number of labourers are earning income between Rs. 801-1200 per month. This is, infact, a sizeable contribution made by the child labourers to support their families. The range of income differs from one labourer to another. The experience they posses, the work they perform reward them more and more. The inequality of income exists because of the variation in the efficiency of the labourers.

As long as the years of experience are more and more, they will be stronger in their efficiency in producing more returns. Apart from this the labourers are provided bonus also on the basis of their income.

11. Working Conditions

The overcrowded match manufacturing units are in no way different from the poor home of nineteenth century England. Most of the children interviewed said that their work places were congested, not properly illuminated and some companies produce noxious odour of chemicals from the chemical dipping section and poor ventilation. To some extent drinking water facilities and toilet facilities are available to the workers.

For the normal working day it is as long as ten hours (8 a.m. and 6 p.m). But some times, children work for 12 hours per day. Children took only short breaks for lunch ranging from 20 to 40 minutes. The workers are, however, free to take any day off since, after all, they are paid only for the work done. We found that children working even on national holidays like Republic Day.

12. Family Income

Family income of the respondents is also one of the factors which greatly determine the extent of child labour. Lower the family income, larger will be the extent of child labour. Table 6 shows the family income of the child labour. About 68 percent of the worker's family income is between Rs.2001-6000 per month. While 20 percent of the worker's family income is below Rs.2000 per month

Table 6 : Family Income

Sl.No	*Village*	*Family Income (Monthly)*			*Total*
		Below 2000	*2001-6000*	*6001 and above*	
1	Maruthanatham	3	15	2	**20**
2	Moolipatti	7	11	2	**20**
3	Shankaralingapuram	2	15	3	**20**
	Total	**12 (20)**	**41 (68)**	**7 (12)**	**60 (100)**

and the remaining 12 per cent of the worker's family income is between Rs.6001 and above per month. A major proportion of the families are earning more than the national average.

13. Expenditure Pattern

Expenditure pattern of the households of the girl children comprise of food items, non-food items and other miscellenous items. Most of their income is spent on food items and other miscellenous items like drinking and gambling, which induce the employment of children with a positive effect. Another important feature is that because of increase in consumption expenditure which leads to greater employment of children.

14. Savings of the Child Labourers

Child labour also posses savings. Most of the girl child labourers are saving money from their income for their personal use. 75 per cent of their income is given to the family while remaining 25 per cent of their income is saved for their own purpose. They use this money for cosmetics, entertainment, jewels, and clothes. It is found from the study that 53 per cent of girls save while 47 per cent of the girl do not save. Their savings ranges from Rs.2000–12000. Girls save money through chit funds in the factory itself.

15. Indebtedness

Family indebtedness is one of the major causes for the acute poverty. It is found from the Table 7 that 53 per cent of the families are indebted while 47 per cent of the families are not indebted. It is evident from the figure that indebtedness is not the main factor to determine the extent of child labour.

Table 7 : Indebtedness

SLNo	*Villages*	*1 Yes*	*2 No*	*Total*
1	Maruthanatham	12	8	20
2	Moolipatti	10	10	20
3	Shankarlingapuram	10	10	20
	Total	32 (53)	28 (47)	60 (100)

Table 8 : Lower Triangular Correlation Matrix

	S_{GCL}	DIST	AGE	EDN_{GC}	EDN_p	CAST	FT	FS	WR	Y	BI	A
S_{GCL}	1.00											
DIST	-0.15	1.00										
AGE	-0.10	-0.001	1.00									
EDN_{GC}	-0.13	0.28	0.44	1.00								
EDN_p	0.05	-0.13	0.10	-0.10	1.00							
CAST	0.10	-0.27	-0.17	-0.57	0.10	1.00						
FT	0.04	0.06	-0.02	0.15	-0.26	-0.15	1.00					
FS	0.28	-0.03	0.12	0.36	-0.01	-0.29	0.06	1.00				
WR	-0.41	0.27	0.30	0.26	0.03	-0.10	0.06	0.07	1.00			
Y	0.07	-0.08	0.07	0.15	0.26	-0.13	0.06	0.27	0.05	1.00		
BI	-0.03	0.08	0.13	0.41	-0.13	-0.15	0.39	0.16	0.52	-0.07	1.00	
A	0.08	-0.05	0.04	0.34	-0.20	-0.23	-0.02	0.52	-0.02	0.20	-0.07	1.00

Results and discussions

The association of the independent variables and the dependent variable is examined with the help of computed correlation coefficients. The linear multiple regression model result is shown in Table 8. The insignificant association (r <= 0.5) among the explanatory variables indicates that there is no multi-collinearity problem. However, the association of the explanatory variables with the dependent variable does not seem to be highly correlated fifted model is considered for the discussion. The selected model gives the highest coefficient of multiple determination possible (R^2) and the large number of significant coefficients.The best of fitted model is:

$$S_{GCL} = 33.24 - 0.20\ EDN_{GC}^{***} + 0.29\ EDN_{p} + 0.70\ FS^{*}$$

(1.67) (2.03) (2.92)

$$-\ 0.20\ WR^{*} + 0.051\ BI^{*}$$

(4.60) (2.63)

$$R^2 = 0.33; \quad F_{(53.6)} = 6.60^{*}$$

*, ** and *** indicate the 1, 5 and 10 % levels of statistical significance respectively.

Note: Figures in brackets refer to 't' values.

It is interesting to note that the educational level and the wage rate do influence the supply of the girl child labour adversely. In other words, the finding supports the hypothesis that the higher the education in terms of years studied, the child is not willing to go for work. Further, higher the wage rate paid per day, the contribution of the girl child on the next day in terms of attending to the work may be unwilling. Higher the family size and bonus index, a girl child would be either forced or attracted to going for the work. Contrarily, higher the level of parent's education could not exhibit positively the non-sending the girl child for the work. This contrary phenomenon may be attributed to the poverty which is exhibited by the uniform and low level family incomes of these households.

Conclusion

Children are an asset for any society. It is the responsibility of society to nurture them through various phases of their development to enable them to make a meaningful contribution to the society. However , the phenomenon of the millions of child labour in Asia, Africa and the Latin America presents a picture of the tragic failure of society to protect and nurture its greatest asset. As long as poverty exists, it will persist in some form or the other. Child labour is attractive to employers because they work in lower wages than the adults. It is generally viewed that illiteracy, poverty, ignorance, unbalanced growth and the inherent defects of the social system are the major reasons for child labour in most of the industries in India. The children of low income families are required to work to a greater extent.

Policy Implications

The constitutional and legal provisions in India view the child as a homogeneous entity whereas, in reality, there exist a marked difference in treatment, disadvantageous to girl children. This forces one to think in terms of revisions in the legal statuses so as to accord preferential treatment to girl child workers.

The state of agriculture in Sivakasi is so deplorable that it is often cited as the major cause for the enlargement of the child labour force. Efforts to irrigate agricultural land should be given prime importance as it would enhance the earning capacity of the households. This would also provide alternative employment opportunities rather than forever depending on the match and other industries.

Along with the overall development, especially in agriculture, society should be sensitised against the evil of child labour. Parents, employers, enforcement authorities, trade unions and social action groups are some of the important categories on whom the sensitisation should be concentrated.

Employers should be convinced about the damage they cause by making children work and should be made to commit that they would refrain from employing children. Fiscal and monetary incentives should be provided by the government to those match factories who do not employ children. These may include tax rebates, provision of soft loans, and preference in raw material sanctions. Along with the practice of providing incentives, there should be a provision for disincentives such as cancellation of licenses of those factories which employ child labour.

Failure on the part of the enforcement machinery to implement child labour legislation has been an important factor in the growth to child labour in Sivakasi. It is imperative that storng measures are initiated to rectify this limitation.

Voluntary organizations can also play a very significant role in eliminating the practice of child labour. They should be primarily concerned with mobilizing public opinion and also conducting awareness camps for the various social groups. Efforts should be made by the government to identify those voluntary organizations which perform their tasks to the best of society's interest and they should be suitably rewarded. Steps should also be initiated to integrate the efforts of the different voluntary organizations.

In Sivakasi, children are drawn into the match industry even without entering primary schools. These children need be given the benefit of literacy and compulsory education.

Special schools under the National Child Labour Project (NCLP) have attracted children since September 1988. This school cover 1800 child workers against the surveyed 14000 children and estimated 45000 children working in the match industries of Sivakasi. But special school have solved only a part of the problem as Rs.3000 has to be spent on a child every year.

To cope with the needs of child workers who are not enrolled in the special schools, non-formal education centers should be started by the government. Classes can be held in the evenings and on Saturday and Sundays availing of the services of local teachers. Classes can be conducted in schools and, community centers. The NCLP director can play a supervisory role in these schools. Books and uniforms for children attending these classes should be distributed free of cost. Financial incentives should also be offered so as to encourage the parents to send their children to such school.

Compulsory primary education, to a great extent reduces the number of children working full time, particularly those working in rural areas.

The coverage by media of child labour will increase awareness and consciousness amongst policy makers and others.

References

Bhat, Ela, *"The Invisibility of Home based work. The case of piece rate workers in India"* in Menefee singh and Anita Kelles – Viitanen (eds.) Invisible Hands, Sage Publication, New Delhi, 1969.

Durairaj, N, *"Child labour in the Match Industry"*, Penisular Economist, 1(2):61-65, 1987.

Espenshade T.J, *"The value and cost of children"* in Population Bulletin, Population Reference Bureau, 32 (1):20-28. 1972.

Geetha Balachandran, *"Legislation on Child Labour"*, Social Welfare, 33(3):20-23, 1986.

Geetha Balachandran, *"Policies on Child Labour, economic and social measures"*, Social Welfare, 33(3):31-32, 1986.

George, K.N, *"Child Labour in the City of Madras"* paper presented in the National seminar on employment of children in India, New Delhi, 1975.

Goyal, R.K, *"Child labour in India"*, Indian Labour Journal, 28(2):173-187, 1987.

Horowitz, David, "*The Abolition of Poverty*", Prager, New York, 225, 1969

Jhabvala, Renana and Jannifer Sebistadt, *"To be self employed ...... and a woman"*, *HIMMAT*, 17(15), 75, 1981.

Juyal B.N. et.al., "*Child labour : The twice exploited*", Varanasi : Gandhian Institute of Studies, 105, 1985.

Karlekar, Malavika, "*Poverty and Women's Work: A study of sweeper women in Delhi*", Vikas Publishing House, Delhi, 287, 1982.

Kiran Bhatty, *"Child labour: Breaking the Vicious Circle*", Economic and Political Weekly, 384, 1992.

Kulshreshtha, J.C, *Child Labour in India*, Ashish Publishing house, New Delhi, 1978.

Mahaveer Jain, *"Perspectives on Child labour in India"*, Awards Digest: Journal of Labour Legislation, 22(7-12), 32-33, 1992.

Mendelievich E, "*Children at work*", International Labour Organisation, Geneva: 257, 1979.

Murthy, P.V.V, *"Bonded Child Labour in Beedi Industry"*, The Hindu, April 11th:5, 1994.

Nair, R, *"Education-why do more girls drop out?"*, *Kurukshetra*:1–5, 1985.

Nasir Tyabji, *"Match industry in Sivakasi,'Sathu towards removal of child labour"*, *MIDS Bulletin*, 16(5-6):325, 1986.

Natarajan S.R, *"Women and Child Workers Safely Match industry"*, Social welfare, 34(3), 4-8, 1987.

Neera Burla, "*Child labour in the Brassware Industry of Moradabad", India*, ILO / ARTEP, New Delhi, 1989.

Neva Burra, *"A report on child labour in the Lock industry of Aligarh"*, Uttar Pradesh, India, Prepared for UNICEF, 1967.

Smitu Kothari, *"There is Blood on those Match sticks"*, Child labour in Sivakasi, *EPW*, 28(5):1191-2002, 1983.

Index